WITNESS TO THE
TWENTIETH CENTURY

WITNESS TO THE TWENTIETH CENTURY

THE LIFE STORY OF A JAPAN SPECIALIST

THEODORE MCNELLY

To order additional copies of this book, contact:
Xlibris Corporation
1-888-795-4274
www.Xlibris.com
Orders@Xlibris.com
26136

CONTENTS

To my children, Douglas and Gale

Also by Theodore McNelly

Contemporary Government of Japan (1963)

Sources in Modern East Asian History and Politics (edited by Theodore McNelly, 1967)

Politics and Government in Japan (1972, 1984)

Introduction to Comparative Government (co-authored by Theodore McNelly, 1990, 1993, 1997, 2003)

Japanese Perspectives on Pearl Harbor (authored in Japanese by Sugihara Seishiro, translated by Theodore McNelly, 1995)

The Origins of Japan's Democratic Constitution (2000)

CHAPTER 1

A WISCONSIN CHILDHOOD

A mong the few things that I recall of my early boyhood is lying on the floor of our living room gazing at a satin pillow. The afternoon sun cast warm rays through the window as I studied the pillow. On it were embroidered three elegantly gowned Japanese ladies about to cross a small red arched bridge. This pattern was repeated again and again in various orientations on the pillow. I was entranced by the bright colors of the ladies' costumes, but I suppose that a mystery was what most fascinated me. There was nothing at the opposite end of the little bridge, so that I was most puzzled, perhaps a bit worried too, about *where these lovely creatures were headed.* Given the elegance of the ladies, I fancied that their destination must be a very fine and beautiful place, and I longed to know what it was like. Thus the beauty and mystery, the exoticism of Japan, were instilled in my consciousness from my earliest years.

Theodore Hart McNelly at an Early Age

My mother had been born in Japan of American missionaries, and she and my grandmother would often refer to Japan. They taught me a useful phrase in the language that we children were fond of repeating: "*Watakushi wa wakarimasen*" ("I do not understand").

I was born in Lancaster, Wisconsin, in 1919, at 6:00 PM, December 27, 1919, one day short of nine months after my parents' marriage (March 28, 1919).

My father was the superintendent of schools in Lancaster, Wisconsin, a country town of perhaps 2500 population that served nearby farmers in southwestern Wisconsin. It was also the capital of Grant county, boasting an impressive domed county building of red sandstone.

Every year or so my father would drive us to Madison to see grampa and gramma Taylor. For a while they had been living in various places in Madison while engaged in building houses. They finally moved into a beautiful house on Regent Street, diagonally across from Randall School. The house, of modest size by today's standards, was unlike the older wooden houses in the neighborhood. It was made of brick, English style. It had been designed by my maternal grandfather, who in his retirement from the ministry, dabbled in real estate and home building. He was proud of the brick, "overbaked" I think he called it, which was dark red splotched with shades of purple and black. The windows were not double hung, as in most American houses, but swung open when you turned a little crank. The panes were leaded. The doorknobs and other fixtures had been brought from England by Uncle Ed, my mother's brother, who had visited England to study the architecture there. Grampa enjoyed explaining to visitors the species of trees and shrubs planted in the front of the house. These were all very exotic to us from Lancaster (or Marinette, where we later lived), where trees were normally of whatever species God had determined.

In the corner of the living room standing on its end was a scabbard containing a Japanese sword. (Many years later, I learned that this was the wrong way to display a Japanese sword; it had warped.) The samurai sword, which my grandfather occasionally unsheathed to impress a privileged visitor, was a souvenir of his service in Japan as a missionary in the 1890s.

Grampa was a dignified individual and very pious. When we visited him, every day there was morning prayer, with verses read from the Bible, followed by our getting on our knees in front of our chairs, listening to Grampa pray and finally everyone's reciting the Lord's Prayer. Grandpa disapproved of playing cards, which he associated with gambling, but he liked to play dominoes with us.

I was the oldest of four children. My sister, Lucille, was a year and a half younger than me. John was four years younger, and Jim was eight years younger.

I remember when Jimmy was born. The nurse was a jolly lady who mispronounced our name: "McNolly." She brought the baby to our house while our mother was still in the hospital. I was very excited by the arrival of the baby.

When we children then went to the hospital, I was delighted to be the first to break the news to my mother that we had a new baby.

The Taylor-McNelly Clan in 1928
From the left: Gramma Taylor, Aunt Harriet Hurd (Gramma Taylor's sister), Teddy McNelly (me), Grampa Taylor, Jimmy McNelly (baby in Grampa Taylor's arms), John McNelly (putting on an act), Mrs. Caroline McNelly (my mother), Lucille McNelly (my sister), Aunt Lois Taylor, Uncle Ed Taylor (my mother's brother). My father is missing from the picture; perhaps he was the person taking it, shortly after Jimmy's birth on May 15, 1928, in Lancaster, Wisconsin.]

When I was still very small, one of my playmates was Edward Wieland, who lived nearby with his grandparents. (Many years later, I learned that Edward was one of my wife's forty-nine first cousins. He ultimately became a lieutenant colonel in the Air Force.) In his capacity as school superintendent, my father hired as a kindergarten teacher a young Florence Wieland, who a few years later married an instructor of electrical engineering at the University of Wisconsin and gave birth to the child who became my wife in 1960.

My mother taught all of us children piano lessons. In our early years we hated it and rebelled at practicing scales and such. We would cry and throw tantrums, but my father always backed my mother up. These lessons greatly enriched our lives and all of us are grateful. Later both my sister and I majored in music at the University of Wisconsin, but both of us failed the sophomore comprehensive examinations and gave up ever becoming professional musicians.

Miss Warren, who taught first grade at South School in Lancaster and who (it seemed) had been teacher to half the population of the town, played the piano when we had music lessons in school. We pointed out to our mother that Miss Warren played all right but did not curve her fingers when she played, as my mother insisted we do. This was just one example of how unreasonable my mother was.

In grade school we had to sing do re mis and tap our fingers on the page (one tap for quarter notes and two taps for half notes). "My country t'is of thee" would be "do do re ti do re mi mi fa mi re do," et cetera. I am not sure that we completely understood what we were doing at the time, but this exercise could not have hurt the students who never had private lessons but who would later sing in high school choruses and church choirs.

One evening I and Curtis Alt (the boy next door who was a year or two older than I) visited a friend's house. The three of us sat on the porch swing while our friend played the mouth organ (harmonica). I was very impressed that he could play the chords as well as the tunes of just about every song we knew. The next day I told my mother about the superiority of the harmonica over the piano. With the mouth organ you did not have to bother with reading music and learning scales. Besides the instrument was very portable as compared with the piano. My mother, a graduate of a conservatory in Chicago, was not impressed by my arguments.

At school, in addition to the do re mis we also memorized multiplication tables. I cannot remember exactly how we were taught to read, but we were often encouraged to pronounce letters one at a time, so that we were trained in the phonetic system. I cannot remember any classmate who failed to learn how to read.

In those days, the father worked and brought home the bacon and the mother stayed home and cooked and watched after the children. There were no children on drugs, and almost no juvenile delinquency. I am not at all sure that the world is a better place today than it was when I was a child.

Once, a week or two before Thanksgiving, my father bought a live goose. One day the goose escaped, and my father and I found it after searching the neighborhood. John, who was about three years old with beautiful long curly hair, became very fond of the goose, which we kept in the back yard. We all felt a bit strange when we finally ate the goose.

Across the street from our house was South School, a grade school. The janitor usually finished his work by early afternoon and would then nap in a chair under a tree. There was a slide in the playground. Every Halloween he would carefully lay the slide on its side to protect it from being pushed over by pranksters. I remember one night when a bunch of us boys were engaged in Halloween tricks. We pushed over the outhouse in somebody's back yard.

Another popular prank was soaping windows. This was before "trick or treat." Then it was just tricks.

Most of the town was Protestant and Republican. When Al Smith was running for president he was derided for pronouncing radio (then a novelty) "raddio." There was also the story that his favorite telephone number was 3909. When you wrote this number on a piece of paper and held it wrong side up against the light it read "pope." The Catholic kids went to the Catholic school. It was said that they put rocks inside the snowballs when having fights with other kids.

The boys liked to make shacks of scrap lumber which we would call club houses. There were some loosely structured gangs. A bunch I was briefly involved with went over to another boy's house and pushed down his shack. His mother was very upset by this.

My father could make kites. He used hardwood sticks instead of the flimsy pine sticks used in store-bought kites. Daddy's kites, made of old newspapers, were not pretty, but they never broke.

We children did not have "allowances." Allowances for children seemed not to be the custom in Lancaster and later in Marinette. If our parents felt that we needed a toy or some other unnecessary thing they would buy it for us, perhaps for Christmas. However when we went to Madison we were each given ten cents to buy whatever we pleased at the ten-cent store. There was no ten-cent store in Lancaster, and a visit to the ten-cent store in Madison with a dime to spend was a rare treat.

Once I bought a fortune-telling ball with my dime. It was a small glass ball with numbers printed all over it. One rolled the ball and read the number that ended up on the top. One then consulted a sheet of paper that indicated a prediction for each number. I was the only boy in Lancaster that owned this marvelous device and it was the source of much fascination. A rich boy offered me 25 cents for the ball, but I refused this offer to make a 150 per cent profit. The fortune-telling ball was my most prized possession.

Mary Carthew lived across the street and was my sister's best friend. Her father was a lawyer, and from time to time the Carthews would drive to Dubuque, Iowa, to do their shopping and take my sister with them. She would boast to the rest of us about visiting the great city. She would say with supreme arrogance, "I went to Dubuque. And we ate at a RESTAURANT. [Our family never ate at restaurants, they were regarded as a waste of money.] And we had CHICKEN A LA KING!" [an exotic delicacy that we never had at home].

One summer, Curtis Alt and I decided to earn money to buy fireworks for the Fourth of July. Farmers would drive their horse-drawn wagons loaded with pea vines through the town on the way to the canning factory. The vines, which included the peas, would dribble off the wagon, and occasionally we would help some of the vines to fall off. We would separate the peas from the vines and put them into quart-size strawberry boxes and peddle them from door to door. The lady would ask, "Are these field peas?" Of course they were, but we would say they were not. In this way we earned several dollars that we used to buy sparklers, fire crackers, and little cones that spouted sparks.

My father sometimes helped farmers with their threshing. They thought that he was just being helpful; actually we needed the money. When we went for Sunday afternoon drives, he would usually comment on the progress of the crops, such as the height of the corn stalks and so on. He had been born and brought up on a farm near Richland Center.

As a member of the Kiwanis Club, father participated in the annual minstrel show to make money for charity. The members, with blackened faces, would sing, tell jokes, and generally clown around.

When we had visitors from out of town, my father would show people the heating system of our house and people would discuss the highways one had taken to get to Lancaster or Marinette.

My father, a versatile athlete, coached football in the high school in addition to other duties. I was reminded by the late Howard Penniman, professor of political science at Georgetown University, that when Penniman had been a high school boy in Lancaster, my father had coached the debate team of which Penniman had been a member. His sister, Clara Penniman, became a professor of political science at the University of Wisconsin, and was a friend to my mother when the latter was living in Madison during her widowhood.

Curtis Alt's older brother had a crystal set—a primitive radio that he had put together. That was the only radio in the neighborhood for a while. Then my father bought a real radio, a Zenith. It consisted of one long box with lots of switches and dials on it with outlets for several headphones and a matching square box which had a large curved horn on the top. The latter was the loudspeaker. There was a third box; I don't know what it was for. For some reason, the loudspeaker was often not used. Instead, father and his friends (they did not have radios) would sit for hours in complete silence listening to the account of a baseball or football game on their headphones.

The rise of the radio yielded an unexpected boon. One day my father brought home a fine console phonograph (a wind-up model) with a great many records. This had been traded in to a dealer for a radio and my father bought the outfit at a bargain. The records, which were made of readily breakable material, included all kinds of goodies, most notably Galli-Curci singing "Lo, Hear the Gentle Lark," John McCormick singing "Silver Threads among the Gold." and a bunch of funny songs sung in Scottish accent by Sir Harry Lauder. We children loved the Harry Lauder records. Years later, during the Second World war, my brother John as a patriotic gesture gave the phonograph and the records to military base near by, where I am afraid the obsolete technology and the artistry on the records may not have been appreciated by the draftees.

Some of the furniture in our house had been built by my father, who was very handy with tools. I remember particularly the Morris chair with an adjustable back and leather-covered cushions. It and the telephone stand were of oak and in "mission style" which was currently fashionable. The buffet, however, was more elegant, surfaced with a glossy reddish brown veneer, with a beveled mirror mounted on the back of the top.

When I must have been in third or fourth grade, a classmate invited the class to a birthday party at his house on the other side of town. My mother gave me fifteen cents to buy a present. I bought a birthday card and glass pistol that had little colored candies inside that could be accessed by unscrewing the cap at the end of the barrel. This pistol was a very lovely thing indeed; no one had ever given me anything so nice for my birthday. When I got to the party I gave the birthday card to the boy's mother and kept the glass pistol for myself. The mother asked me if I had brought anything beside the card and I said no.

MADISON

After my father had served as superintendent for eleven years in Lancaster, the school board did not renew his contract. Unable to find immediately a new job in education, he became a textbook salesman, traveling from town to town in Wisconsin selling books for a small publisher to school officials. So in the summer of 1929, we moved from Lancaster to Madison, where my father made his headquarters. He hated selling, so he continued to seek another job in school administration. He also began work on a masters degree in education at the University of Wisconsin.

We rented a house on Lathrop Street in Madison, about a block from grampa's house on Regent Street and close to Randall School, where I attended fifth grade. I particularly remember the music teacher, who carried around a portable windup phonograph in an oaken case. She played records on it and we were supposed to remember the names and composers of these pieces. I really liked "Danse Macabre" by Saint-Saëns, which, as the teacher told us, depicted ghosts and skeletons coming out of their graves, tuning up their fiddles, and dancing wildly in the cemetery.

Several friends whom I knew in fifth grade at Randall I would meet again six years later at Madison West High School. One of these was Aldo Leopold, whose father taught at the University of Wisconsin and was a famous conservationist. I also remember a neighbor boy who liked to play Germans vs Americans fighting a war, and taking turns tying one another up, which I thought strange. He and his parents lived in the basement of a neighbor's house. Across the street there was a bully whom I was afraid to confront. His father was a physician who had been arrested for conducting "illegal operations."

Grampa sometimes took us children on walks to nearby Lake Wingra where we would "go on a boat ride," i. e., sit on a rock on the shore and look at the waves, enjoying the illusion of moving on a boat. In a gruff but very gentle voice he would sometimes sing Stephen Foster's "Uncle Ned," ending with the words, "Lay down de shubble and de hoe, Hang up de fiddle and de bow, For there's no more work for poor Uncle Ned, He's gone where the good darkies go."

At about this time, grampa's niece (a cousin of my mother) was living in a small bedroom at the top of the stairs in grampa's house. We children were very fond of Dorothy Taylor, who was a secretary downtown. She had formerly taught school but did not like it. She knew how to play the ukelele and would play and sing "It Happened in Monterey" for us. To us children the words were romantic indeed, which told of Old Mexico a long time ago and ladies' lips as red as wine that stole somebody's heart.

She was studying Spanish in night school. One day mother told us about a terrible fight between Dorothy and grampa. It seems that she came home very late at night, having been on a date with her Spanish teacher, Larry Delgado. Not long after that, she married the Spanish teacher. They bought a cottage on the shore of Lake Mendota and had a daughter, Leonda. The couple divorced and years later when Dorothy's sister Edna, a school teacher in Platteville, died, there was a dispute over the inheritance of Edna's property. Around 1985, my wife Myra and I met Leonda, now a grandmother, when she was visiting her son in Virginia. Leonda said that I was the closest relative that she had on her mother's side. Leonda and I are second cousins. She is a lovely lady who has had a difficult life, and I was much impressed with her. She has become well acquainted with her father's family. It appears that Delgado was not her father's real name; he was not Hispanic at all, but had been involved in intelligence work.

CHAPTER 2

MARINETTE

While we were living in Madison, my father landed a job as principal of the Junior-Senior High School in Marinette, Wisconsin. He was fond of telling how, when he was being considered at Marinette, the superintendent of schools pointed out to the school board, which included Scandinavians, that although Mr. McNelly was Scottish, he was nevertheless competent. After living in Madison only one year we moved to Marinette in the summer of 1930.

Marinette was a town of about 13,000 souls on the south side of the mouth of the Menominee River, which emptied into Green Bay, a part of Lake Michigan. There were a little more than one thousand students in the Junior-Senior High School, which meant that one of every thirteen inhabitants of the city attended the school of which my father was principal. Next to the Marinette Junior-Senior High School stood Lourdes, the Catholic school. There was, to my knowledge, no relationship formal or informal between the public and the Catholic school; they might just as well have been on different planets. Except for one thing: the public school students were very conscious that they had fewer holidays than the Catholic kids, whose lives were made easier by saints days.

The students all walked to school in those days. Nor did individual students drive to school in their own cars. Nor did yellow busses clog traffic during rush hours. Massive "school bussing," such as we now know, came into being after the Second World War.

On the north side of the river was a city of the same size, Menominee, Michigan. It was said that in 1900, the two cities together exported more lumber than any other port in the world. When we moved to Marinette in the middle of the Great Depression, mama said it seemed that the depression had begun there several decades before, when lumber ceased to be produced in such great quantities. It was not unusual for the city and its surroundings to be clothed in smoke from nearby forest fires. Rumors, which were repeated in the press, asserted that some of the forests had been deliberately ignited by unemployed people wanting temporary jobs to put out the fires.

Diagonally across the street from our first house in Marinette was a huge red brick French Catholic Church. Evidently many of the local inhabitants were French Canadians. Probably more numerous or conspicuous in Marinette were the Swedes and the Norwegians.

The rivalry between Marinette and its neighbor, Menominee, on the other side of the river was intense. I clearly recall that everything on the Menominee side seemed to be nicer than what we had in Marinette. Each town had one large department store, but Lauerman's in Marinette was shabby and run down as compared with Lloyd's in Menominee. The Menominee High School band, with its formidable trumpet section, could play louder than our band. There seemed to be fewer forest fires and less smoke on the other side of the river, and everything there looked prettier.

One bright winter day, my father and I went ice skating on the river. The ice was very thick and deep blue in color. We skated for several miles up and down the river, and although I was a poor skater, I shall never forget the beauty of the experience.

One year, smelt, which are a small fish, began what was to become their annual run up the river to spawn. People would line up on the interstate bridge and let down square nets to pull up the fish. In a few hours they might catch a bushel of fish. Smelt is not bad tasting, and people would peddle them door to door for as cheap as three cents a pound. The smelt run was a boon to the city, and one year a Smelt Festival was held. The queen of the festival was not a great beauty, but an attractive tomboy who was an excellent ice skater. She used to play hockey with the boys on the river in the winter, something that I could not dare to do as I was not a good skater.

My father had always derided golf as a silly game of chasing a little ball around. However, on the urging of his friends on the faculty and in the Kiwanis Club, he took up the game. The Marinette golf course was beautiful. Pine trees served as the background for the greens.

Father was very fond of fishing, camping, and hunting. He designed an unusual camping trailer which was built in one of the garages at the high school. The trailer consisted of an upper and a lower half. When being pulled behind the car it was kept with the upper half lowered completely over the lower half (like a box lid). After one had parked the trailer, one would raise the top half so that the trailer was tall enough to stand up in. The top half was raised and lowered by means of a crank, cables, and pulleys. The mechanism was not easy to operate, but daddy made quite a bit of use of the trailer for his camping expeditions.

Once the family was driving on a highway with the trailer attached to the car. Another car began to pass us, but an oncoming vehicle was approaching rapidly. My father, who was a fast thinker, drove our car, with the trailer behind it, into a broad ditch on the side of the road. The trailer came unhooked but we were not hurt. The car attempting to pass us was damaged and the occupants injured. They were a doctor and a patient he was taking to the hospital. At the time that this happened we all thought that we were going to be killed. Although we never mentioned it, for a long time afterwards we would think of our close encounter with death.

At the edge of Marinette was a settlement called Minnekonnee. The families of poor fishermen lived in primitive shacks made of packing crates and scrap lumber. I never saw the inside of one of these dwellings, but they must have been very primitive and cramped, and very cold during the long Wisconsin winters. It was a depressing shanty town and I think we drove by it only two or three times at the most. One of the LaFollettes gave a campaign speech in Minnekonnee, and the view of middle-class folks was that it was not a place where any respectable politicians would go.

Wisconsin was a Republican state and whoever won the Republican nomination in the primary election was certain to win the general election. My parents were staunch Republicans. I remember that once when the La Follettes (of the progressive faction of the Republican Party) won the primary election my mother wailed, "Oh now I will have to vote for one of those terrible La Follettes!" I pointed out that she could vote for a Democrat, but that was unthinkable for her. Democratic politicians in Wisconsin were scorned as "post office Democrats," i. e., Democrats who hoped that a Democrat would be elected president and then they would get post office jobs. In 1932 when the Democratic Franklin D. Roosevelt won the presidency, Democrats won the state offices of governor, etc.

My father adamantly criticized Roosevelt and the New Deal. He equated it with fascism or communism. He made no secret of his disapproval of the National Recovery Act (NRA) and the Agricultural Adjustment Act (AAA). His view was vindicated when the Supreme Court declared this legislation unconstitutional. Nonetheless, when Franklin Roosevelt came to give a speech in Green Bay one summer, we drove to Green Bay to see the president. I don't remember hearing FDR giving a speech, but I clearly remember seeing him driven by in an open touring car. I also remember hearing some of FDR's "fireside chats" to the American people on the radio. He had a splendid speaking voice, mellifluous like that of a professional radio announcer, with a fine cultured enunciation. Other politicians, including many of his Republican critics, did not have his class. But my parents never wavered in their loyalty to the Republican Party.

BAND MUSIC

One summer, a man came from a musical instrument manufacturer to sell instruments to the school. I and the son of the superintendent of schools were given respectively, a clarinet and a cornet. John Hulten and I then took lessons in how to play from the high school band man, Clyde Russell. Russell could play any instrument in the band and was famous for his lyric tenor voice. It was said that he had once sung on WTMJ, the *Milwaukee Journal* radio station.

My clarinet was made of metal, finished to look like silver. I could read music fairly well, having been given piano lessons by my mother, and had little difficulty learning to play the clarinet passably enough to perform in the high school band. However, I rarely practiced on it. Although one of the boys in the band played vastly better than I, I was assigned first chair clarinet by Mr. Russell, possibly because my father was the school principal.

The people in Marinette were, on the whole, poor. One girl in our band played an ancient clarinet inherited from a relative. It used the Albert system of keys rather than the Boehm system, which had made the Albert system obsolete, but it was the only instrument she had. During ball games, the band sat in the bleachers, and when we had to leave temporarily it was the custom to leave our instruments on the bleachers. One day the girl returned to her seat and found that someone had apparently stepped on her clarinet. The barrel was cracked and the instrument was ruined. The owner wept because she would no longer be playing in the band.

The annual football game between Marinette and Menominee High Schools was the event that evoked the greatest sense of intercity rivalry. I played clarinet in the high school band and remember one of these games. It was bitterly cold, and there were snowflakes in the air. Between halves, we had to march on the field, and my mouth and fingers were so cold I could not play my instrument.

One summer, the Menominee high school band director needed a couple of players to fill out the Menominee Boys Band, which would play daily concerts for a week on Mackinac Island, a famous summer resort in the straits between Lake Michigan and Lake Huron. So I and a cornetist from Marinette were invited to join the Menominee band.

One night before our trip to Mackinac Island, we gave a concert at a nearby town to earn some money to help with our trip. I was in a car driven by the solo clarinetist. It was night and the road was full of curves. For a cheap thrill the driver briefly turned off the headlights. When he turned them on there was a high cliff in front of us where the road suddenly turned. If the driver had not turned on the lights when he did we would have crashed into the cliff.

After some rehearsals, we took a bus to Mackinaw City. There was (and still is) no bridge to the island and I remember first seeing the Grand Hotel from the ferry. The unusually long building was white, about five storeys high with a porch with columns three stories high that extended the entire length of the imposing structure. Automobiles were banned from the island; transportation was by bicycle or horse-drawn wagons.

We performed every day in a sunny park and lived in a local hotel. We ate our meals in a side room of a restaurant. The food was not very good, and after formal complaints had been registered, it improved. To make pocket money, several senior members of the band organized a dance orchestra. I was amazed how the pianist and the others seemed to be able play anything without using any printed music. Our solo clarinetist played skillfully, but I was scandalized by his wide vibrato, which made the clarinet sound something like a saxophone.

The band director had an old friend in Sault Ste. Marie, Michigan, famous for its locks connecting Lake Huron and Lake Superior. The friend owned a large hotel and invited the band for a visit following our performances on Mackinac Island. We slept in the annex of the hotel. We gave a concert in Sault Ste. Marie as a return gesture. Some of us went hiking in the woods near the city and walked across a railroad bridge, entering Canada without at first realizing it. There was a tricky place on the bridge where one had to dangle by his hands over the river. The band leader was briefly terrified that one of us might fall in the river.

The camaraderie among the boys in the band was very strong. We thoroughly enjoyed our congeniality. We were all white American middle-class boys bound by a common interest in music and we thought we were about as fine as human beings could be.

Two melodies our band played have clung ineradicably in my memory for over sixty years, and I recently tried to identify them. I stumbled on to one of the tunes in an anthology of songs (Hugo Frey, ed., *Robbins Mammoth Collection of World Famous Songs* [New York: Robbins Music Corporation, 1937], p.146-147). I associated the melody with the words "Moonlight Madonna." The lyrics by Howard Johnson in my song book do not include these words but bear the title "You're My Poem of Love." A search in the Internet discloses that the author of the melody, Zdenek Fibich (1850-1900) was a leading Czech composer. With lyrics by Paul Francis Webster, the melody was published in 1933 under the title "My Moonlight Madonna" and became quite popular. I have located the original piano version of this melody by Fibich, entitled "Poème aus der Idylle 'Ein Sommerabend,'" in the key of B flat major. It is printed in Germany by B. Schott's Söhne of Mainz, copyright 1950.

The other memorable melody was that of "In a Monastery Garden," A Google search informs me that its composer was Albert Ketèlbey (1875-1959), an Englishman who also composed "In a Persian Market." In 1999, Bosworth (of London) published *Ketèlbey Classics for Piano*, which includes the above cited pieces with editorial comment.

It is a source of wonderment to me that the human mind is able, with no conscious effort, to cling so tenaciously to a piece of music. Of course individual taste, social structure, and technology largely determine what one listens to, and the intrinsic characteristics of a piece of music—the product of a composer's inspiration, largely determine its memorability. Contemporary music often seems to lack discernable melodies and understandable lyrics. One of the finest concerts I have ever heard was given in an assembly program in the Marinette High School auditorium by the eighty-five voice a cappella choir of the Oconto Senior High School. (Oconto is a city not far from Marinette.) The choir had performed for the Wisconsin State Teachers Convention and had become justly famous. I had not thought it possible for human voices to sing such elaborate and difficult music with such beauty.

THE TENT COLONY AND THE MUSIC CLINIC

During the year that we were living in Madison, daddy had enrolled in the University of Wisconsin to earn a Master's degree in education. After we moved to Marinette, once we all went to Madison to be with daddy, who attended the summer session at the university. But we did not live in a house, but in the tent colony.

The McNelly Family, About 1932
From the left: Father holding onto John, Lucille holding onto Jimmy, Teddy,
mother (In front of Grampa Taylor's house, Madison, Wisconsin)

The university tent colony was located on a wooded hillside along the shore of Lake Mendota, near Picnic Point. Permanent wooden platforms had been erected in the woods, on which the summer school students could pitch their tents. Occasionally attached to the tent would be a shack made of construction paper over a wooden frame. The tents were provided with electricity, but there was no indoor plumbing. There were public restrooms with showers scattered about. There was one building open at the sides which were screened that served as a place for students to study. Just about every evening my father would go there to study and write his papers. (The university tent colony no longer exists, apparently a victim of contemporary affluence.)

We children really liked the tent colony. We could go swimming any time we wanted in the lake. A neighbor girl whose family regularly came to the tent colony made and sold home-made ice cream that was grainier than the store-bought variety but tasted just as good. Life in the tent, I fear, was less pleasant for my mother, who had to cook and do the laundry under primitive conditions. I wore white duck trousers (*de rigueur* in my set) to the music clinic every day, and they were a burden for her to keep washed and pressed.

While we were living in the tent colony, I was admitted to the band of the All-State High School Music Clinic. This enterprise, sponsored by the university, lasted three weeks each summer, and the members of the band and orchestra were recruited from among students in Wisconsin high schools. Every morning as the sun gleamed through the trees I would ride with my father to the clinic sessions at the university and would return to the tent colony with him in the evening.

I was one of the poorest players in the clarinet section and was assigned to the third row. During sectional rehearsals we were each required to play scales. Whenever my turn came I was frozen with panic and unable to remember to play the B flat in the F major scale. I was assigned to the last chair in the third (last) row of clarinets, a distinction I repeatedly earned and eminently deserved. One day a girl came to class late and as punishment was demoted to the last chair in the section, so I was moved up one chair. She was very upset by this and asked if I would change chairs with her because she had played last chair clarinet the summer before. When the band picture was to be taken she did not wish again to be sitting in the last seat in the clarinet section. I was mean and said no. As a result, I played fifty-first chair in the clarinet section consisting of fifty-two musicians. Because the band included over a hundred players, I doubt if many people could discern from the photograph that my disappointed friend was sitting in the last chair.

The experience at the Music Clinic did not necessarily improve my skill as a clarinetist. At the clinic I was told to use stiffer reeds for my instrument. I had not had any private lessons on the instrument since the first few months that I had first owned it, and after being told to use stiffer reeds I was never properly instructed how to trim them and to control my breath. As a result, the instrument became hard to blow and I did not enjoy playing it. I rarely practiced at home on it; and although I continued to play in the high school band, I never progressed beyond a low plateau.

The first time that my father took his comprehensive examination for his M.A. he failed it. This was of course a tremendous disappointment, and there were rumors of a quota requiring that every year a certain percentage of the candidates would be failed. On his second effort, a year later, daddy passed the examination. His M.A. thesis, which cousin Dorothy typed for him and which I have found on file at the university, described a survey concerning a problem in education. He had sent questionnaires to school administrators which they returned to him and he analyzed.

Late in 1932, when it became known that Mr. Hulten, the superintendent of schools, would leave Marinette to accept a position elsewhere, my father earnestly hoped that he would be promoted to superintendent. It was a great disappointment when Mr. G. E. Denman, who had a doctorate in education, was appointed to the position, beginning January 1933. (Daddy was awarded his Master of Philosophy degree in education on October 11, 1933.) The new superintendent was a good sport, and even though he was not used to hunting, joined my father and his friends on a camping trip.

SCHOOL

I was a disappointment to my father as I had no interest at all in athletics. I turned down his invitations to go fishing, which I regarded as boring. Sometimes when I was with him and we met a friend or acquaintance, he would comment on my frailness and my need to gain weight in order to amount to something. My mother said I looked peaked, and concerned about my health, my parents required me to play in junior high football. This proved to be a terrifying experience. Mr. Exworthy, the unathletic geography teacher who seemed to know nothing about the game, coached us in tackling practice. This was before face masks. I was supposed to throw myself headfirst into the legs of the guy running in front of me and I was sure that my teeth would be knocked out. I could scarcely wait for the end of the football season.

I decided to participate in an oratorical contest to be presented in the auditorium. Miss Gretchen Laird, who was in charge, gave me a speech to memorize. As I recall it was "Merchants of Death," about how munitions manufacturers conspired to bring about wars in order to enrich themselves. This pacifist theme was then popular, as perhaps most Americans believed that it had been a mistake for the United States to become involved in the World War (i.e., World War I).

Being the school principal, my father happened to be one of the judges of the contest. A much older boy won first place. I got second place. But it was extremely clear to me that my father was genuinely impressed with my performance, and he seemed to respect me more after that.

I learn from old year books that the home room system applied at Marinette, and that each home room consisted entirely of students of only one sex. The home rooms were organized to facilitate group activities. My sister was elected as one of the two presidents of her home room.

LIFE IN MARINETTE

The constellation of my friends varied from grade to grade. Charles Cohen, lived across the street, went to the Presbyterian Church, and played the trumpet. Morris Mundt played in the band and we discussed becoming civil engineers. engineers. Warren Mullen played the baritone horn and told of student pranks at the university his brother attended. Gene Farnsworth was a bright and lovely girl descended from a famous fur trader who had married an Indian princess. Although I always made the honor roll, I could get nowhere with my clumsy efforts to impress the beauteous Eleanor Kopischke, the star pupil in my first-year Latin class.

I recall two great scandals. One was the divorce of the band man at Menominee High School (the band man under whom I had played). People would tut-tut and express great shock that this man who was prominent on both sides of the river, had gotten a divorce. Divorce in those days was regarded as disastrous and scandalous.

The other great scandal involved our pastor. Because there was no Presbyterian Church in Marinette, we went to the Congregational Church, which my mother regarded as the next best thing. The church building was a huge wooden structure painted white. Many of the town's leading citizens belonged to this church. My father was made a trustee, although he rarely, if ever, attended services as he preferred to go hunting or fishing on weekends. My mother directed the choir, and occasionally the minister dropped by the house to drive her to the church. He wore his oily hair closely slicked back over his head, and he sometimes led the singing in our Sunday School. He had a lusty voice and we sang tunes like "Brighten the Corner Where You Are."

His daughter, who seemed sexy for her age, had been in my sixth grade class, and a friend had a very strong crush on her. One day a prominent girl student in the high school was missing. Truancy was taken seriously, and she was discovered at Lloyd's Theater in Menominee with the minister's son. This is all I know about the scandal, but it was regarded as sufficiently serious that the minister had to resign his post, and he and his family left town in disgrace.

To earn pin money, mother usually had one or two students to whom she taught piano or voice. One of her students gave her bicycle to me. I loved riding the bike with Charles Cohen, a neighbor friend, but was always embarrassed by the fact that my bike was a *girl's bike*. One day the bike disappeared from our house, but I was not greatly disturbed by this because of my ambivalent feelings about the vehicle. The consensus was that it had probably been stolen by some neighbors who had a shack in their back yard where they were believed to repaint stolen bicycles. The family was large and poor. The father once ran for the office of country registrar of deeds. The principal argument printed on his fliers was that he had a large family and badly needed the job.

I remember an argument that we once had in a class at school. One student said that it was all right for poor people to steal from the rich. This seemed to be the view of a substantial minority in the class.

My father was an ardent admirer of Theodore Roosevelt, after whom he named me. Roosevelt was a great sportsman and it was this that probably appealed to father. We had a set of something like twenty volumes (filling two shelves) of the complete works of Theodore Roosevelt. I found Roosevelt's letters to his children charming to read. We also had a set of the *World Book Encyclopedia*, given to my father when he had lost his Lancaster job and someone was trying to recruit him to sell the encyclopedia. Without television to distract us, we children loved to browse through the volumes, which had lots of good pictures.

When we moved from Lancaster to Madison, my father sold our house in Lancaster. When we lived in Marinette, we never bought a house because the rent was so cheap. After moving from the house near Garfield school, we lived in a bungalow that badly needed painting, but the cost of painting it was prohibitive for the owner as we were paying only $35 a month rent. At the end of the living room was a flight of stairs going up to the second floor. To save on coal bills, my father hung a large rug over the stairs to prevent heat from going upstairs. (It was thought that because we were sleeping under heavy blankets, it was not necessary to heat the upstairs.) Water was heated by a device connected with the furnace. This meant that we did not have running hot water in the summer, which in Marinette was short.

An art dealer who had displayed his wares at the high school had given my father a framed print of a painting called "Avenue of Trees." It hang in the living room, and to make conversation, some visitors would observe that no matter from what angle you looked at the picture you were still looking straight down the road. The painter, I now understand, was Meindert Hobbema, 1638-1709. (See Rockwell Kent, ed., *World-Famous Paintings* [New York: Wise, 1939], plate 32.)

Marinette is not far from the Land of Lakes. Lake Noqueby was newly opened for development. A boy scout camp, consisting of rudimentary cabins, was set up on the shore, and one summer I was sent to that camp. It was an enjoyable experience for me, a tenderfoot. When sides were being chosen to play baseball, I was usually the last person chosen, as I was no good at the game. We did many interesting things, including an all-day canoe hike with cold fried egg sandwiches for lunch. We had a "snipe hunt," which was actually a trick the senior boys played on the uninitiated. They would leave the unsuspecting victim to wait in one spot in the woods until fairly late at night to spot snipes and let the others know when they saw the bird. The older boys would then be partying somewhere else.

One of the requirements was to learn signaling. Most of the tenderfoots chose to learn semaphore, which required two flags. I was alone in opting wigwag using the Morse code, which could be transmitted by the use of only one flag. Dots were indicated by waving the flag to one side and dashes indicated by waving the flag to the other side. The Morse code could be used in telegraphy or by flashing lights. It seemed more useful than semaphore. Later, I practiced it with the man who lived behind us, who also new Morse code.

We had a stunt night. I earned a music badge to wear on my belt for playing "I'm Forever Blowing Bubbles" on an ocarina. The instrument emits a plaintive tone that I enhanced with a vibrato. In a skit given by some of the boys, one boy held a pistol against the face of another boy and fired. The victim cried out in pain that he could not see and was sent to the doctor. The evening was pretty well ruined. Later we learned that the gun had been loaded with a blank cartridge, but it was held so close against the victim that it had temporarily blinded him.

Every morning a bugle awakened us at six. We would run into the lake completely naked for our morning dip. There was a cottage next to the camp that my father rented for several days, so that my family was living in the cottage. The scout master then announced that all of us would have to wear swim suits because Buddy Donaldson's girl (Lucille) had moved in next door.

The Sunday afternoon drive became a strong tradition in the family. Sometimes we would drive quite a distance, and the children would sleep on the way home. In those days, there were no seat belts, and the front seat consisted of a single bench so that three people could sit easily in the front, and three in the back, accommodating our family of six perfectly. Today bench seats are no longer in style, possibly because middle-class families are smaller than they used to be.

During our drives, it was daddy's invariable custom as a one-time farmer to comment on the progress of the farmer's crops. Sometimes daddy would say that we would have to speed up to get home before we would run out of gas.

I became interested in astronomy and read a number of books on the topic from the city library. The library was located near the interstate bridge and like the church was a reasonable walking distance from home.

The Century of Progress Exposition, a World's Fair, was held in Chicago in 1933-1934. An arrangement was made whereby high school children might reside and eat at University of Chicago dormitories to attend the fair. My parents signed me up for this program, and took me to the railroad station to see me off. They gave me $3.00, which was a lot of money for me, to use during the three or four days at the fair. On the train to Chicago I was accompanied by a classmate who entertained me with lore about roller coasters. The meals in the gothic dormitory were elegant. Each day one took an electric train to and from the fair. I found the exhibits interesting, but never stumbled onto Sally Rand's famous fan dance. By the last full day I had run out of money and just hung around the dormitory.

FATHER

My brother John recalls that by 1935, father began suffering badly from rheumatism. Daddy said that he didn't think he had long to live—a statement that disturbed John.

We children all got the mumps, one after the other. In those days if there was chicken pox, mumps, or measles in a home, the house was quarantined. A conspicuous sign was posted on the door warning people not to enter the house. My father had never had mumps as a child, was not immune, and became sick with the rest of us.

After that experience, my father seemed pale and sickly and it was decided that he would need an operation on his gall bladder. The surgeon was a prominent individual in the city who had studied medicine in Germany. I noticed that just before going to the hospital daddy told mother where his valuable papers were located. I took this as a bad sign.

After daddy's gall stones were removed, it was decided to remove his appendix as well. Something went wrong and he died on June 27, 1935. By strange coincidence my father's death followed by one week that of our next door neighbor, a popular young lawyer. Our families were friends, and they had a son about my age. After these deaths, both of the bereaved families moved to Madison.

The yearbook of the Marinette High School class of 1936 contained the following obituary

IN MEMORIAM
Stephen Sumner McNelly
Born September 30, 1885
Died June 27, 1935
OUR PRINCIPAL
FRIEND AND ADVISOR
1930-1935

The overcoming of handicaps, problems, and obstacles featured his
entire life. Patience and perseverance characterized his dealings with those
whom it was his privilege to guide and direct. *[sic]*

In his untimely passing the Class of 1936 lost a true friend and wise
counselor. Even though we were the denied the benefit of his wise guidance
during our Senior Year, we will always remember with benefit to ourselves
the courteous and friendly patience which so often assisted us, individually
and as a class, over our many difficulties.

I have quoted this memorial, in spite of an apparently infelicitous rhetorical lapse, as it suggests that my father had projected to some people that he had had much difficulty in overcoming his handicaps, but that his earnestness and persistence were highly appreciated. Although he could speak and write eloquently—he had directed the high school debate team in Lancaster, Wisconsin—his blunt manner of speech sometimes betrayed his background of rural poverty.

My father's effectiveness as a school administer stemmed from his strength of character. He was always completely honest with people. He was a strict disciplinarian, but this was accepted because he projected affection and sympathy towards those he disciplined. He was athletically talented, inspiring respect, and occasionally, a wholesome fear among rowdies. He was not interested in church at all. More than once he stated his ideal to me: to make the world a better place. My father did just that. In the cynical world we live in today, not many people seem to aspire sincerely to this ideal.

I must add that my father was a happy, outgoing individual. He certainly did not regard himself as "handicapped," and took joy in his athleticism and friendships. He was an active Kiwanian. His suits were made by one of the town's leading tailors. I am not aware that he had enemies in Marinette or that he held grudges. He loved and took pride in his family, and we all enjoyed our activities as a group. His closest friends, with whom he went hunting and camping, included Lee O'Leary, one of the athletic coaches, who also taught science and citizenship and had previously been on the faculty in Lancaster, and Karl Evert, head of the science department. Several times our family went on outings with the family of Stafford Byrum, the assistant principal.

As he had been in poor health, daddy's death was not a complete surprise to the family, but he was only 49 years old at the time. The first page of the *Marinette Eagle* for June 27, 1935, carried a portrait of my father and the headlines "S.S. M'NELLY PASSES AWAY EARLY TODAY: Local Educator Fails to Survive After Operation; Rites Saturday." The article stated that his condition was not regarded as serious and "his death was unexpected and a shock to the community."

A Masonic memorial service was held in Marinette on the morning of July 1, and that afternoon, after the body had been taken to Madison, a memorial service was conducted under the auspices of the Masonic Lodge of Lancaster. A family friend drove us to Madison, Wisconsin, where my father was buried in Forest Hill cemetery. As we drove into Madison, I was impressed by the beauty of the city, where the greenery of the trees arched over the streets, in contrast to the drabness of Marinette.

There were four children in the family; I, then only fifteen, was the oldest. This was before social security had taken effect. It was out of the question that our middle-class family would go on welfare, whatever that was in those days. My mother immediately announced that we would move to Madison and live with grampa and gramma.

I had spent the sixth grade in the grade school, and the seventh, eighth, ninth, and tenth grades in Marinette Jr.-Sr. High School—a total of five years in Marinette Thus in 1935 the McNelly family, consisting of my mother and four school children, all moved to Madison to live with gramma and grampa Taylor. Grampa Taylor was retired and almost 73 years old.

For several years afterwards I had a recurring dream that I saw daddy walking in the street. I had inherited from him his beautifully tailored gray plaid overcoat, and sometimes wore it. It made me uncomfortable to be wearing his clothes, but we had to economize and it was a much better garment than we could afford to buy. After my father had been dead for two years, I attended a lecture in the auditorium at Bascom Hall at the university. As the coat was too bulky to keep at my seat, I put it with the pile of other students' coats on the front of the stage. At the end of the class, when students went to retrieve their coats, my father's elegant coat was missing. I did not make a serious effort to find it, and my mother did not press the issue.

In the 1990s, after my retirement as a professor of political science, I became acquainted with Professor Howard Penniman of Georgetown University, a leading authority on comparative electoral systems. He told me that while he was a student in Lancaster, Wisconsin, he had participated in the debating team coached by my father. I also learned that my mother, during her long widowhood in Madison, had become friendly at church with Howard's sister, Clara Penniman, an authority in public administration who for a while chaired the Department of Political Science at the University of Wisconsin.

(One of my wife's forty-nine first cousins is Marinette Jordan (née Wieland), who as a child lived on a farm outside of Lancaster and is a longtime friend of Myra. I too, of course, was a Lancastrian but also was a former resident of Marinette, Wisconsin. In 2001, Marinette Wieland Jordan and her husband Jack, who traveled a great deal, made a special trip to investigate Marinette, Wisconsin, and gave Myra and me a fascinating booklet about Queen Marinette, the canny half-Indian half-French wife of a fur trader. (See Beverly Hayward Johnson, *Queen Marinette: Spirit of Survival on the Great Lakes Frontier* [Amasa, Michigan: White Water Associates, Inc., 1995].) It was from this remarkable woman that the city of Marinette got its name. A popular girl in my class in Marinette, Gene Farnsworth, was said to have descended from a famous fur trader named Farnsworth, who reportedly married Indian princesses. A princess involved was Marie Chevalier, who was half Indian, half French, and famous as Queen Marinette. Queen Marinette and William Farnsworth bore three children. Marie Antoinette Chevalier, Queen Marinette's paternal grandmother, was called Marinette.

The origin of Marinette Wieland's given name is a mystery.

My Marinette friend, Gene Farnsworth, married Eldon Mueller in 1942, had two children, and died in Madison, Wisconsin, in 2002 [Madison *Capital Times,* April 26, 2002].)

CHAPTER 3

MADISON

In the summer of 1935, the bereaved McNelly family briefly lived with grampa and gramma Taylor in grampa's lovely home on 1727 Regent Street. After several weeks, the McNellys and Taylors moved to an old house grampa owned at 1716 Jefferson Street. The Jefferson Street place was a large Victorian frame structure with a porch that wrapped around the entire front (the southeast side) and part of the southwest side of the house. Towards the rear and on the southwest side of the house there was an additional porch accessible to the kitchen (the "kitchen porch"). On the back northwest corner of the house was a small third porch that had been enclosed and served for storage. (I must confess that when I was actually living in this house, I was not particularly conscious of the points of the compass that I have here been referring to.)

The Jefferson Street House
(The "George Nielson/Ralph and Amy Vernon House")
1716 Jefferson Street, Madison, Wisconsin

The front door of the house was at the northern end of the front porch and led into a hall, at the right side of which was a stairway leading to the second floor. On the left side of the hall was a door that opened to the front parlor. The door at the far end of the hall led into the dining room. On the southwest side of the wrap-around porch was a second door, facing front, which opened to our living room. Large wooden sliding panels could separate the living room from the dining room, but these panels were normally kept open. In one corner of the living room was an ancient gas fireplace, but the gas had long since been sealed off as a safety measure. The ancient fixtures on the ceilings of the living and dining rooms had once provided gas lighting, but had been converted for electric lights. Sliding panels could be used to separate the living room from the front parlor. For a while, the front parlor served as my grandparents room, but at some point they moved their beds to one of the upstairs bedrooms.

The kitchen in the back part of the house was quite large. A door on one side led to the kitchen porch, another led to the dining room, another opened on a large bathroom, and another opened to the enclosed back porch. Finally there was a door opening to the dark narrow back stairs that wound their way to the second floor. At the top of the stairs a door opened to the small back bedroom and another door to the upstairs hall. These back stairs were a perennial source of delight to children, who liked to climb these stairs, run through the upstairs hall, and down the front stairs, then back again to the kitchen and the back stairs. For some years the back bedroom was my preserve.

As I recall there were, including the back bedroom, four bedrooms on the second floor. A stairs led to a full attic. This attic was spacious and had full sized windows on the front and sides, and could have been finished off to serve as a roomy third floor, but this had never been done. Instead, we used the attic to store unused furniture, my grandfather's many old books, bedsteads, mattresses, and other effects from our two families.

For example, the attic contained mementos brought back from grampa's missionary days in Japan, including native costumes in which we children might pose for photographs. Also I once found in a trunk a small nickel-plated revolver that allegedly had been used during the Boxer Rebellion by Edwin Hurd Conger. Conger had been my grandmother's first cousin, who after serving as a congressman from Iowa, became the American minister to China during the Chinese uprising in 1899-1900. I would have liked to include that little revolver with its historic associations in my own collection of orientalia, but no one knows what happened to it.

The Jefferson Street house, called the "George Nielson/Ralph and Amy Vernon House," is pictured and described in a pamphlet issued by a preservation society as it is one of the older houses in the city of Madison. We learn that George Nielson was a carpenter-contractor when he built "this fine Queen Anne style house in Wingra Park in 1892 as a speculative adventure." (Timothy F. Heggland, *The Greenbush-Vilas Neighborhood: A Walking Tour* [Madison, Wisconsin: Madison Landmarks Commission and the Brittingham-Vilas Neighborhood Association, 1991], page 22.)

The Jefferson Street house was only four blocks from Vilas Park and Lake Wingra, where in the summer we could go swimming, see the zoo, hear Sunday band concerts, see fireworks on the Fourth of July, and, in the winter, ice skate. Our house was three blocks from Monroe Street, a principal thoroughfare where there were bus stops and stores and where my grandfather every few days would go shopping.

Grampa would study the grocery ads in the newspaper comparing prices and so on and would then walk to Monroe street pulling a children's red wagon, which he used to carry groceries. Sometimes one of his grandchildren would tag along. To save money he would occasionally negotiate to buy entire boxes of canned food that we could store in the basement.

Grampa at one time had owned a Chevrolet, but he had not driven for many years and when we lived with him, he did not have a car. When the family moved to Madison we advertised our pretty red Pontiac for sale in Madison. Our asking price was $250, but we settled for $225. The family did not feel greatly handicapped for being carless. Grampa had long since given up driving, gramma did not drive, my mother and the children did not drive. The schools, Randall, West High, and the state university, were within walking distance. So were our church and the shops on Monroe Street. The bus system was reliable and cheap so that to go downtown we would just hop on a bus on Monroe Street.

We children, who had to get up early for school, ate our meals together in the large kitchen. Normally the evening meal, dinner, was eaten in the dining room. Grampa refrained from coffee as he did from alcohol, and usually drank hot water, into which he put some sugar and cream. Formal dinners were anteceded by grace. Birthdays were celebrated with ice cream eaten with soda crackers. (The ice box was not cold enough to preserve ice cream, so someone had to buy it at a nearby drug store just before we ate it. I would have preferred cookies rather than soda crackers, but we never bought cookies and mother seldom made them.) Gramma Taylor sometimes helped Lucille or mama with the dishes, although as her eyes became weaker she occasionally missed a spot or two.

The size of the house made it possible for our grandparents to have privacy for themselves when they wanted it. I cannot recall problems involved with sharing the single bathroom upstairs, but of course the large bathroom attached to the kitchen must have helped.

Mother did the laundry in the basement, where there was a tub supplemented with a hand wringer and a washboard. Laundry was hung out to dry in the back yard. To heat the house in winter, we had a coal-burning furnace. The coal had to be shoveled from the coal bin to the furnace. If one was neglectful, the fire might go out and one would be faced with the extra effort of restarting the furnace. Coal was delivered by a truck that would drive next to a window over the coal bin, and the coal would be fed onto a shoot that carried the coal through the window into the bin. As may be imagined, bits of coal and coal dust made it impossible to keep the basement clean.

Winters in Wisconsin are cold, long, and snowy. Although one might experience here and there a really hot day in the summer, on the whole the summers are lovely, and it is then that one wants to be in Wisconsin. The summer school at the University of Wisconsin, whose campus embraces much of the southern shore of Lake Mendota, owes much of its attraction to the climate. Students may walk out of their dormitories in their swimsuits to the beach. Madison, of course, is bounded by three lakes: Mendota, Monona, and Wingra. Downtown Madison, including the state capitol, is located on an isthmus between Lakes Mendota and Monona. The lakes are connected with one another and several other bodies of water by streams and locks.

GRANDPARENTS

Once every few weeks, gramma and grampa would take the bus to the library downtown and draw out books. Gramma would read Thackeray or Hemingway, which she would discuss with friends in her book club or bridge club. Grampa would get books on foreign policy.

Gramma was a very quiet person, quite the opposite of her husband, who strongly expressed his views on moral and political topics. I picture her seated on her low armless Queen Anne chair, rapping her fingers on the side of the seat. Gramma did not seem to interact with the rest of us much beyond helping with the dishes. She had had a genteel background. She would frequently comment that she could see no advantage of having "modern conveniences," such as electric vacuum cleaners, and the like, because in her day they had servants who did the work. When we took rides and looked at newly built houses, she would say she wondered how people could live in such small houses. When she was a little girl, she wanted to milk a cow, but was warned that if she learned to milk cows she would end up milking cows for the rest of her life.

She was very conscious of her connection to the Galesburg Gales, her mother being a daughter of George Washington Gale, the founder of Knox College and Galesburg, Illinois. Through her father, Professor Edwin Lucius Hurd, she was a descendant of three *Mayflower* passengers, William White, White's wife, Susanna, and his son, Resolved. She was also a descendant of Thomas Seldon, a founding father of Hartford, Connecticut, in the early 1600s. The Gales, Seldons, and the Ferris-wheel Ferrises had intermarried to constitute the local gentry of their corner of Illinois. (The great Ferris wheel, which could accommodate up to 1440 riders at the Chicago World's fair in 1893, had been designed by George Washington Gale Ferris [1850-1896] an engineer in Galesburg, Illinois. Gramma would sometimes mention Zona Gale, the authoress and member of the Board of Regents of the University of Wisconsin. I had gotten the impression that Zona was related to the Galesburg, Illinois, Gales, but my researches have not yet disclosed such a connection. Zona was born in Portage, Wisconsin.)

Gramma liked to play bridge with her friends, and, perhaps as customary among the wives of clergymen, was a member of the local chapter of the WCTU (Women's Christian Temperance Union). Grampa did not approve of cards, which he associated with gambling, but was available for checkers or dominoes, and we played with him occasionally.

One day we children were told that gramma had suffered some kind of breakdown although we children were unaware of any of her symptoms. A doctor advised that she be taken to some institution for care (perhaps it was a nursing home). My grandfather took her to the place recommended, but gramma was so repelled by what she saw that she insisted on going back home where she would be with her husband, daughter, and the rest of us. The subject of gramma's breakdown never arose again, but during the last few years of her life she was an invalid.

A principal cause of discord within families is often said to be disputes over money. But I cannot recall any financial disputes. Before my father had died, we children did not receive allowances, and we certainly did not expect any later. My strong impression is that in those days only a minority of children received allowances. Because of the depression, the general tendency even among children was to be grateful if one had adequate food, clothing, and shelter. The fathers of some of our friends were unemployed, and we wondered how they were able to manage.

My father had died intestate, and I have no idea how much money he left. After my father had sold our Lancaster house he was receiving monthly payments on the mortgage. I do not know when the payments stopped coming. My mother sometimes complained that in order to get the money from time to time she had to apply to a judge and explain what the money was to be used for. According to Lucille, my father left little other than teacher's insurance. At some point, my mothers cousins in Texas, retired school teachers, sent my mother a substantial gift of money. Of course grampa Taylor had retired comfortably off, being the owner of three houses and a bit of land in the country.

Although we children thought of ourselves as poor compared to some families, we were never in want. We could take it for granted that mama or grampa always had the money needed for food and clothes and doctors and dentists. We were aware also of the many advantages we enjoyed from simply residing in the west side of the best city in the state of Wisconsin.

I remember when I got my first pair of rimless glasses. I had them only one or two days when, without thinking, I pulled my sweater over my head without first removing the glasses. Both of the lenses were broken. I felt dreadful and expected my mother to give me a severe dressing down. She did not. She accepted the incident as if it had been a completely unlucky accident. She was very fair.

CHURCH

While we were in high school and the university, Lucille and I both sang in the choir that my mother directed at Westminster Presbyterian Church. The church, on Monroe Street, was only three blocks from the Jefferson Street house. We were also active in the Young People's Society. This neighborhood church was much more accessible than the much larger Christ Presbyterian Church, which was located in downtown Madison near the capitol. Since we did not have a car, the neighborhood church made sense.

For several years I attended a Sunday School class for boys conducted by Mr. Artman, a prominent man in the church who sold insurance. There were eight to ten of us high school boys in the class. We never discussed religion or the Bible, but just chatted about sports or other goings on at West High. Although the Sunday class itself struck me as a waste of time, occasionally we had midweek meetings at somebody's house, where again we would just gossip or listen to a crime show on the radio. I sang at the funeral of one of Mr.Artman's daughters, and his daughter Eleanor attended music school at the University of Wisconsin about the same time that I did and sometimes she played the organ at our church. (Later Eleanor taught in Dearborn, Michigan, in the same school where my future wife Myra taught.)

While I was attending the music school at the university, I was able to improve my piano playing to the point that I could play four-part hymns. I volunteered to play the piano for the Sunday School. I also briefly taught a class of little boys. One of the lessons concerned the opening up of the Red Sea when Moses and his followers were fleeing from Egypt. One of the children insisted that he did not believe this story. I cannot remember how I responded to the little boy, but after class I resigned from my involvement with the Sunday School.

My sister was less than a year and a half younger than I. As a result, we went to the same schools, including for a while, the School of Music at the University of Wisconsin. We both attended the meetings of the Young People's Society at Westminster Presbyterian Church, and sang in the church choir. (Lucille was a contralto, and sang the important role of Lady Jane in Gilbert and Sullivan's *Patience*, when it was performed at Madison West.) When I began attending the university I did not participate in the activities of the "Pres House" (the Presbyterian Student Center), an elegant Gothic building that adjoined the campus. It was more convenient for me to continue at Westminster.

The young people's society met every Sunday night. We would have a "hot dish supper," a casserole contributed by someone's mother. We would meet in the church basement or in somebody's house, often the pastor's house. Mrs. Kuhnert, the pastor's wife, took a great interest in us and tried to encourage a romance between me and one of the girls.

Sometimes we would have a speaker. Once it was a Negro student from the University who told us how he felt being a Negro in white society. Another time, a man who worked at the Forest Product Laboratory told about how his expertise led to the arrest of Bruno Richard Hauptman, the convicted kidnapper and murderer of the Lindbergh baby. After a formal meeting we might listen to a Sunday night show on the radio or play monopoly.

Attendance would range from as few as six or seven to as many as twenty. One evening a pair of tall handsome girls, dressed identically in red dresses, joined our group. They were Jeanne and Jacqueline Sweet. We soon learned that although their mother referred to them as "the twins" actually they were about a year apart in age, Jacqueline being the younger. They had rather different personalities. Their brother, Elliot, was a few years younger than his sisters. The three Sweets all became active in the young people society, Jacqueline and Elliot sang in the choir. Lucille and I found the Sweets very interesting and congenial. The Sweet girls sometimes came to our house, and the girls would dance together.

I dated Jackie a few times. She liked boys who were substantially older than herself, and ultimately married a Ph.D. student of a professor Glenn Koehler, whose daughter, Myra, became my wife in 1960. (The Hegbars adopted two children. At one time Jackie was completely blind for weeks, awaiting a cornea transplant. The Hegbars divorced, and Jackie died in the 1990s. During the war when I was visiting Madison, I had a movie date with Jean.)

I especially remember Sunday nights after our young people's meeting, washing dishes at the Sweet house while listening to the Jack Benny show, depicting the comic adventures of that famous tightwad, and the Bing Crosby show.

The young people's society was more popular among girls than among the boys. This worked to my advantage, because I did not have much competition in attracting the interest of the girls.

Lucille was a much better pianist than I. She was not particularly interested in classical music and shared with me a dislike for practicing scales. She could read popular music readily. Sometimes friends of hers who also played the piano came to visit and the girls would take turns playing popular tunes. None of them played by ear.

One of Lucille's friends, Sondra, an attractive blond—I have changed the name here—also played the piano and one summer she and Lucille spent a lot of time together on the beach at Lake Wingra, hoping to make the acquaintance of boys. Later my sister became cool towards Sondra, and Sondra stopped coming around to our house. There was a rumor that Sondra had "gone the limit." One New Years I made a double date to go to a movie with Sondra. After that my mother said that I should not go with Sondra because it would hurt Lucille's reputation.

Lucille was an attractive and lively girl who had no problem about catching the attention of the boys. Once, several years after moving to Madison while she was attending the university, a boy from a wealthy Marinette family dated Lucille. He did not ask for a second date. My sister speculated that he did not date her again because she had let him kiss her on the first date.

At least three of the boys in my Sunday school class dated her at one time or another. A new boy joined our church group. His father had been a band man at a high school in the state, but had lost his job and the family was now living near us in Madison. I liked the boy, who was working at a filling station, and several times he dated Lucille. One night he came to the house to pick up Lucille for a date as they had previously arranged. But Lucille said that she did not want to go out with him that night. He was very hurt by this and I thought she was behaving atrociously. Her purpose, however, was to be sure to be at home on the chance that Charles Oakey would call her up.

Charles was in my Sunday School class and would occasionally call up Lucille on the spur of the moment to see her. He was a second-string player in the West High basketball team, and members of the class would occasionally discuss Charles's performance on the court. Lucille really liked Charles. They married in 1942.

In Madison, I sometimes mowed lawns for several of the neighbors and the money I got I could use as I pleased. I got fifty cents for each time I mowed Mrs. Jones' lawn. After six mowings, I took my earnings to the bookstore and bought a dictionary entirely in French, *Le Nouveau Petit Larousse*. This purchase symbolized the level of my competence in the language and the seriousness of my commitment to French studies.

One summer, a man in our church who was connected with the FBI hired a number of boys more or less informally to work for his agency for several weeks. As I understood it, the local FBI had not used up all of its yearly appropriation, and to ensure that its appropriation for the following year not be reduced, it needed to spend some money immediately. About ten or twelve boys then were hired to destroy marijuana. In that part of the Wisconsin marijuana was growing wild in farmers' fields. It was called "Indian hemp" by the farmers, and its quality as a recreational drug was not widely understood.

The boys were divided into two or three groups. Each group would ride in a car driven by one of the boys. The cars as a group would randomly drive about the countryside keeping their eyes open for the plant, whose distinctive leaves were identifiable from the road. There was one mature man with us—an old reprobate who tried to regale us with tales of his adventures with ladies of questionable virtue. When we spotted the plant, we would get permission from a farmer to cut it with our scythes or sickles. The son of a professor of English at the University (who happened to be living in an English-style house that had been built by my Uncle Ed) drove the car I was in so recklessly up and down hills and around curves that I transferred to a different car.

(It was my wife Myra who recently reminded me of this adventure, for it was in the course of cutting marijuana that I first met her brother Karl, one of the cutters, before I became acquainted with Myra in a very different context.)

GRANDFATHER

It is probably the case that my grandfather was a much greater influence on me than on the rest of the children. I lived in the same house with him from the ages of 15 to 22. I was a young adult and we would talk about politics, economics, and moral questions that he seldom discussed with my younger siblings. Once we were talking about "moderation in all things." In order to clarify the point, he showed me the Greek version of the Old Testament. As a divinity student, he had studied Old Testament Greek. Of course, as a missionary to Japan, he had mastered at least the spoken Japanese language. I have in my library some of his ancient Japanese language textbooks and some of his sermons, typed or handwritten not in Japanese or Chinese characters but in Roman letters.

While I was attending the university, my grandfather bought me a beautiful dark blue double-breasted suit. I had not expressed any particular interest in having a suit, and was quite surprised by the gift, as grandfather was not in the habit of throwing money around. I am not conscious that he ever gave such a gift to the younger children. I am sorry to say that I did not take as good care of the fine garment as I should have. I once let myself be caught in the rain, which shrank the seams. I think that the suit was a gift motivated solely by my grandfather's love for me.

I once had an apparently telepathic experience relating to my grandfather's death. I was studying in my room, when very suddenly, completely out of the blue, with no forewarning of any kind, the thought occurred to me that my grandfather was dead. This thought was a complete surprise and so startling that I felt that it demanded serious attention. I thought about it for several minutes. I had heard of such miraculous events and was aware that scientific thought tended to scoff at them. With a strong conviction that I had actually had a premonition and that it should be taken seriously, I decided that I would test its validity. I went downstairs to check up on Grampa. Somewhat to my surprise, but to my great relief, he was sitting in his favorite wingback chair contentedly reading the *Wisconsin State Journal.* That experience made a lasting impression on me and has made me skeptical of hunches and premonitions.

Today, in retrospect, it seems that this experience demonstrated the unconscious awareness of my dependence on my grandfather. While he, of course, was the paterfamilias and controlled the family economy, our relationship matured while I attended the university, and we frequently engaged in friendly but occasionally heated discussions of politics and moral questions.

I was living at home (Jefferson Street) at the time of my grandfather's death in January 1942, at nearly the age of 80. In all the time that I had lived with him (seven years) I cannot recall his ever being ill. Once helping him set up a ladder to install a storm window, I was struck by how very strong his arms were. He seems to have got suddenly ill and then died of pneumonia after two or three days. He did not go to a hospital. During his last day or two he breathed with a very loud rasp, which I took to be a "death rattle." He seemed to be fighting to stay alive, and did not want to die. Gramma survived him by 18 years, dying in 1960 within two months of the age of 95.

By the standards of some of our Madison friends, our family was parsimonious, but actually we got along OK, did not perceive ourselves as being poor, and we benefitted enormously from the love of our mother and grandparents. We all attended a good church, an excellent high school, and a first rate university. Our lives were rich in music, scholarship, religion (although religion seems to have become unrespectable in many quarters today), and friendships.

In the fall of 1942, as described elsewhere, I left home to teach at Kemper Military School. Except for a few vacation periods, I did not again reside in Madison until the first eight months of 1951, when I was writing my Ph.D. dissertation for Columbia University.

MADISON WEST

When I arrived at Madison West High School in the fall of 1935, as a junior I met friends whom I had known at Randall School and almost immediately felt at home. Based on the size of the class of 1937, the total enrolment (both junior and senior high) would have been 1500, a large school for those days, but not notably larger than the Marinette Jr.-Sr. High.

I signed up for band. The regular director, Richard Church, was on leave to complete graduate work in music, and his place was taken by Douglas Steensland. Steensland asked what position I had played in Marinette. I said first clarinet. So I was seated next to Bob Woollen, who was an excellent clarinetist, way out of my humble league. In the second semester, Church came back and I ended up first chair third clarinet, which was exactly where I belonged. Church made the band sound a lot better than Steensland did.

The West High band did not have legitimate uniforms when I joined it; instead we wore blue sweaters with white duck pants. During my senior year, the members of the band were all measured for and received tailor-made uniforms. Church's costume was all white, as was the drum major's. The band members' uniforms were "of West Point style in blue and gray with gold trimming and white belts." The hats were tall and topped with panaches. Church commissioned some of the players to preside over certain sections. Bob Woollen is shown wearing double chevrons in the 1937 yearbook's band photograph. Several others are shown wearing single chevrons, including "Lieutenant" Theodore McNelly, positioned at first chair third clarinet in the extreme lower left hand corner of the photograph. I was not a good clarinetist, but presumably helped others who could not read music very well.

Once at the beginning of a practice, Church had one of his officers stand up, denounced him for disgracing his uniform, and ceremoniously ripped the chevron off the boy's uniform. I never knew what the boy had done to deserve this treatment.

I enrolled in beginning French (not having taken the subject in Marinette), and from the first day of class, Miss CarolineYoung started saying things in French to us. For a number of days she dramatized the following monologue:

"J'ouvre le livre. Je cherche la photographie. Je trouve la photographie. J'admire la photographie" As she said all this, we did not have in front of us the printed text and were at a loss about what she was saying, but after week or two it began to make sense. ("I open the book. I look for the photograph. I find the photograph. [She takes the photograph out of the book and gazes at it.] I admire the photograph.") Also the textbook contained oral material written in a phonetic alphabet which gave us a much more accurate notion of French pronunciation than we would have assumed from the actual French spelling. (Much later I would practice teach French using the "direct method" emphasizing the oral approach, and I would simply think back about how Miss Young used to do it.)

Miss Young's dynamic and humorous approach to teaching made one forget that actually she was not a young woman. She had us all of us draw maps of France, not by tracing or copying but by using the coordinates of latitude and longitude as references. (France has a roughly pentagonal shape. In 1953 as I was flying over France, I could identify Normandy from the air, thanks to having drawn that map for Miss Young.). We read an extremely elementary history of France, bearing the name of the famous historian Ernest Lavisse (who would probably have rolled over in his grave if he saw the school-child French into which his great work had been condensed). We read a sentimental novel by Georges Sand. During second year French Miss Young charmed us with her stories and pictures of the chateaux on the banks of the Loire, which had been the scenes of love affairs, murder, and intrigue during the French renaissance. Everyone had to choose one book in French and write a report on it. When immersed in the study of French pronunciation and vocabulary I yielded to the exoticism of the foreign tongue and became oblivious to the prosaic world around me. (French grammar was no problem after two years of Latin in Marinette.)

Of course I sang in Miss I. Lunt's large a cappella choir. (An a cappella choir sings without any instrumental accompaniment. A pianist played with us when we were learning a new piece of music.) The a cappella choirs of West, Central, and East High Schools would band together every winter to perform music for the Christmas pageant in the rotunda of the state capitol in Madison. The West High chorus was also involved in the two operettas that were given at West when I was there, *The Mikado*, and *A Kiss for Cinderella*. I was too busy for piano lessons any more but my mother began to coach me in voice.

During my junior year, the chorus and the orchestra were mobilized for Gilbert and Sullivan's *The Mikado*. Everyone in the cast was charged $5.00 to rent elegant costumes from a company in Chicago. Ray Holcombe directed the acting, Richard Church and Miss Ilah Lunt directed the music. I was chosen to play Pooh Bah, Lord High Everything Else, in the *Mikado*. Pooh Bah was an egregious snob who claimed a pre-Adamite ancestry. So I affected a snooty English accent and hammed up the role as best I could. Holcombe taught the principals little dance routines to accompany our songs.

When the Mikado asked where the prince was, Koko replied "Lodi," which brought down the house, as Lodi is a humble village much closer to Madison, Wisconsin, than it is to Tokyo. Bob Woollen, who played Koko, the Lord High Executioner, and I were cited in the *Wisconsin State Journal* for our comic performances.

We gave two performances of the opera, Friday and Saturday, March 27 and 28, 1936. Up to this point, probably because I had shown no interest or aptitude in athletics, I had made no great impression on the boys in Mr. Artman's Sunday School class. But on the Sunday after the great show, my classmates lined up one after the other and shook my hand. I'm sure that Artman put them up to it, but I think they were sincere. I had been accepted.

We gave James M. Barrie's *A Kiss for Cinderella* during the senior year. It was a spectacular extravaganza with a cast of 125; I had a speaking role.

I note from the 1937 student yearbook that at the district music tournament held in Wisconsin Dells that year, I and three other members of the chorus were awarded first division for solos that we sang. (My solo was "When I Think upon the Maidens," by Michael Head, for which my mother had coached me.) These first division singers then competed in the state solo tournament, held in Madison. At that tournament I placed second division (certainly not up to West High standards), but the other three soloists from West all placed first division. I envied Hugh Rundell, who was blessed naturally with a lovely round baritone voice and had sung the title role in *The Mikado*.

THE MUSIC CLINIC

In the summer of 1937, I took another stab at opera. The All-State High School Music Clinic, in whose band I had performed less than stellarly several years before, staged Arthur A. Penn's *The Lass of Limerick Town*, an old-fashioned operetta full of singable tunes. The director, W. H. Manning, professor of music at Utah Agricultural College, who had a terrible voice, would demonstrate how to perform our songs with lots of expression. I was one of the principals, playing the role of Judge Hooley. There were two sets of principals. The nine Madison boys and girls among the principals, including me, are separately pictured in the university's newspaper, *The Summer Cardinal* (July 29, 1937). I note in the program the name of Orville Shetney, my Lancaster acquaintance, among the principals. Irving Sklar, a classmate at West, was also one of the leads. At the Parkway theater on the Capitol Square in downtown Madison the first performance used the first set of principals, the second performance used the second set, and the third performance used the best members from either of the sets. I was chosen for the third performance.

When I had an important solo selection to sing, without waiting for instruction by the director, I chose to move to the very front of the stage and face the spectators directly. I had the impression that I had everyone's full attention and that I was really connecting with the audience. At the closing performance of the Music Clinic an announcement was to be made about the ten winners of four-year tuition scholarships to the University of Wisconsin. I entered the contest without any real expectation that I would win. I rounded up an accompanist (I have forgotten whom) at the last minute and sang a piece (I cannot remember what) for the selection committee. I assumed that my performance in opera would also be taken into consideration. I was dumbfounded when I learned that I was one of the ten winners. I had thought that certainly among the hundreds of students in the band, the orchestra, the chorus, and the opera of the clinic there would be dozens and dozens who were better musicians than I. But I won anyway. I must have done something right. I cannot help but feel that the training in music and dramatics that I had received from my mother and at West High School had made the difference.

As later explained, in my junior and senior years at the University of Wisconsin, I lost a semester's worth of academic credits in the course of changing from my music major to a French major, and was faced with the prospect of not completing my degree at the same time that my classmates from Randall and West would be graduating. Instinctively, I made a special effort to "graduate on time" rather than spend an extra semester at the university. Why did I make that special effort? I believe that it was because I had so strongly identified with my class of 1937 at West.

Why had that class come to mean so much to me? I had not been one of those who belonged to an exclusive fraternity, I had not attended parties at hotels, I had not even gone to a prom or other school parties. I was not among those singled out for the best academic records. I was not elected to the president of anything. I didn't go on dates.

Part of the reason for my identification with the class was that I had become well acquainted with so many of my classmates and genuinely liked them. Being a member of the band and of the a cappella choir certainly helped. Miss Lunt called roll orally at chorus rehearsals, so that I came to associate the names of many of the students with their faces. The fun we shared when the band and choir took the train to Wisconsin Dells for the district music tournament helped to cement friendships.

But the real secret of my identification with the class is disclosed on page 28 of the 1937 yearbook: In its description of the group of seniors (including Bob Woollen) who graduated in February, we find a statement "second only to music in the interest of our class was sports." The school was not about jocks; it was about music! It was no disgrace to be a musician (or a scholar, for that matter) at West, and I fit in perfectly.

Of course I knew some students better than others. Perhaps the ones I was most conscious of, aside from the Sweet girls whom I knew in church, were Lawrence Ketchum (an avid photographer), Bill Balch (who was seeking his way), Kathleen Campbell (just about the prettiest girl I ever knew), John Clark (a fellow thespian), Helen Jane Dinsmore (Yum-Yum in the *Mikado*), Dick Garner (another actor), Phil Lescohier (an old friend from Randall School), David Perlman (sergeant of the band and second only to Bob Woollen on a clarinet), Hugh Rundell (a star baritone), David Saunders (a very congenial soul), George Schafer (a flutist), Mary Jane Samp (also a fan of Miss Young), and Bob Woollen (a superb clarinetist with a flair for dramatics).

All four of the McNelly kids went to West, as did two of their spouses (my wife, Myra Koehler, of the class of 1942, and Lucille's husband, Charles Oakey, of the class of 1937), serving as constant reminders of the place.

My sister Lucille, during her senior year at West (1938) performed the role of Lady Jane, the lead comic, in Gilbert and Sullivan's *Patience*. I recall Lucille singing the tunes around the house, and those tunes are still familiar to me. Marion Blum (later to become Mrs. Elliot Sweet) was appointed to coach Lucille how to hold a bass fiddle, plump Lady Jane's matching accessory.

My wife, Myra, (whom I did not meet until 1950) had been concert mistress of the West High Orchestra, directed by Richard Church, during her senior year (1941-42).

My graduation from West in 1937 did not permanently end my official relationship with the school. In 1941-1942, while working on my M.A. in French at the University of Wisconsin, I taught French part-time at West High. I note from yearbooks that Mary Jane Samp and Bob Woollen, like me members of West's class of 1937, taught Spanish and music respectively at West the same time that I taught French there.

In July 2002 the efforts of my wife Myra and of me to attend the 65th annual reunion of West High class of 1937 ended when I fell with a broken a hip in the Cleveland airport.

CHAPTER 4

THE UNIVERSITY OF WISCONSIN

The overwhelming proportion of Madison West graduates went on to college. Indeed, that high school was actually a college preparatory institution.

As one of the ten winners of Music Clinic scholarships, I was granted tuition for four years at the University of Wisconsin. (In 1937 tuition was $27.50 per semester.) I was not required to major in music, but would have to participate in band, orchestra, or chorus, and maintain an overall average of C+ or better. Even if I had not won this scholarship, I would probably have attended that university. As a resident of the state, I would not have had to pay out-of-state tuition, and I could attend the school even while living at home, without paying room and board. As none of us was gainfully employed and were not on welfare, which would be unthinkable for us in the middle class, I suppose that without really being conscious of it I and the other children were actually all along being supported by our aged grandfather, to whom we children seldom showed much gratitude.

I enrolled in the university as a freshman in 1937, pursuing the pre-law sequence. A recommended requisite was English history. The English history course was taught by the eminent Paul Knapland, who talked with a labored Norwegian accent. The lectures were in the auditorium of Bascom Hall. The lectures seemed awfully pedestrian and although I could easily have earned an A with a bit of effort, I got a B with very little effort. Because the course turned me off, I enrolled in the School of Education majoring in music in the sophomore year. (Ironically, when later I became a graduate student and professor in political science I was intensely interested in seventeenth century British political history because of its importance to the theory of American democracy.)

MUSIC SCHOOL

While attending the university my sister and I continued to sing in the choir that my mother directed at the Westminster Presbyterian Church. After Gladys MacGowan, the organist, died, Orville Shetney and Eleanor Artman, friends of mine in the university music school, played the wheezy reed organ, which was equipped with a noisy electric pump.

During the summer following my freshman year at Wisconsin, I accepted an invitation from the Music Clinic to participate in the production of a light opera, Balfe's *The Bohemian Girl*. This seemed to me like a strange arrangement, because the Music Clinic had been established for the education of high school students, not college students. (However, I understand that it is not unusual for musical groups occasionally to recruit outsiders, especially for lead parts, called "ringers," for their performances.)

The *Wisconsin State Journal* carried photos of each of the three casts of leads, each to participate in one of the three performances of the opera. Each cast consisted of four boys and two girls. I notice that Orville Shetney, who like me had won a Music Clinic Scholarship and had just finished his freshman year in the university, was also in one of the casts of leads. The newspaper noted that this was only the second year in which the Music Clinic sponsored an opera.

In those days the Music Clinic lasted three weeks. In 2004, its seventy-fifth anniversary year, it runs for only one week and no longer presents operas.

During my sophomore year Lucille joined me in the Music School. We both began working towards B.Sc. in education, because this degree was about the only four-year program that would lead to a job. Our father having been a teacher and school administrator, it was not surprising that teaching was our aim. It would be virtually impossible to make a living as a musician, but public school music was an option for many musicians. My sister was very reluctant to get involved in teaching, but in the context of the depression when jobs were scarce she reluctantly agreed to mother's and my arguments.

Of course, the first two years at the university largely focused on courses required of all the students in the university, and to shift from one major to another during this period did not involve the loss of too many credits. Although I was deeply involved at the Music School, my interest in French, my minor field, grew perhaps at the expense of my work in music.

When I was a sophomore, I tried out for a role in the French play sponsored by the French Club (le Cercle Français) and directed by the vivacious Mlle Marcelle Henry of the French Department. I was assigned the role of Crainquebille, in the play by that name by Anatole France. Although I had studied French for only three years (two years at West and one at the university), I had become moderately fluent, and was able to earn a favorable mention in the *Daily Cardinal,* the university newspaper (November 30, 1938), for my performance: "Ted McNelly, sophomore 'find' in French dramatics, led an all-student cast in the title role of the old pushcart peddler who, over an incident in the Paris streets, stumbles bewildered into the pompous, insensible maze of justice and then out again, to find himself friendless and unable to make a living."

When I was a junior, on May 4, 1940, I played the role of Mario, the brother of Silvia, in Marivaux's comedy, *Le Jeu de l'amour et du hazard* (The Game of Love and Chance), sponsored by the Department of French and Italian. This classic play had first been performed in Paris in 1730. Most of the cast consisted of faculty (including André Lévèque and Alex Kroff) and graduate students. Preceding the curtain raising there was a musical program. Alfred Galpin, of the French faculty, played some Couperin pieces on the piano, and I sang Lully's "Bois épais" and Giovanni Martini's "Plaisir d'amour."

Marivaux *Le Jeu d l'amour and du hazard*
From the left: Alexander Kroff (Arlequin), Helen Hall (Lisette), Theodore McNelly (Mario), André Lévèque (M. Orgon), Lily Salz (Silvia), Nathaniel Rasmussen (Dorante)

Before I had entered the Music School, there had been a great debate in the university about the deanship of the School of Music. It was widely believed in music circles that the new dean should be the eminent Canadian band director and cornetist who had been conductor of the Music Clinic band. However, to the chagrin of many, a Mr. Carl Bricken was chosen by a search committee headed by a professor of law.

Bricken was a composer and, with some new faculty he brought in, placed heavy emphasis on ear training. Thus our harmony class consisted largely of dictation. The instructor (for a while it was Bricken himself) would play a short Bach chorale on the piano. We were supposed to write down the notes as he played them.

The majority of the students had a lot of trouble with this. For example, I could ponder the first measure of the music and using my knowledge of harmony calculate what the notes were. But while I was fussing over the first measure, the piano continued playing and I could do nothing about the rest of the chorale except for the final chord, which would be a major or minor chord corresponding to the key signature of the piece.

It should be said, however, that one or two students who had absolute pitch, including Gerald ("Jerry") Borsuk, a talented pianist who had studied under Sigfrid Prager and had played oboe in the band at West High, had no trouble at all with dictation. The only mistakes Borsuk made occurred when he failed to properly distinguish between the tenor and alto notes when those two parts crossed. But my problems in this area were the least of my difficulties in the music school.

As my talent in music was confined to voice and I was not really proficient on the piano or any other musical instrument, I seem not to have been taken very seriously as a musician by my fellow students and faculty. For example, I was not inducted into Sinfonia, the music honorary society. Orville Shetney, whom I had known in Lancaster, who was a baritone, a pianist, and player of the bass fiddle, was more in the swim of things. He gave the impression of being very thick with Paul Jones, the organist and director of the chorus that sometimes performed in foreign countries. As a Music Clinic scholarship student I was required to participate in the university band, orchestra, or chorus. The university chorus, which I opted to sing in, was directed by E. Earl Sweeney, my singing teacher. It rehearsed weekly and performed only once or twice a year. The rehearsals seemed boring and I thought we were just going through the motions.

My experience with Professor Raymond Dvorak was illustrative of my problems. The students in his conducting class all played in our class orchestra, which we took turns conducting. I was not a good clarinetist, had given up playing that instrument, and had taken a class course in violin under Georges Szpinalski. I was issued a metal violin, painted to look like wood. Although I played it poorly, I opted to play violin in the Ray Dvorak's conducting class.

Dvorak was famous throughout the state as the conductor of the University Band, which performed at football games. He justifiably took pride in his ability to play orchestra scores on the piano.

Dvorak was not reluctant to criticize our conducting. After a friend of mine conducted, Dvorak asked him, "Do you know what you did?" My friend said no. Dvorak said, "Your beats were very unclear, Your conducting is very sloppy. You play the oboe without a clear rhythm. Your piano playing is the same." Dvorak attacked not only the boy's conducting but also his instrumental skills and his fundamental musicianship. I had not noticed anything terribly wrong in his conducting. My friend was reduced to tears in front of the rest of the class. Dvorak similarly criticized one of the girl's conducting; she too had tears in her eyes at the end of his devastating critique. I thought Dvorak had a mean streak. He had not been very critical of my performance. I think that this was because he did not know me.

As part of the final exam, the student was given an orchestra score to study for five or ten minutes and then had to conduct it for Dvorak, who would play it on the piano. The score I was given was a medley, full of time changes and a variety of rhythms, and I did poorly in this exam. At the end of the term, in accordance with the custom, I went to Dvorak's office to ask him what my term grade was. He said C plus. This was the lowest grade I ever got at the university. I was not particularly surprised, and said thank you. He said, "I don't know what you're thanking me for. I gave David Machtel a D. He was a singer too."

David had sung the romantic lead in the *Mikado* I had sung in at West and had a magnificent natural tenor voice and years of training. To my knowledge he was the best singer in the university. I was left with the feeling that Dvorak had a prejudice, not uncommon among conductors, against singers.

I could not help wondering if Dvorak, who was a very serious musician, was frustrated because he was not director of the University Symphony Orchestra. Instead he directed the university band that played at football games. Bricken took over the symphony orchestra when he became head of the music school and had it play his compositions.

In 1948, Dvorak lost an arm and seriously injured a leg in a train accident and earned the sympathy of the people of Wisconsin. In the fall of 1950, Ray Dvorak returned to the podium of the Wisconsin band with an artificial arm and a repaired leg. He retired in 1968.

A bright point in my music school experience was class piano. Walking past the music school, one was apt to hear the strains of Chopin's C sharp minor waltz. Notwithstanding its daunting key signature, double sharps, and ledger notes, Mr. Coon managed to teach and motivate his students to play this difficult piece passably. (Unhappily, after decades of lack of access to a piano, I lost the knack for playing it and seem unable, despite earnest and painful effort, to resuscitate it.)

Gunnar Johansen, the piano virtuoso, was an artist in residence at the university. One year I attended his concert series of the complete works of Chopin. My grandfather attended a few of these sessions, emphasizing that he was more impressed by Johansen's memory (he played the concerts entirely by memory) than by the music itself. I never had any personal contacts with Johansen.

My career at the school of music ended with the sophomore comprehensive examination. Bricken seems to have believed, perhaps rightly, that many of the students in the Music School were hopeless. He introduced a scheme for examining students in their sophomore year to eliminate the duds. Since I had begun majoring in music in my sophomore year, I took the sophomore comprehensive examination during what was my junior year. The exam consisted mostly or entirely of a performance. I rashly decided to sing one or two classical Italian bel canto numbers, accompanying myself on the piano. The accompaniment was simple enough and I did not stumble, but I am sure that my concern with the accompaniment did not help my uninspired singing. A week or so later both Lucille and I received letters from the University advising that we (like almost half of the sophomore class) had best find our "niche" elsewhere than in music. (Although I had flunked out of the music school, my four-year Music Clinic scholarship was still good, because I was maintaining a better than C+ average in all of my courses.)

My sister has reminded me that she transferred to a French major and remained in the university through her junior year. But having lost 30 credits she thought she was wasting her mother's money so she dropped out of school without completing her senior year.

CHANGING MAJORS

I had already decided to earn an M.A. in French, so I changed my major to French. In the course of transferring, I would be about 12 credits short of graduating on schedule, i.e., at the end of four years in the university. I wanted to graduate with my class, which included friends I had known at Randall School and at West High. I had been making arrangements for a scholarship to study in the summer at Laval University, a French-language institution in Quebec. I gave up this project and in the summer of 1940 attended summer school and took correspondence courses to catch up with my class. I took American Government and beginning German in the university correspondence program and took English novel and advanced French in the summer session.

In the English novel course, we had too many books to read, but they were wonderful. I was introduced to the writing of Anthony Trollope among others. I am grateful to the professor for introducing me to some great writing.

The American government course, taught by correspondence, was based largely on "Ogg and Ray," the unrivaled standard textbook on the subject, by Frederick Austin Ogg (of the University of Wisconsin) and P. Orman Ray, *Introduction to American Government*, the first edition of which had been copyrighted in 1922. Later editions of this book would become the basis of the relevant course I would teach many years later in the University of Maryland overseas program. This course required me to write short essays in the answers to questions. I used this requirement as an opportunity to learn touch typing from a manual. By the end of the course, I had typed over two hundred pages of material, and to this time I can type without looking at the keys except for the numbers. My final examinations in American Government and German were taken under supervision without possibility to refer to the textbooks. (I was able to make some use of German when, in the overseas program of the University of Maryland, I resided in Germany for a total of three years.)

In my senior year the French and Italian Department presented Molière's *Le Bourgeois Gentilhomme,* a *comédie-ballet* with music by Lully. I played the role of a student of the music master (performed by Alex Kroff). Professors Germaine Mercier and Julian Harris directed the production, which involved a corps de ballet and an orchestra. The principals in the cast were mostly professors and graduate students. Professor Galpin arranged much of the music and directed the orchestra and singers. The play was performed in Wisconsin Union Theater on May 10, 1941.

I sang in two musical soirées sponsored by the French Club in the Play Circle (a small theater) in the Memorial Union. In November 1940, I sang "Les pas d'armes du roi Jean" by Saint-Saëns, accompanied on the piano by Professor Julian Harris. In January 1942, also in the Play Circle, I sang Massenet's "Ouvre tes yeux bleus," and Hedwige Chretien's "Que je t'oublie," again accompanied by Professor Harris. Professor Samuel Rogers, who taught the course in the French novel (he introduced Proust to me), was one of the pianists on the program. My violin teacher, Mr. George Szpinalski, also participated in the soirées, but one evening I was shocked by the strong smell of alcohol on his breath.

THE WISCONSIN PLAYERS

I tried out for a part in Franz Lehar's *The Merry Widow,* sponsored by the Wisconsin Players. Richard Church, whose day job was conducting band and orchestra at West High, conducted operettas at the university. I thought I did poorly at the tryout, but Church, who had seen me in the *Mikado* at West, always seemed to like me and for that reason, I guess, I got the role of St. Brioche. My sister has reminded me that she sang the role of Sylvaine (Khadja's wife) in *The Merry Widow.* The day before the performance one of the major principals became sick and Russell ("Rusty") Lane, the director, took over that role at the last minute. I had the impression he was ad-libbing throughout and I was terrified that clues were going to be missed.

In 1944, Richard Church became professor of music at the University of Wisconsin. For twenty-two years he conducted the University of Wisconsin Symphony Orchestra. Following an automobile accident he died in February 1976 at the age of 68.

On April 8, 9, 10, and 12, 1941, I sang the role of Peachum in the *Beggar's Opera.* An Englishman, Ronald E. Mitchell, had just become a dramatics teacher at Wisconsin and his project was to revive the play by John Gay, using the original eighteenth-century music by John Christopher Pepusch. Peachum, whose role I played, was the "patron of a gang of thieves, and receiver of their stolen goods. His house is the resort of thieves, pickpockets, and villains of all sorts. He betrays his comrades when it is for his own benefit, and even procures the arrest of their leader, Captain Macheath" (William Rose Benet, ed., *The Reader's Encyclopedia* [New York: Crowell, 1948], p. 831). A classmate in the music school, a pianist, played the harpsichord accompaniment for our production.

The *Wisconsin State Journal* carried portraits of all six of the principals, and indicated that there would be four performances of the play. The part of Macheath was played by Ben Park, a Madison boy who like me had been involved in the Music Clinic Opera program.

An interesting fact emerged while we were working on the *Beggar's Opera*. We heard that German dramatists were producing an adaptation of this opera. This was the *Dreigroschen Oper* (Three Penny Opera) produced by Bertolt Brecht with music by Kurt Weill. (Kurt Weill's song about Mack the Knife became popular in the United States in the 1950s. I learn from the Internet that Laurence Olivier performed in a 1953 motion picture version of the *Beggars Opera*. In about 1995, our family witnessed a remarkable production in English of the *Three Penny Opera* produced by the North Carolina School of the Arts, in Winston-Salem, North Carolina, where my son was studying for his masters degree in music. Later I managed to acquire a video of the first German movie version and a Vienna edition of the complete piano score of the *Dreigroschen Oper* bearing a 1928 copyright.)

After the *Merry Widow* and the *Beggars Opera* I completed the requirements for admission to Wisconsin Players by serving on the properties committee for one play and doing a bit part in another (*The Merry Wives of Windsor*, which was presented on April 9, 10, 11, and 12, 1940). I became eligible to carry a Wisconsin Players key as well as that of the Phi Kappa Phi, an honorary society.

Although I had sung principal roles in six operettas—two in high school, two in Music Clinic, and two in the University of Wisconsin, I never gave serious thought to a career in opera because my voice teacher was uninspiring and I was unfamiliar with grand opera. I had never seen a performance of grand opera, other than *La Traviata,* performed by a group in Madison directed by the venerable Sigfrid Prager. (I was then in high school and played clarinet in the stage band in the opera.)

THE MÉDAILLE DE BRONZE

As previously mentioned, when I was a junior, I played the role of Mario, brother of Silvia, the heroine, in Marivaux's *Le Jeu de l'amour et du hasard.* Later we broadcast excerpts from the play in the French program regularly broadcast by the University of Wisconsin radio station WHA.

In the spring of 1940 the French Department sponsored a contest, in which the winner would be awarded a medal by the French Ministry of Foreign Affairs. I signed up to take the written and oral examination to compete for this and I won the contest.

At a special dinner held at the French House attended largely by faculty members, René Weiler, the French consul general in Chicago, awarded me the medal on behalf of the French government.

The *médaille de bronze* with my name inscribed on it was accompanied by a certificate for framing dated June 13, 1940. That was the date on which German troops occupied Paris. There was gloom in the French Department office when I picked up the certificate.

In my senior year, on May 10, 1941, the Department of French and Italian sponsored an elaborate performance of Molière's *Le bourgeois gentilhomme,* including a ballet and music by Lully. (This play had first been performed at Chambord in 1670.) I played the role of a music student.

When I was a student at Wisconsin, the French House consisted of a drab Victorian residence located on a corner on University Avenue, on the opposite side of the street from the university campus. Some female students resided there. At the meals, French was supposed to be used exclusively. I ate there once or twice, but the French spoken there was uninspiring. The French Club met there. We would sing French folk songs and occasionally the latest French popular songs. According to the class of 1941 yearbook, I was president of the French Club, but I have no memory of how I came to be chosen for that position and what my official duties were.

After World War II, money was raised for a new French House to be built on the shore of Lake Mendota, adjacent to the campus. I looked over the "new" French House in 1996, noting the surrounding thick vegetation and the pier extending into the lake. I peeked through a window and noted that the building was in need of new furniture.

PRACTICE TEACHING

As I would get a bachelor of science degree in education, it was necessary to do some practice teaching. My minor teaching fields would be in music and English, but my major teaching field would be French, and I would be doing my practice teaching in French at the Wisconsin High School, which was administered as part of the university with professors in the School of Education doing the supervision.

My professor for the teaching of French was Laura B. Johnson, who was a strong advocate of the "direct method." The direct method emphasized practice in actually speaking the language and acquiring the ability to understand the spoken as well as the written language. Traditionally the emphasis in the teaching of foreign languages was grammar and translation. The main weakness of the traditional approach is that the students often never learned to speak the language.

The main weakness of the "direct method" was that the students were apt to neglect grammar and might be unable to translate texts accurately.

I tended to favor the direct method, as that had been used by Miss Young, my wonderful French teacher at West, who began speaking and dramatizing little bits in French from the first day of class. I was motivated to learn the spoken language from the very beginning, and after three years of French in high school and college had been able to play the lead in the French play at the university.

I have long suspected that the traditional method has been favored by teachers of foreign languages because they are often not competent in speaking the language. By talking at length in English about subtle points of French grammar and focusing on translating, they do not have to be able to speak the language.

This problem was evident in our little group of four or five practice teachers. I was the only one who could speak French with any fluency. I believe that the others would never be able to teach using the direct method. They may not have taken enough courses in French at the university to speak it. At the same time, there were several students in our high school class at Wisconsin High who had some fluency in the language. The daughters of a political science professor, for example, spent their summers at school in Switzerland and had learned French there. I was a strong supporter of the direct method and enjoyed using it with this class.

However, one day I was naughty. Miss Johnson was away. I had the feeling that many of the students were lost and that even the speakers of the language did not have a very clear idea of what they were doing. So I spent the whole day discussing grammar. And the students seemed to appreciate it.

I thought even while teaching at Wisconsin High that a high school attached to the university was a mistaken idea. A very high portion of the students were the children of professors, not the kind of students that made up the majority of the children that we would later find ourselves teaching. The high school students in the real world would likely not be as talented or motivated as the children at Wisconsin High, and the teachers should be prepared to deal with this less favorable environment as well as with their own weak preparation in French. Perhaps other people felt the same way about Wisconsin High as I did, because decades ago it was abolished.

I had the highest regard for Dr. Johnson, and had a brief correspondence with her when I went to Japan after the war.

REQUIRED COURSES

I was required to take a certain number of credits in science as part of the undergrad curriculum at Wisconsin So I signed up for courses in physiology and astronomy.

The physiology course was taught be a professor in the school of medicine. The thick textbook was printed on pale green paper, which was believed by the publisher to reduce strain on the eyes. The professor gave his lectures in an auditorium and the exam papers were graded by graduate assistants. In the laboratory among other things we had to administer shocks to the legs of the frogs that we had murdered. We had to learn the scientific names for the various parts of the body. In 1996 when I developed diabetes, some of my old lessons in physiology came back to me, but I wished that I could remember more.

The professor was somewhat beyond middle age. He was an M.D. and talked about physiology as one who had a very direct acquaintance with the topic. He also let drop bits of his personal philosophy. He said that he would not greatly mind dying because he had had a family and done just about everything worthwhile and was willing to call it quits. This struck me as fatalistic and pessimistic, but I suppose there are plenty of old people who take this attitude. Everyone is going to die in the end and it makes a certain sense to be reconciled to that fact rather than feel in constant dread of death.

(During the final days of my grandfathers death in early 1942, I had the impression that in spite of his strong religiosity he had no desire at all to die and wanted to continue living. His mind was acute at the age of 79, and I suspect that he felt a strong responsibility for his wife, his daughter, and his grandchildren, whom he had been taking care of, and he looked forward to seeing us grow up to adulthood.)

A footnote in our astronomy textbook referred to Professor Stebbins' research on variable stars. At the second meeting of the class, two girls in the back row engaged him in an argument about which way the earth rotates. They insisted that it rotated in a Western direction. He became incensed when they refused to accept his contention that the opposite was true, and the top of his bald head turned crimson. He finally said that he hated to be dogmatic but that the earth rotated eastwardly.

Professor Stebbins must have been completely nonplused and disgusted with our class, because he never came back to lecture us again. A younger, more understanding man took his place. He assured us that the concept of the "celestial sphere" was difficult for beginners to comprehend, but that we would gradually come to understand it after we had had a few more lessons. I am happy to say that he was right.

The lab consisted of going to observatory once a week at night. The first lab consisted of looking at the sky with our naked eye and identifying constellations. I think we looked through the telescope. The third week we could not have lab because the extreme cold had made it impossible to rotate the dome of the observatory. A new schedule for lab was promulgated. The lab would meet the first night of each week Monday through Thursday that was not excessively cold. It turned out that because of the extreme cold that winter there were no more lab sessions.

(In those days colleges usually began their first semester in late September, winding up the end of January, with a two-week break for Christmas vacation.

This schedule was partly to blame for the scarcity of astronomy lab sessions. In the 1970s universities started the first semester in the beginning of September and ended the semester before Christmas. The second semester began in early January. This had the advantage of ending the second semester in the middle of May before the weather became favorable for student demonstrations. Under the new schedule campuses became much more manageable. From a scholarly point of view, however, Christmas vacations were no longer taken up with writing term papers for the first semester. This made life easier I think for the students, who could now have a more pleasant winter vacation.)

Every male freshman at the University of Wisconsin was required to take either physical education (PE) or Reserve Officer Training Corps (ROTC). I chose physical education. The first semester I took swimming. In those days the men's gym was located in the Armory, an imposing red brick Victorian structure on the lake shore. The swimming class was conducted completely in the nude, without jock straps or anything else that would hide our masculinity. The instructor wore a jock strap, which seemed a bit unfair but understandable since he had to stand in front of all of us to give us his lecture. I often wondered how a girl would have reacted if for some reason she had wandered into the pool area and contemplated our full frontal nudity. (I am not sure that it was safe for us to practice diving without athletic supporters.)

I have forgotten what subject I signed up for my second semester of PE. After the first meeting of the class I noticed that I had athlete's foot. I went to the infirmary for treatment, and as I left the doctor's office I asked if it would not be prudent for me to avoid spreading the disease by attending the PE class, where we had to change clothes in the dressing room. He agreed with me; so I did not attend class again until the last day of the semester, bringing a medical excuse. Apparently the grad assistant, who was disgusted with me, found it inconvenient to pursue my case, and I was given the necessary credit in PE.

Apparently my conscience troubled me for decades afterwards. I had a recurring nightmare that while lined up in the stadium to receive my diploma, someone comes up from behind me, taps me on the shoulder, and reminds me that I had failed to fulfill the PE requirement and will not be able to graduate. This nightmare assumed additional credibility, because, as elsewhere explained, I had lost many credits as a result of flunking out of the Music School, credits that I barely replaced by going to summer school and taking correspondence courses. A minor mistake in my arithmetic could have resulted in my failure to graduate on time. My Bachelor of Science Degree was conferred on June 23, 1941.

My grades were evidently not good enough, given my problems in the music school, for Phi Beta Kappa. I was, however, chosen for membership in the Phi Kappa Phi for outstanding scholarship and leadership in campus activities. My Phi Kappa Phi certificate indicates that I was elected to the society on March 11,

1941. (The newly elected members were required to pay for the initiation banquet and the key.) The *Capital Times* published the names of the 84 students elected to the Phi Kappa Phi, including 17 Madison seniors. Among the Madisonians, including me, were my friends at West High: Richard Garner (actor and tympanist), Sue Hadley, James MacDonald, David Perlman (clarinetist), and Mary Jane Samp (a fellow student of Miss Young). The class of 1941 yearbook, *The 1941 On Wisconsin Badger,* did not includes honors and high honors lists, but did list members of Phi Beta Kappa, Phi Kappa Phi, and other honorary organizations

On examining my class yearbook, I find the names and pictures of one Lancaster acquaintance, Orville Shetney; a friend at Randall School, Philip Loscohier; two friends from Marinette, Gene Farnsworth and Philip Martineau; and a number of friends and acquaintances at West High, including Betty Blankenship (Mortar Board) Beverly Bliss, Richard Garner (Phi Beta Kappa, Phi Kappa Phi, Iron Cross), Sue Hadley (Phi Beta Kappa, Phi Kappa Phi, Mortar Board), Kenneth Kerst (who became Soviet expert and a diplomat), James MacDonald (who became a lawyer and finally a professor of Law at Wisconsin), Charles Oakey (who became my brother-in-law), David Perlman (Phi Kappa Phi), Mary Jane Samp (Phi Kappa Phi, Mortar Board), George Schafer (the flutist), and Bob Woollen (the clarinetist). The Iron Cross and Mortar Board were small honorary societies for men and women respectively. (I was a member of the Phi Kappa Phi, which was made up of 85 members of the graduating class of about 1230 students.) Although I was not a close friend of most of these people, for some reason, it seemed very important to me that I "graduate with my class."

Nowadays in this era of affluence, students seem not to give much thought about "graduating on time." Recent statistics show that the average student takes five years to get a bachelor's degree instead of four, as was customary in my day. Perhaps today's students enjoy college life too much, and are too affluent to have to go out and earn a living right away. Some of them have to work full—or part-time in order to pay for their automobiles. In my day only students from wealthy families had cars.

By successfully completing the requirements for the degree of "Bachelor of Science (Education)" at the University of Wisconsin I automatically was qualified for and received (for the payment of a $2.00 fee) a one-year license dated July 1, 1941 from the state Department of Public Instruction to teach French, English, and music in the public schools of Wisconsin.

TEACHING AT WEST HIGH

I had been planning to pursue graduate work in French, and deeply impressed by a bulletin from Columbia University that pictured its elegant buildings in New York, I applied for a fellowship to go there. My French professors at Wisconsin referred to "le grand Columbia" and were sympathetic, but my application came to naught. Instead of moving to New York, I entered the M.A. program at the French department in Madison.

As before, I lived at home. By this time, Miss Young was no longer teaching at West High, and Miss Morgan needed someone to help with French there. I was hired as a part-timer to teach one class of French and supervise one period of study hall at West. (I note in the 1941 West High year book that Miss Young was teaching at West as late as 1941. Thus I was in a sense, her successor!) It became my custom to ride to school every day on a shiny red bicycle.

The junior high study hall got off to a bad start because in the beginning I found the students cute and smiled at them. As a result, with my unthinking encouragement, they became cuter and cuter and much too noisy. The junior high principal, Mr. Leroy Luberg, came by and we restored order, fortunately, on the first day, and I had no problems later with that.

The French class was second year French, and I enjoyed teaching it. I structured the course as Miss Morgan wished, and I taught it pretty much the way it had been when I had taken the course under Miss Young. I did, however, try to take advantage of the my university connection. The university Student Union presented the French version of the new Disney movie, *Snow White and the Seven Dwarfs* (*Neige Blanche et les sept nains*), and I had the students go see it. The names of the dwarfs had been translated into some very cute French words, *Grincheux* for Grumpy, etc. (I now have mixed feelings about contributing to the Disneyfication of French culture.)

As a class, we read a novel and in addition, every student was required to read one additional book in French (on an approved list) and write a report on it. This was what I had done in second year French and my students did it too. I believe that this was a substantial accomplishment for second year students.

One of the students, Jeanette Kennett, resided in one of the three houses owned by my grandfather. Her mother complained to me that the book her daughter was reading for my class was too long, and I agreed, permitting her to report only on the first half of the book. Around 1990 this girl (who had been a classmate of my wife) and her husband came visiting in Maryland, bringing with them their *granddaughter*.

Another of my students at West was Jeanne Parr, who had long beautiful hair and later became a professional model and the mother of the TV actor Chris Noth.

My wife's 1942 West High year book, page 14, has a picture of Mr. Christopherson and me talking with "Senorita Samp." The senorita was Mary Jane Samp, class of 1937 and former student of Miss Young. Mary Jane had returned to West to teach Spanish. Robert Woollen was back at West at the same time, advising the Music Club. I was not unique among West alumni who had returned to West to teach.

While teaching at West, I was hired by M. Halleux, a Belgian violinist in the Pro Arte string quarter (in residence at the university) to tutor his son in English. After one or two lessons we gave up because André Halleux had already become thoroughly acclimated to West High and the English language and didn't need tutoring. He was president of the West High French club, of which I was the faculty adviser.

GRADUATE WORK

My favorite French teacher at the university was Professor (I think we called her Madame) Germaine Mercier, who taught French literature. She spoke English fluently with a strong Parisian accent. She gave essay exams. I would look at her questions appalled at how difficult they seemed. But once I started to write, everything would come back to me and I did fairly well. In 2002, while rummaging through my disordered library, I stumbled across a paper-bound book in French, *Pilote de guerre* (the title of the English translation is *Flight from Arras*), by Antoine de Saint Exupéry, published in 1942. My translation of the inscription in French handwritten on the flyleaf follows:

> Madison, Wisconsin. To Mr. Theodore H. McNelly. Congratulations to
> the winner of the French contest organized among the students of the
> advanced courses in conversation and composition, French 124 and French
> 127. Germaine Mercier, University of Wisconsin, May 1942.

The book is based on the famous author's experience in 1940 as a reconnaissance pilot. He was reported missing in action in 1944. (His airplane, a Lightning P-38, was discovered in the sea near Marseille in 2004.)

While I was a graduate student in the Wisconsin French Department, on May 9, 1942, I took a part in a performance in French of Beaumarchais' *Le Barbier de Séville*. (Rossini's opera by the same name was based on the Beaumarchais comedy.) I played the role of Don Bazile. Among my mementoes I find a hand written letter:

Central State Teachers College
Stevens Point, Wis.
May 19, 1942

Mr. Theodore McNelly
    Department of French
    University of Wisconsin

Dear Mr. McNelly:
    The directors and members of the cast of "Le Barbier de Séville" are
to be highly commended for an excellent performance. Will you please

tell them that they made our trip to Madison one that was most worth while.

We were delighted with Mr. Kroff's characterization of Figaro . . . . And it is our unanimous opinion that your Don Bazile "stole the show." That was a professional's interpretation if ever we saw one.

Sincerely, [Here follow the signatures of 30 students.]

A Scene from *Le Barbier de Séville*
Theodore McNelly wearing a large hat and seated in the center, plays the role of Don Bazile

In addition, I acted in a humorous skit in French that we performed at several colleges in Wisconsin. All of this while teaching part-time at West High. I seem not to have had much time to study French medieval poetry for Professor Zdanowicz's seminar.

In the summer of 1942, I submitted two seminar papers in lieu of an M.A. thesis, which had previously been required, for the partial fulfillment of the degree requirements. I passed the oral examination with little difficulty. I was so relieved and happy with this accomplishment that I coasted down the steep paved alley behind our house on my bicycle with my hands removed from the brake levers. I could not stop the bicycle at the bottom of the hill and crossed a street—fortunately there was no traffic there—and ran head first into a hedge. I was very lucky not to have been hurt. My M.A. degree was conferred on September 6, 1942.

WAR

It will be recalled that after the Germans conquered Poland in the fall of 1939, over two years elapsed before the United States was embroiled in World War II. The mood of the country did not support our active involvement until the Japanese attacked Pearl Harbor, on December 7, 1941.

Around 1937, I attended a lecture at the university by an eminent German politician. He said that Hitler hoped to annex Austria and part of Czechoslovakia, and the like. I thought this was unbelievable and fantastic. Certainly the British and the French, who had beaten Germany two decades before, and the League of Nations would never permit Germany to get away with such blatant aggressions. I suspect that my skepticism was typical of the mind set of that period.

My grandfather asked me to type a letter to the *Wisconsin State Journal.* His letter insisted, "There will be no war in Europe." The newspaper did not print the letter.

Around 1940, a fellow student in my harmony class, invited all of the members of the class to her house for an evening party. Her father, who had come from Germany, was the minister at a Lutheran church in Madison. He said that the English and the Jews were doing their best to drag the United States into the war. Some of us protested, but I suppose there was some truth in what he said. The subject of the Germans' bad treatment of the Jews was raised. One of the girls at the party said that she had recently visited Germany. She said that considering what the Jews had done to Germany, one could understand the German point of view. (This was before the American public was made aware of the "Holocaust;" indeed, the Holocaust had not yet reached its full fury.)

After war had broken out between Japan and the United States in December 1941, it was thought that it might be necessary to replace me at West High, and I was sent to the home of Professor Cheydleur of the Wisconsin French department to recruit his daughter to take over the second semester of my French class. However, I was not drafted at this time and I finished the academic year with my class at West.

As I was winding up my M.A. in French, a world war was raging and the thought of continuing graduate studies that would include French medieval poetry had no appeal to me. I wanted to leave home, work for a living, and live independently. The going annual salary then for beginning high school teachers in Wisconsin was $1,200. When I was offered a position to teach French and English at Kemper Military School, in Boonville, Missouri, at a salary of $1,350 plus room and board, I took it.

This chapter on the University of Wisconsin would not be complete without a note concerning my brother John's long and distinguished association with that institution. During his senior year (1945-1946) he was the editor of the

Daily Cardinal, the university's student newspaper. He later served as a reporter for the United Press, edited a weekly newspaper in Santa Barbara, California, earned a Ph. D. in journalism at Michigan State University, and ultimately became Evjue-Bascom professor in the School of Journalism and Mass Communication at the University of Wisconsin. After retiring, he and his wife continued to live in Madison and maintained many friendships among alumni and former faculty of the university.

CHAPTER 5

KEMPER MILITARY SCHOOL

W ithout being interviewed by anyone, and without any direct knowledge of
what Kemper looked like (although it had a good reputation), I accepted
the offer of the job at Kemper. For some reason, perhaps it was just curiosity, I
decided to visit Kemper in the summer before classes began. This involved a long
train ride in a coach made frigid by the air conditioning. This was in the summer
of 1942.

Boonville, Missouri, according to the map, is located on the Missouri River,
midway between St. Louis and Kansas City. I anticipated that the Kemper campus
would be beautifully situated on a hillside overlooking the majestic river. Instead,
I found the campus at the opposite side of the town on the edge of some low land.
There was a pond there, called Kemper Lake. (Conceivably, the lake had been
created by draining a swamp.) The buildings consisted of barracks painted dark
gray. Several residences adjoining the campus had been painted gray and converted
into barracks for the overload of students.

It was dreadfully hot in Boonville, and when I visited the administrators there,
I politely refused to take off my suit jacket even though they suggested it (they did
not wear jackets). In those days casual dress was not the style.

Because of a shortage of space in the barracks, I was given an allowance to live
in a room in the town. This suited me, as it would relieve me of the responsibilities
that would inevitably arise from residing with the cadets. I would eat my meals
with the cadets, however.

I found (or I may have been assigned) a room in what had formerly been a
large private residence next door to the Boonville theater. The theater was a stately
brick structure painted white with columns in the front. It had once been an
opera house. The theater (the only one in town), changed movies twice a week,
and I believe that in this pre-television era I saw just about every movie that came
to town. One movie particularly stands out. It was *Tennessee Johnson*, and dramatized
the story of President Andrew Johnson, Lincoln's successor who was impeached
but not convicted. The lead was played by Van Heflin.

The cadets ranged from seventh grade to the second year of college. I was assigned to teach high school English and French at the college level. I had no trouble at all with teaching French, my favorite subject. But during my second term I found the English lessons (the lesson plans were prescribed by a colleague in charge of the English courses) extremely dull and I had difficulty in holding the interest of the students.

My French class included the cadet captain, the highest ranking cadet in the school. He was a tall blond young man who earned virtually straight As, was a principal basketball player, and was highly esteemed by everyone in the school. Some years after I left Kemper, I heard that he had become shell-shocked during the war. I do not know whether he ever recovered.

Late every afternoon, we would have retreat, the cadets and faculty would assemble, and the American flag was ceremoniously lowered while a bugle played. It was wartime, and I found the ceremony moving. The American flag was taken seriously in those days. American boys were giving their lives for the defense of the country that the flag represented. Flag burners did not exist and if any showed up with their cute demonstrations, they would have earned no sympathy.

For the cadets Kemper was much more than just a school. They were living separated from their families, so that the school served as their families. Kemper with its many rules and 24-hour schedule was a way of life for the cadets and for the faculty, especially the faculty who lived in the barracks with the cadets. Many of the younger cadets very much missed their mothers and one or two at the beginning of a semester, would flee school and return home. I understood, however, that once a boy began classes, the tuition could not be refunded just because the boy left school.

I ate every meal with the cadets. The dining room was filled with long tables. Twelve people would sit at each table, and at the head of each table a faculty member would preside. In front of him were a dozen plates, and he would dish out the food into the plates one at a time, the plates then being passed along to their recipients. I soon became skilled at dishing out equal portions for everybody.

The food was quite acceptable. However, on Tuesdays we had "chili mac" (macaroni in chili sauce). This dish was not popular among the faculty, many of whom would then eat in a restaurant in town. On Sundays we always had chicken and dumplings. This was regarded as a treat and was the chef's pride. It was served because Sundays were visitors days, when some of the cadets' parents would dine with us before watching the parade and other ceremonies on Sunday afternoon.

The days of the cadets (and to a lesser extent the faculty) were very full. They would arise early in the morning. The last half of each afternoon was devoted to drills and athletics. From 7:30 to 9:30 P.M. they were supposed to study in their rooms. Faculty members took turns walking through the barracks to ensure that they were indeed studying. Smoking was strictly forbidden. Any infractions would be reported.

About once every other week I had the duty of making the rounds of the barracks in the evening. I took a special effort to walk quietly so that the students would have no forewarning that I was coming around. I am happy to say that I found extremely few violations, but I acquired the nickname of "hawk-eye."

Kemper had the reputation of maintaining the strictest discipline of any leading military school. I am not sure that this was necessarily to its credit, especially if the rules are applied without the application of common sense. At the time that I was hired, it was understood that I was a teetotaler. The contract specified that I would "abstain entirely from the use of intoxicants." After our first faculty meeting, before any classes met, one of the deans invited me to his house for wine. I was very surprised.

I suspect that one reason why so many private schools are military schools is that by imposing some of the burden of discipline onto the cadet officers, it was cheaper to manage the students.

On Sundays the cadets were required to attend one of the local churches. Only the two or three Jewish students were excused from this. They were served by a local individual who performed some rabbinical function. I got to know one of the Jewish boys because on Sunday we were working on scenery for a play. He was bright and resourceful and also worked on the school newspaper, which served as a kind of advertisement for the school and was closely supervised by the school administration.

One Sunday I attended the Presbyterian Church. The minister gave a scholarly sermon. In the middle of it he made the passing remark that perhaps the reason Jews were suffering so much in recent times was that they had rejected Jesus.

Another Sunday, I was invited by the Christian Church to sing a solo. Throughout the service, the minister referred to male members of the congregation as brothers, affixing the title brother (or sister) before people's names. Brother McNelly was thanked for his solo.

One day two workmen came into my classroom to wash the windows. I was struck by the fact that two men were required to do this simple task, and figured that that was the southern way of doing things. They pointed to the portrait of Lincoln hanging on the wall in the front of the room, but which I had not given any thought to. They said that "that" (meaning Lincoln) was the cause of everything that had gone wrong nowadays.

One thing that I did not like was the hazing. All the new students were called "rats" and subject to continuous humiliation. For example, they would be made to polish a senior student's shoes, then the shoes would be deliberately muddied and the rat would have to repeat the project several times. Every year, several of the rats could take it no longer and escaped to go home. They would usually be sent back, as the school had the policy of collecting tuition in advance.

On the far side of town was a boy's reformatory. A story that went the rounds at Kemper was that a boy being sent to the reformatory was sent to Kemper by mistake. He attended Kemper over a week before he realized that he was not in the reformatory.

Like the other civilians on the faculty, I was given a simulated military rank of lieutenant. I wore khaki shirt and trousers and a little brass insignia on my epaulets. Some of the faculty and all the administrators had some kind of reserve rank in the U.S. Army and wore regular army uniforms all the time. Saluting or returning salutes was required for everyone.

The military school has pluses and minuses. On the one hand some of the boys were the sons of Kemper cadets, and it was a family tradition to go there. The students got individual attention. If a cadet student did failing work in a class on a particular day, he was given a special assignment to be done at supervised make-up sessions. I remember one of my French students complaining about having to do make-up work for my class on Sunday afternoon when his parents were visiting. I confess I felt sorry for him, but that was the way the cookie crumbled.

I had the impression that some of the cadets thrived in the environment. As cadet officers they get direct experience in leadership. I much admired some of them. One boy told me that he had been sent to Kemper by his parents because the public schools in his Arkansas hometown were inadequate.

It was popularly believed in those days that if a boy habitually misbehaved, one way to straighten him out was to send him to a military school. We had a few of these types around, but if they got out of hand at Kemper, they could be expelled. One boy told me that if he had not been sent to Kemper he would probably have ended up in jail. His father was the district attorney in his county, but the boy had been apprehended with a friend for counterfeiting, and was incorrigible. This boy, however, took to making scenery with great enthusiasm (I was the drama coach), and I felt that we were doing him some good.

The full schedule and strict discipline on the whole no doubt had a way of suppressing individualism and one can well imagine that some boys would find it hard to adjust.

My extracurricular activity was to serve as coach of dramatics. At the start of the term, the dean told me that he hoped that the level of the dramatics at the school would be improved. For example, in the past, the annual play had been a comedy in which administrators of the school would be imitated by the student actors engaged in farcical behavior. I was given to believe that although this annual farce was amusing, it was not sufficiently serious to be instructive and that I would be expected to have the students present a serious play. As a result, I bought and paid the royalties for a play called *Submerged,* which involved a bunch of sailors in a submarine that had crashed to the bottom of the ocean and there were discussions as to how they were going to escape. It was a good play that struck the imaginations of the boys I had recruited for the project. The play was a success when it was presented to the cadets, and we accepted an invitation to present it at the local high school.

Just before Christmas vacation, a stunt night was scheduled. The dean called me in and said that he expected that the students would want to perform a skit in which faculty members would be imitated. He volunteered to help coach any student who wanted to imitate him. I was astonished, as this was the same dean who had previously indicated his disapproval of that kind of dramatics. Apparently this skit had become or was becoming a beloved tradition of the school. With several bright volunteers, I oversaw the preparation of a skit that made fun of the school and its administrators. We thought that what we wrote was very funny and clever, and it was well received by the cadets and everyone else when it was performed.

Colonel Hitch, the superintendent of the school, was a conservative very serious individual. His wife was the daughter of the preceding superintendent. He and the other administrators all drove black Buicks. He explained to me that there was nothing wrong with his previous Buick and he liked it but his wife insisted that they drive a Buick of the current year. He took a special interest in my musical background and invited me to sing at one of the assembly programs. I sang "Then You'll Remember Me," from the *Bohemian Girl.*

I was permitted to practice on the Hammond Organ in the auditorium when no one else was using it. I had taken several lessons on the Hammond organ the preceding year in Madison.

I enjoyed knowing the other young members of the faculty. They were mostly Missourians of about my age who had done graduate work at college. The music teacher organized a quartet of faculty members. I am afraid that I did not fit in well because I was determined to show off the beauty of my high baritone voice by drowning out the other men. The director had to keep reminding me not to sing so loud. I cannot recall that we ever performed anywhere.

The English program was overseen by a very pleasant blond fellow, a local boy who knew all about the history of the school. He said that the stock in the school was very closely held among the administrators and that it paid very well. It was his ambition one day to become one of these stockholders. He had several girl friends, one of whom he expected to marry. I assume that he ultimately achieved his ambition.

I was instructed to follow the lesson plans that he gave me for the conduct of my English class. This is just as well, because I had never practice taught English. One day I assigned my students to write a personal letter—one that they might ultimately send to a friend or relative. After class one student came to me with a problem. He did not know what to say in the letter he was writing to his girl friend. I suggested that he might say that recently one evening he was strolling along Kemper Lake (the pond near the school), that the moon reflected in the lake and that this romantic scene reminded him of her. He thought that was a good idea, but what else should he say?

I asked him what interests or hobbies he and his girlfriend had in common. Nothing in particular, he said. He added that the girl was now pregnant and that her father had contacted his father in connection with what should be done next.

For several days, rumors swirled around the school about one of the cadets who had propositioned another boy. It was said that the offending cadet would no longer be attending Kemper, and that his father had come to Kemper to take him home.

One of the instructors was a middle-aged man who had earlier in his life taught music. It seems that he had gone to people's homes to give them piano lessons. As he told it, the lessons were not confined to the teaching of scales or Czerny exercises, but rather involved romantic (to put it mildly) encounters.

One day a group of cadets showed up at the infirmary, alarmed because their urine had turned a decided green. It seems that the day before, one of the cadets had passed out round white balls that he said was candy. It turned out that it was not candy, but a harmless medication that doctor's used for diagnostic purposes. At another time several cadets suddenly showed up with bright red hair. They had dyed their own hair as a joke. These incidents confirmed my view that only God could have created little boys.

Kemper was an all-male institution. There was not a single female on the faculty. There may have been some women secretaries but I have no recollection of them.

Some of the faculty, and possibly some of the older cadets, dated girls who attended the two women's colleges in Columbia, Missouri, where the University of Missouri was also located. Columbia was only about thirty miles from Boonville, but gas rationing during the war put a cramp on intercity romances. Once I saw a big football game in Columbia between, I think, Missouri and the University of Kansas.

Every year at Kemper there was a great ball (I can't remember the occasion celebrated), at which the parents, girlfriends, faculty, and administrators were all invited. People would come from all over to this great event. I had no plan to go as I did not have a girlfriend to escort. One night I was watching a movie at the neighboring theater, when a girl sitting next to me struck up a conversation. On the spot it was decided that I would take her to the party. I bought a used tuxedo from the wife of a faculty member who was serving in the army. It developed that one of the cadets was taking the sister of my new girlfriend to the party. So the four of us made up a double date went to the ball together in his father's car. His date I must say was very pretty, but the sister, my date, was ordinary looking. The upshot was that we had a lovely time. Nearly all of the men were dressed in military uniforms, some in blue dress uniforms, and the girls all wore beautiful formal gowns. I have never seen such a grand party before or since. I did not pursue any farther my acquaintance with the girl I dated that night. But I did date once or twice the cute kindergarten teacher who lived in the same rooming house as I.

Close to my rooming house, which was on the main street, was a restaurant that remained open till late at night with a juke box that dispensed Henry James playing the trumpet. There I became acquainted with a member of the faculty who was married. I suspected that he spent time in the restaurant because he was having trouble at home. Also I learned from him much of the scuttlebutt about the school.

The war was on and the school was having trouble keeping the faculty, who were continually being drafted or enlisting for the army. Also there were discipline problems that some of the teachers were having. Indeed, my informant told me about problems with keeping order in his class and his difficulties with the administration. However, I thoroughly enjoyed my teaching at Kemper, and had had no experience with the kind of problems he was talking about.

In the spring of 1943 I got a letter from the Office of the Chief Signal Officer in Washington to work in the area of cryptanalysis. It sounded like an interesting job, but I delayed answering the letter because I liked my Kemper job so much. However, by the middle of the second semester I was having problems similar to those I had been hearing about. I was very reluctant to report trouble makers, who would be subject to severe punishment, and was at loss how to handle the situation. One or two other faculty members had run into this kind of difficulty and quit.

The Washington job now looked more attractive. I saw Colonel Hitch and announced my decision to resign my job at Kemper. (My smoking greatly annoyed him during our conversation.) When the word spread among the students that I was about to quit, my problems worsened and I heard a rumor that I would be put in the drink, meaning that I would be tossed into the lake, a ceremony that was said to be customary for faculty who were about to leave. Happily, the rumor, at least in my case, was without foundation. (I note in my Kemper contract the provision: "This contract may be canceled by either party if its terms are violated by the other party, or on fifteen days notice.")

So I left Kemper during the middle of the second semester. I have no idea what happened to my high school English classes and my college class in French.

I had enjoyed my friendships and teaching during the first semester at Kemper and value the experience. But my later stint with the Office of the Chief Signal Officer would have a more critical influence on the rest of my life.

CHAPTER 6

ARLINGTON HALL

On March 15, 1943, while teaching French and English and coaching dramatics at Kemper Military School, I received a detailed two-page letter from the Office of the Chief Signal Officer, offering me a position in the Washington, D. C. area. The letter was mimeographed, with short insertions typed, but the mimeographed portion included the interesting paragraph:

> The work for which you are being considered is of a highly secret nature involving duties connected with cryptographic activities, procedure and practice therein, under supervision. For this reason, it is desired that you do not discuss this proposed appointment with any unauthorized person. In this position you will be actively engaged in a phase of the war work which has a direct contact with the armed forces. *It is hoped that in arriving at your decision you will give full consideration to your responsibilities at this time* [emphasis added].

I suppose that the reference to my "responsibilities" implied that I should be engaged in essential war work if not serving (possibly as a draftee) in the military services. There was a war on, and I could not but take this job offer seriously. I was flattered by the job offer, especially since I had not applied for the position—indeed I had never heard of the Office of the Chief Signal Officer. I thoroughly enjoyed teaching and my friendships with congenial young members of the faculty. The annual salary $2190 for the 48-hour-a-week job in Arlington, Virginia, was not particularly attractive, and I either declined the invitation or delayed replying to it (probably the latter, as it would have seemed most prudent to keep my options open). However, some unpleasant incidents arose at Kemper, and I changed my mind about going to Arlington. In my files, I find an official action report dated April 10, indicating my appointment to the new position effective April 16.

About two months before the end of the second semester at Kemper, I resigned my job at Kemper much to the distress of the superintendent, Colonel Hitch, who liked me (he had asked me to sing a solo once at a school assembly). I sympathized with Colonel Hitch because the instability of his faculty in wartime must have been a constant worry for him. So I would move to Arlington, Virginia, a suburb of Washington D.C.

Edwin ("Uncle Ed") Taylor (my mother's only living sibling), Aunt Lois, and my cousin Carol lived in the D.C. metropolitan area. So did my mother's cousin, Mrs. Carol Brown Orlowsky and her husband and daughter, Carol Jay. I would not be completely bereft of family connections in Washington. Because Uncle Ed and Aunt Lois both were to show me and later my wife so many kindnesses, I should explain who they were.

Grampa Taylor, who had built some houses in Madison during his retirement, had helped his son Edwin and Edwin's wife get started in remodeling houses and building new houses in Madison. Before World War II Ed and Lois, who had studied architecture at the University of Michigan, built about a dozen beautiful custom brick English-style homes in fashionable neighborhoods in Madison, and then moved to Washington, D.C., where they designed and built prize-winning homes. Among their clients were J. Willard Marriott, Sr. and J. Edgar Hoover (whose home is shown in *Life* magazine, May 12, 1972, and Curt Gentry, *J. Edgar Hoover: The Man and the Secrets* [New York: Norton, 1991], pp. 519-520).

During the war, when building materials were in short supply, they had to quit home building. They bought a farm in Potomac, Maryland, outside of the District of Columbia, speculating that that particular rural area would become fashionable after the war. After the war they designed and built several fine homes on their farm land, which was divided into five-acre lots in the heart of the Potomac horse country. All their houses were individually designed, and they did not go into the business of building entire developments. Sometimes they resided in one of their recently built houses until it was sold.

Aunt Lois's father, R. Kent Beattie, a former botany professor at Washington State University, was a plant pathologist in the Department of Agriculture. He had spent many months in the Far East in connection with his study of chestnut blight and Dutch elm disease. He had worked closely with Japanese experts and studied Japanese language and culture. He brought back from Japan maps and gazetteers, which during the Pacific War he shared with the U.S. Army. In 1943, the Army Map Service published a book entitled on the cover *Beattie's Gazetteer*, the contents of which are an 888-page gazetteer of Japan in Japanese, which Dr. Beattie had bought in Japan. This book was particularly valued as a reference for romanizing the spelling of Japanese place names, which on Japanese maps are printed in Chinese characters. Both doctor and Mrs. Beattie liked to talk about Japan, China, and Indochina, where they had traveled extensively, and I enjoyed hearing what they had to say. (Dr. Beattie died in 1960 after donating his papers to the Smithsonian institution and to the Washington State University Herbarium.)

In Arlington, my initial work title was Research Analytic Specialist with a civil service rank of P-1. In January 1945, with the same title, I was promoted to P-2 with an annual salary of $2600. Much of the time, in spite of a frugal life style, I was living from paycheck to paycheck, once having to pawn the gold chain of the watch I had inherited from my grandfather.

My place of work, formally known as the Signal Intelligence Service (later Signal Security Service, and finally Army Security Agency at the end of the war), was located on the campus of what had before the war been a girls junior college ("finishing school") known as Arlington Hall, a name that continued in use as a synonym for the Army Security Agency. (Similarly, I much later learned that in England, Bletchley Park came to be used to denominate the famous Government Code and Cypher School [GC&CS], where a huge staff of scholarly types managed to decrypt the supposedly unbreakable Enigma code used by the Germans.) The main building of Arlington Hall was an imposing yellow-brick Georgian structure with tall white columns in the front. Behind it were some sprawling one—and two-storey temporary buildings painted grey.

The housing office of the Agency had a file listing available living quarters, and through that I learned of a succession of single rooms to rent in people's homes. For various reasons, I was unable to live for very long periods in one place, and I would today be at a complete loss to provide the list of my addresses. Most of these places were in easy walking distance of the Agency, but for one or two I had to take a bus. As I had no cooking facilities, I ate my breakfasts as well as my lunches at the large cafeteria at the Agency, where I found the food quite satisfactory. I usually ate my evening meal at nearby restaurants or at a drug store in Georgetown on nights when I attended a class at the university.

CRYPTANALYSIS

I was immediately enrolled in a small class (about ten students) in the cryptanalysis school. Here we were taught about substitution ciphers, transposition ciphers, codes, and superenciphered codes and techniques for their decryption. A substitution cipher involves the substitution of a different letter for each letter of a message. Ciphers normally are made sufficiently complicated that, for example, the letter A may be represented by the letter Q at one time and later A will be represented the letter M, etc., so that A is never repeatedly represented by the same letter. A transposition cipher involves the systematic scrambling of the letters of a message. Of course substitution and transposition may both be used to make a message harder to decrypt.

A code (as contrasted to a cipher) involves a code book, which may supply four- or five-digit numbers to represent entire words or entire phrases of a message. For example, the number 74789 might be used to signify the entire expression

"This is urgent; please reply immediately." The receiver of the message simply looks up the number 74789 in the code book to find out what it means. In order to make a code more difficult to be solved by a cryptanalyst, the numbers that are used may be enciphered. This device would be a superenciphered code. The cryptanalyst would have to both solve the method of encipherment and recreate (or manage to obtain somehow) the code book.

Because in any language some words and letters appear more frequently than other words and letters, messages that have been enciphered or encoded are not absolutely random conglomerations of letters or numbers. By collecting a sufficient number of messages using the same encryption method, it is possible mathematically to discern patterns, and from these the cryptanalyst, translator, or intelligence officer may make educated guesses about the original texts of messages (plain text), and figure out the encipherment method or recreate a code book. It helps, of course, to surreptitiously photograph, steal, or capture code books and cipher machines.

Since 1946, when I left the business, cryptography has gotten to be vastly more complicated than what I have just described.

The work was not dissimilar from doing difficult cross-word puzzles. Our class worked on substitution and transposition ciphers and on superenciphered codes. However, I was completely stumped by the last of our exercises and after two weeks of full-time effort was still unable to solve the problem, although some of the students in the class succeeded. The course ended after six weeks. The bright pretty blond (her husband was an airman) who sat next to me was promoted to an advanced class because, unlike the rest of us, she was highly trained in mathematics.

I was then assigned to work. My section, consisting of perhaps not more than ten people, was reading the enciphered messages of a country with which the United States was not at war and which was not an American ally. A pretty blond girl was assigned to teach me to use the little cipher machine, a task in which we found mutual enjoyment. The head of the section was a man whom I had known slightly when I was an M.A. student and he was a Ph. D. candidate in the French Department at the University of Wisconsin. He once gave a dinner party for all of us at his house nearby.

In the 1960s, about two decades after the end of the war, I received a telephone call at our home in Takoma Park, Maryland, reminding me that I should not discuss with anyone the work that I had been doing during the war. Although much had already been published about the role of cryptanalysis in the American victory over Japan, I took this telephoned warning seriously and until 2000 never mentioned to anyone, including my wife, the name of the first country whose messages I had been involved in reading. However in 2000 a book by David Alvarez (*Secret Messages: Codebreaking and American Diplomacy, 1930-1945*

[University of Kansas Press], page 167) revealed the story of the Arlington Hall's Finnish project. (The Finnish project was not mentioned in James Bamford's best seller, *The Puzzle Palace,* published by Houghton Mifflin in 1982.) Finland, the victim of a Soviet attack in 1941, had enjoyed much sympathy in the United States, and American-Finnish relations remained friendly even though Finland was, in effect, an ally of our enemy, Germany. According to Alvarez, Arlington Hall first began reading the Finns' most confidential communications in May, 1943.

The Hagelin cipher machine used by the U.S. army and the governments of minor countries throughout the world is pictured on page 429 of David Kahn's *The Code Breakers* (Scribner, 1996). The machine shown in this picture finds a vivid place in my memory.

JAPANESE STUDIES

I had been in the Finnish section for only a few weeks, when someone tapped me on the shoulder and asked if wanted to learn Japanese. This was the first time that I had heard Japanese mentioned at Arlington Hall, although I later learned that Japanese was the principal business of the institution. As I had all my life been interested in learning the language (I had studied some Chinese characters on my own), I enthusiastically agreed to enter the Japanese school at Arlington Hall.

Edwin O. Reischauer, a Harvard professor, who was the American ambassador to Japan from 1961 to 1966, describes in his autobiography how he set up the Japanese language school at Arlington Hall in the summer of 1942. (Edwin O. Reischauer, *My Life between Japan and America,* Harper and Row, 1986, pp. 91-94)

The school consisted of a number of small classes located in the main building (the yellow-brick edifice). The class to which I was assigned was probably the smallest there: only six students. Each morning we had successive sessions of instruction in reading, writing, and speaking Japanese. Occasionally there were lectures on special subjects. I especially remember a lecture on the Russo-Japanese War by Mr. Lloyd Faust that so fascinated me that I entertained fantasies about becoming someday a professor and giving a similar lecture. (One day Mr. Faust pointed out to us William F. Friedman, the famous cryptanalyst who had broken Japan's principal diplomatic code, known as *Purple,* in 1940.)

The afternoons were devoted largely to studying or reading assignments and learning how to write Japanese characters. The class included a bright young enlisted man who had already learned some Japanese in the ASTP (Army Specialized Training Program), a personable second lieutenant, two attractive former college girls, and a young Jewish woman, who was not shy about expressing her impatience with the rest of us, who seemed to be slow learners. The young lieutenant left us before the completion of the six-month course. (It was later reported that he had been attacked during a brawl in Australia.) Needless to say, the members of this tiny class came to know one another very well in the course of working together for six months.

The instructors included a Korean, who taught conversation (with, I suspect, a Korean accent), a Mr. Kerr (a former missionary to Korea), a sweet elderly lady who had worked in the American embassy in Tokyo, and several others. We used a textbook on written Japanese that had been developed at Harvard University by Edwin O. Reischauer, and Serge Ellisséeff.

After completing the Japanese course we were assigned to the translation of decrypted Japanese messages. I feel free to describe the nature of my then secret work because Reischauer has freely revealed it in his autobiography, page 91. I and the people around me were primarily concerned with messages written in the Japanese Army transport code. A typical decrypted message would indicate the name of a transport vessel, the places and dates of its departure and arrival, and an inventory of its cargo. Evidently the decryption and translation of these messages played a major role in the virtually complete destruction of Japanese shipping by American aircraft and submarines.

The translators were divided into teams, with about eight or ten people sitting around a table on which a few Japanese-English dictionaries rested. The teams consisted of army officers, enlisted men, and male and female civilians mixed together. A few of the civilians and military had lived in Japan before the war and had learned the language there. Off-hand, I cannot remember seeing anyone of Japanese descent at Arlington Hall with the possible exceptions of Richard McKinnon and his stunning Eurasian sister, the children of a Japanese mother and an American teacher of English in Japan. The large Kenkyusha Japanese-English dictionary, of which we were supplied photocopies, included an amazing number of euphemisms for extramarital activities, and these were frequent sources of innocent merriment.

GEORGETOWN UNIVERSITY

As I aspired to become a diplomat assigned to Japan following the war, I decided to go to night school for advanced work in international relations. I talked with several employees of the State Department to get their views. One of them said that although he himself taught a night course at one of the local universities, he thought that my best bet would be to study at Georgetown University, which was famous for its School of Foreign Service. As I already had an M.A. degree from Wisconsin, I entered the graduate school at Georgetown, majoring in political science.

I attended classes several nights a week at Georgetown, taking courses in comparative politics, Thomistic philosophy (required at Georgetown), political theory, and international administration. I would take a bus that brought me to the far end of Key Bridge, linking Virginia to the D.C. From there I would walk up the hill to class, often stopping at a drug store for a bowl of chili. I liked all of my professors, who were interesting to hear, but unfortunately, I often had difficulty, at the end of a full day's work, in keeping awake during their lectures.

I shall never forget Professor Goetz Briefs' magnificent lectures on Adam Smith and "zee inwizible hant of Gott." (In the 1980s Professor Ferdinand A. Hermens kindly gave me a copy of the December 1983 issue of the *Review of Social Economy,* which is entirely devoted to essays on "solidarist economics" by the late Goetz Briefs [1889-1974]. Professor Hermens, who was internationally famous for his critique of proportional representation, and his wife kindly hosted Myra and me at their apartment on Rockville Pike one afternoon. He told me of his experiences in Germany under Hitler's rule. He died in 1998.)

Professor Boyd-Carpenter often concluded his lectures with this observation: "Gentlemen, it all comes down to this: man is a hunter and woman is an acquisitionist." At the time I regarded that statement as ridiculous, but with the passage of time I have come to appreciate its essential truth.

I wanted to enhance my competence in Japanese, and wrote applying to study at the Navy Language School in Boulder, Colorado. I had heard that the Japanese course there was eighteen months long as contrasted with the six-month course I had taken Arlington Hall. Upon completion of the course, one was made an ensign. The course was reputed to be very difficult and there was a high rate of drop outs because of "eye trouble." I received no reply from the Boulder school, possibly because they were reluctant to recruit from the staff at Arlington Hall.

FRIENDS

During the three years that I worked at Arlington Hall, I met many interesting people there, including Andrew Rice, whose twin brother and sister, Peter and Pam, had been high school students in my practice-teaching French class at the University of Wisconsin. Peter was a close friend of my brother John. They once built a small sailboat together based on plans in *Popular Mechanics* magazine. They sailed it during the summer of 1941, but in the fall during Freshman week a great storm arose. The boat was moored near the Memorial Union. Someone telephoned our house about the problem but mother was unable to warn the boys in time, and the storm reduced the boat to scrap lumber.

The Rice children's father, William Rice, was a professor of law at the University of Wisconsin, and was working during the war in the War Labor Board in Washington. I was invited to several parties at the Rices' rented home in Maryland, which Pamela and some of her friends attended. In 1944, completely unknown to me at the time, Peter, a crew member of a submarine, was killed during the fighting in the Pacific Ocean. In 1946, Professor Rice, unopposed in the primary election, ran unsuccessfully as a Democrat for Congress. My brother John did publicity for him and they worked hard to resuscitate the Democratic Party in Wisconsin. My mother, a rock-ribbed Republican, was distressed by the subversive influence of the Rices on John. In 2002, John still owned the mast of the famous sailboat, which he used as a leveler when building a patio in his backyard, and a picture of Peter Rice hangs in his study.

An English teacher of mine at Wisconsin, Samuel Chew, also worked at Arlington Hall. A few years ago, I learned that he had been one of the principal cryptanalysts engaged in the solution of the Venona messages (Soviet correspondence between KGB agents in Washington and the KGB headquarters in Moscow, critical, among other things, in the discovery and conviction of the ring of atomic spies headed by Julius Rosenberg). Just before I left for Japan in 1946, Dr. Chew warned me that the Japanese were treacherous people, and that I should take care against being stabbed in the back.

Edwin O. Reischauer, as a major and later a lieutenant colonel, maintained liaison with the State Department and Pentagon and often worked on Japanese communications at Arlington Hall, where I first came to be acquainted with him. His sister-in-law, the widow of Robert Reischauer, who had been killed by a bomb in Shanghai during the Sino-Japanese War in 1937, also worked at Arlington Hall. She was very outgoing, and at a large dinner party at a Chinese restaurant downtown, she would go from table to table holding up samples of food on her long chop sticks and recommending them to the rest of us.

Occasionally groups of us would visit China Town, on H Street in downtown Washington. On at least one occasion our favorite restaurant was closed by officials because of sanitary violations.

The people in my section worked in a very long room in one of the temporary buildings, where, after several months, everyone came to know everyone, and there was much socialization both on and off the job. I was involved with a small informal group that we nicknamed the Oochoochoo Goonattach (Chattanooga Choochoo spelled backwards). My friend Luhrs Stroud was a leading celebrant, and some of our parties were noisier than they should have been. Three lovely and intelligent young cryptanalysts (with whom I successively fell in love), Flora Kearney, Louise de Haven, and Lucille Dahlgren (who later married Luhrs), graced some of our get-togethers.

One co-worker at Arlington Hall was Chad Walsh (1914-1991). He was said to be an outstanding scholar of literature, although I had never before heard of him. The January 19, 1991, issue of the *New York Times* contains a long obituary of Chad Walsh, indicating that after two years in Washington as an research analyst for the Army Signal Corps, he joined Beloit [College] as an assistant professor. Walsh's "vast literary output" included books on C.S. Lewis, religious and children's books, and volumes of poetry. He reviewed books by C.S. Lewis and Aldous Huxley for the *New York Times* and was a leading advocate of Lewis's philosophy. In addition to being a professor English at Beloit for several decades, he was ordained as an Episcopal priest in 1949 and during summers served as a guest preacher throughout the United States. The *New York Times* article seemed to imply that he had been converted to Christianity in 1944, about the same time that he was working in Arlington Hall.

One notable acquaintance at Georgetown University was Sotero Laurel, the son of José Laurel, who had become president of the Philippines under Japanese rule. It was amazing that the son of this Japanese puppet was residing at the Philippine mission in Washington. Sotero had a car, and one evening a bunch of us students rode with him in search of a good restaurant. (Sotero later became a prominent politician in the Philippines, and I once stumbled on a book written by him.)

One summer, I auditioned for the choir at the Washington National Cathedral and joined the bass section. We had rehearsals every Wednesday night and performed in both morning and afternoon services on Sundays. The choir was all male—the sopranos and altos being recruited from the boys school in the cathedral close. Our choirmaster, who doubled as organist, was a brilliant young man who had recently been studying in Europe. He was an exacting musician who tolerated no imprecision, and we all admired him. We sang magnificent music, and I always felt a thrill as the great cathedral organ boomed during our processions and recessions. (As I was paid $50 a week for this extremely pleasant work, I lost my amateur standing as a musician.)

I later joined the amateur choir of the Foundry Methodist Church on 16th and P Streets and also participated in meetings of its young singles group, which, among other things, sponsored dances with live music every month. It was common for a small group of us to congregate after church to go to lunch together. Once a young man from Madison joined our luncheon group. He was Vernon Kirkpatrick, who had recently graduated from the University of Wisconsin Music School (although I had not known him there), and I was much impressed that he had been hired as an oboist in the National Symphony. (I now know that shortly after I met him he married a Lucille Tipple, a bassoonist, who was a neighbor and life-time friend of the Madison woman, a violinist, whom I married in 1960.) The girls in Foundry Methodist Church were lively and attractive, and some played in a small orchestra sponsored by the church. I became acquainted with Ruth Jones, an attractive tall blonde from rural Iowa. She insisted that the two of us were related, but I never understood the details of the relationship and my subsequent genealogical researches never produced her name.

The Foundry Methodist Church was a leading Washington institution. I learned later that during the war Syngman Rhee, the Korean politician, regularly attended the church. The pastor claimed to be personally acquainted with Chiang Kai-shek. (In 1993 and 1994, both President Clinton and his rival Senator Robert Dole, attended this church with their wives. In December 1994, after the pastor had expressed in a sermon his support for U.S. intervention in Haiti, which Senator Dole had opposed, the Doles ceased worshiping at Foundry.)

In 1946, following the example of some of my friends, I applied for a position in General MacArthur's Tokyo headquarters. At the old Navy Building in downtown Washington, I was interviewed by Commander Charles Nelson Spinks, who was then in a naval uniform. I emphasized not only my experience at Arlington Hall but also my status as a graduate student in political science at Georgetown. Dr. Spinks recruited me to serve in the Civil Intelligence Section in Tokyo, where I later encountered him.

While my transfer from Arlington to Tokyo was being arranged, I was given a physical examination for the military draft, and classified 1-A, apparently for immediate induction in the Army. However, without my asking for it, the Army Civil Affairs Division obtained a deferment for me, and I retained my civilian status when I went to Tokyo.

CHAPTER 7

A SLOW BOAT TO YOKOHAMA

It was August 1946. To cram for my final exams at Georgetown and to pack for my impending journey to Japan, I took a week off from my job at the Army Security Agency. At the last moment it became evident that I could not possibly finish packing without some help, so I called up Jim MacDowell, a friend at Arlington Hall. We took the bus to Georgetown and got a bite at Blitze's Cafeteria. I then walked over to GU to write my semester exam while Jim did the following: bought me a footlocker, took it to my room in Arlington, packed and labeled it, took my footlocker, trunk, and three pieces of luggage to Union Station, checked them all on my ticket to NYC, helped his taxi driver to change tires (he had a flat tire en route), and finally met me at GU. This all in three hours flat. (Jim also undertook to mail my books and magical equipment home to my mother in Madison, express C.O.D.)

At GU I put my suitcase next to the wall while I wrote my final exam for Professor Boyd—Carpenter's class. When I told the professor that I was on my way to Japan, he said he wished I had mentioned this to him sooner, as he was a friend of Prime Minister Shidehara, and we could go into the railroad business together.

(The professor was an old Japan hand, full of memories about his dealings with Chinese warlords in the 1930s. He treated his students with unusual kindness. He once invited us to his house for dinner, where some of the guests remarked that Roosevelt had gotten us into the war because he had wanted to be remembered as a great president. Another time, Boyd-Carpenter invited the entire class to dinner at the Mayflower Hotel, where an orchestra played while we had a wonderful dinner, topped off by frozen custard, a novelty to me.)

Jim and I got to Union Station at 9.30, and found that the train I was to take would be made up at 10:00 but would not leave till 2:00 AM. Charles Crosby, my old Madison friend, was at the station and the three of us had a little celebration. I went to bed aboard the Pullman car at about 11:30. In New York the next morning I checked into a hotel near Times Square. I did some sight seeing and saw

Clarence Day's "Life with Father." While in New York, I met my mother's cousin, Carol Orlowsky and we took a double-decker to her pleasant apartment in the Queens.

At an orientation meeting I learned that the trip to Japan (via the Panama Canal), originally scheduled to take twenty-eight days would actually take fifty-one days. The passengers consisted of 350 women and 70 men. Our voyage had to be postponed for several days as the ship was being painted. I dated Carol J. (Carol Orlowsky's daughter, my second cousin) to go swimming in the Atlantic. Carol J. had just been elected "Miss Personality" at her high school and although she was only 17 years old she had done some professional modeling. She was tall and shapely.

After six days in New York on per diem, I took a taxi to Brooklyn and checked in at the POE (Port of Embarkation). Much of the day was spent loading the *U.S.S. Wisteria*, a Liberty Ship that had been serving as a hospital ship. Stevedores unceremoniously threw onto the ship our luggage, including portable radios, which were smashed. Finally we walked single-file up the gang plank. Our ship and our companion ship, a slightly smaller vessel, the *U.S.S. Acadia*, were loaded at about the same time. At night we lifted anchor and oohed and aahed at the pretty lights along the shore. We were finally on our way to Yokohama via the Panama Canal.

All the passengers were Department of Army Civilians (DACs), many destined to Tokyo to work for General MacArthur. There were five female passengers for every male passenger, a ratio that became increasingly salient during the progress of our journey. The voyage was by no means unpleasant. In the Carribean Sea, we enjoyed watching for flying fishes.

In the course of writing my memoirs, I got massive help from the letters that I sent to my mother during the trip to Japan and my work in MacArthur's GHQ. I am especially struck by the fact that both shipboard and afterwards in Tokyo, I frequently went dining and dancing with American girls, some of whom I have since completely forgotten. A week or so after the *Wisteria* left New York, I wrote the following letter to my mother:

> Dear mother:
>   I had a glorious time in Panama running around with [Arvilla] Chick. The boat docked in Crostobal Friday night. I took Chick to Colon (next to Cristobal) It is full of night clubs and bars, as there are many sailors stationed and passing through. We went to the Copacabana. They had a big orchestra with lots of singing and dancing acts. A man would announce the acts in Spanish then a woman would announce them in English. Signs on stores are usually in two languages. There are lots of silk clothes from China, Parker 51 pens, white shirts for $2.00, alligator handbags, filigree jewelry in gold and silver—all hard to get in the States.

Saturday night we took the bus from Colon to Panama City. In the mountains we saw many primitive huts with palm-leaf roofs, no walls, and built on stilts. Ciudad Panama is most colorful. Houses are painted orange, blue, red, etc., and all have balconies. You can see right in them as they are built for lots of ventilation. We saw the Cathedral of Panama City, the president's palace (gleaming white with a patio and pool; inside were three white long-legged birds). The tropical vegetation is most interesting. We ate at the Hotel Columbia on Plaza Bolivar. They did not give us a menus so we were pleasantly surprised to see the meal turn out to be a steak dinner. The waitresses (one Negress and one Indian) spoke Spanish, but enough English to tell us how much the meal cost. The streets are full of open shops with picturesque names and men, women, and children selling tickets for the National Lottery, which has daily drawings. I bought some T-shirts to wear around on the boat, as much of the time it is very hot . . . . We are having a dance on the sun deck tonight.

I go on to say some nice things about Arvilla Chick, a tall slim teacher of political science and student of law, who looked very good in shorts and who endeavored to teach me something about economics in exchange for Japanese lessons.

Most of the male passengers were assigned to upper and lower bunks in crowded rooms. Shortly after the canal passage, one couple on board was married by the captain. When the newly weds were assigned a private compartment all to themselves, it was said that it was not love, but rather a desire for decent sleeping quarters, that motivated the marriage.

We were scheduled to tie up in Honolulu for about ten days for repairs on the ship's engine. By the time we arrived in Honolulu, some pairing off had occurred. A few couples registered in hotels. Many of us went dancing one night at the famous Royal Hawaiian Hotel. As we had been scantily attired aboard ship, it was a shock to see one another in respectable clothes. One day some of us took a narrow-gauge train to the opposite end of the island to swim. On the way back a boy with a ukelele entertained us with his singing.

We had a great luau at Ala Moana beach, with pig roasted in a pit, poi, and native dancing and music. The dancing looked dangerous as the performers hopped around sharp knives and the like. It was rumored that this was the first great luau since the end of the war, and that a photographer from *Life Magazine* was taking pictures of the proceedings. (Later pictures of our passengers and of our ship were published on several pages of *Liberty Magazine* dated February 15, 1947.)

There were romantic evenings in Honolulu. One of the passengers encountered her old beau (a sailor) in Hawaii, and stayed there to marry him. Another passenger was arrested in Honolulu for prostitution. I envied her skill on the *Wisteria's* piano.

She played popular sheet music recklessly with occasional wrong notes, but with a feeling for the words and tune that made it listenable.

Honolulu was not entirely songs and games. I spent a day at the University of Hawaii library doing research for a term paper for GU. College students of Japanese extraction whom I saw on the bus spoke English with a discernable Japanese accent.

Aboard ship, the meals were good with steak several times a week, turkey and chicken on Sundays. The sunsets on the Pacific Ocean were breathtakingly beautiful. In the evening after dinner we would go up to the bow to admire them. Afterwards we played cards, went to the movies, or just loafed on the hurricane deck and looked at the stars. The weather was pretty warm, so most of our time we spent out of doors. Because of the heat in the cramped sleeping quarters, some of us slept on the deck.

During the fifty-two days spent aboard the *Wisteria* (including time in Hawaii) there were organized activities. There were regular religious services, both Protestant and Catholic, overseen by the ship's chaplain. Some of us established the "Hysteria University," where we took turns lecturing on our specialties. I lectured on Chinese characters. Someone else told us how MacArthur was converting Japan into a democracy. From my knowledge of Japan, I thought the idea of Japan becoming a democracy was ridiculous. A former soldier led a group in calisthenics every morning.

I became friends with Albert Coleman, a music teacher who could play anything on the piano by ear. Some of us wrote a song about the *Wisteria*, to the tune of "Dirt Behind the Bunks." It was published in our souvenir booklet. My contribution went like this:

> *Wisteria, Wisteria,* What happened to the spoons?
>   *Wisteria, Wisteria,* We're eating like baboons.
>   We'll chopsticks use,
>   To stir our coffee and our booze.
>   *Wisteria, Wisteria,* You're a lollapalooze.

There were eighteen men in my cabin, with just enough room to get in and out. I wrote some of my letters while lying on my bunk. The few lounges on the ship were inadequate, so people played cards in the hallways and spent much of the time on deck. It was so hot one night that I took my mattress and blankets to the sun deck and put them on a couple of deck chairs so I could get some sleep. It was impossible to have any privacy to speak of as everywhere you went there were people. From time to time bridge tournaments were organized, and some people would play all night.

Wilson, a cabin mate, edited the ship's daily mimeographed newspaper. He was frequently seen with Esther Wright, a statistician friend of Chick's.

After we drew into the port at Yokohama, we had to remain aboard the *Wisteria* a whole day. Around five or six in the evening we were loaded on a special train for Tokyo. We pulled into a very dark Tokyo. Among the few city lights was a vertical electrical sign on which Japanese characters descended from the top to the bottom of the sign, chronicling the news. It reminded me of Times Square with an exotic twist. I had been studying Japanese for several years, and this sight thrilled me.

The trip to Japan had taken fifty-two days; we had left New York in midsummer (August 15) and arrived in Japan in midfall (October 5). (About fifty years later I flew from Tokyo to Washington, D.C., arriving in Washington ten minutes before the departure from Tokyo.)

After several weeks in Tokyo I went to collect my salary. The paymaster counted out for me $940.00 in $10 denominations of Military Payment Certificates (MPC). Never before or since have I seen so much cash at one time. The six days in New York and the fifty-two days aboard the *Wisteria* had been a paid vacation. (We were supposed to use MPCs for purchases at the PX and for our room and board.)

Some months after arriving in Tokyo I mentioned to a lady in our office that I had come to Japan on the *Wisteria*. She exclaimed, "If I had been on that ship I would be ashamed to admit it!"

CHAPTER 8

THE OCCUPATION OF JAPAN

In an earlier chapter, I told of my famous fifty-two-day voyage to Japan aboard the *U.S.S. Wisteria*. I will now tell about what I did after arriving in Tokyo in mid-October, 1946.

It was easy to understand why General Douglas MacArthur chose the Dai Ichi Mutual Life Insurance Building for his headquarters. On the same street (called "Avenue B" by the Americans) were a number of other modern six- or eight-storey office buildings (some of them were requisitioned for use by Occupation authorities) as well as the famous Imperial Hotel designed by Frank Lloyd Wright. The Dai Ichi Building was faced with rough-hewn gray granite and was graced with a row of square columns that extended upward to almost the full height of the building. Unlike its neighbors it was uncompromisingly contemporary in design. An American flag flew from the top of the structure. Today the dignity of the edifice is diminished by the much taller buildings that have since been erected in the neighborhood.

Late every morning, MacArthur's limousine would arrive at the front of the building, where a crowd of Japanese and Americans were waiting to watch the general enter the building. His residence was the American Embassy, not far away, which had been occupied by Ambassador Joseph Grew for ten years before the war broke out. In those days, the embassy grounds, which included a lovely swimming pool and white buildings in classical architecture, were attractive. But in the 1970s some of the buildings were torn down and a tall mustard-colored office building has compromised the original charm of the compound.

(In 1980, I asked the doorman at the Dai Ichi Building if I might see MacArthur's former office, which had been preserved intact. I went to the sixth floor and enjoyed the privilege of trying out the general's small tattered revolving chair. From this chair [or should it be dubbed a throne?] General MacArthur had ruled the Empire of Japan.")

On my first day of work I was interviewed in the Dai Ichi Building by Colonel Russell Duff and told him about my background, having learned the Japanese language, worked in the Army Security Agency, and studied political science at night at Georgetown. He said he thought I could do just about anything, and I was assigned a desk.

My desk (actually it was an ordinary office table) was in a large room on the first floor in the front of the Dai Ichi Building. My back faced a large window on a major street. Across the street was a moat, on the other side of which were the grounds of the imperial palace.

(Years later I told a Japanese friend that my job in the Dai Ichi Building was the best job I ever had. "Yes," he said, "You were closest to the emperor then.")

I was assigned to read a carbon copy of a long report that had been prepared by our intelligence. It was a detailed narrative of the February 26, 1936, military mutiny, which had threatened to establish a military dictatorship in Japan. I was already familiar with the story but enjoyed spending several days reading it. After a few days, Colonel Paul Rusch gave me an individual tour of the facilities of the Civil Intelligence Section (CIS), some of which were located in other parts of Tokyo.

I should perhaps mention that when I entered the CIS in the fall of 1946, I was unaware of the past turbulent history of that organization. For example, I was unaware that—and here I am oversimplifying—it had once been a special staff section headed by General Elliott R. Thorpe and been part of the headquarters of the Supreme Commander for the Allied Powers (SCAP, one of MacArthur's titles), and that later it had been taken over by the anti-Communist General Charles A. Willoughby and incorporated as the Civil Intelligence Division into his G-2 Section (a general staff section, under the Commander-in-Chief, Armed Forces Pacific Area Command (CINC-AFPAC, MacArthur's other title). (See Takemae Eiji, *Inside GHQ: The Allied Occupation of Japan and Its Legacy* [New York: Continuum, 2002] pp. 161-168.) In spite of these changes, the term Civil Intelligence Section continued to be used for the section.

Also, I was unaware that in the fall of 1945, the famous Canadian historian, E. Herbert Norman, who had been a communist as an undergraduate at Cambridge University, had served as chief of Research and Analysis Section, Counter-Intelligence under General Thorpe. (Roger Bowen, *Innocence Is Not Enough: The Life and Death of Herbert Normon* [Armonk NY: Sharpe, 1986], p.118.)

I was told that I would be assigned to a Lieutenant-Colonel Slade, and we would be entrusted with the establishment of a new branch. A few days later, Colonel Slade arrived. He had been involved in combat intelligence. He was a mild-mannered individual who before the war had taught Spanish at West Point.

We were directed to devise the procedure by which documents (including English translations of letters written by Japanese to MacArthur) coming into Operations Division of the CIS would be disseminated to appropriate branches, and how reports from the 441st Counter Intelligence Corps would be answered.

This latter organization had stations scattered all around Japan. It seems that the CIC was very unhappy that we were not providing them with instructions as to how to proceed following their submission of reports to us. Colonel Slade and I would set up a new branch—Evaluation, Control, and Dissemination Branch— which would process incoming documents, assign them to the appropriate branches of the Operation Division, and oversee appropriate responses.

Because of Colonel Slade's experience in intelligence, I anticipated no difficulties. He would outline the scheme, and I could write it up. During his first few days, he was much preoccupied with preparing for the imminent arrival of his family, locating a house for them, ensuring that the heating was adequate, etc. After a week or two his wife and one child arrived. The wife was a very attractive lady. Colonel Slade complained about his rank; it seems that most of his fellow classmates at West Point had full colonelships and he had been unjustly denied a promotion.

We were to head up the proposed new branch and were told that a half dozen or so civilians and enlisted men were to be assigned to the operation. Colonel Slade would be the chief, and I would be the "coordinator." We discussed where the desks would be located, and the locations of waste baskets and pencil sharpeners. I assumed that he knew pretty much how our tasks would actually be accomplished.

He was absent from the office entire days or half days attending to the logistics for his family, and our paper describing the office procedures for our new branch was not being written. After about three weeks had passed, Colonel Slade, with a note of panic in his voice, announced that we were required to submit our report the following Monday. In order to meet this deadline, he and I spent that evening at the Peers Club (which had been taken over for use by American military officers) to iron out our proposal.

Within five minutes it was clear that neither of us had any idea as to what to write in our report. When he offered me a beer, I accepted. Up to that moment I had been a complete teetotaler. In Marinette I had become a member of the Loyal Temperance Legion, a young people's auxiliary of the WCTU (Women's Christian Temperance Union). I had taken a solemn oath to consume no alcoholic beverages, and had never broken this oath. But overcome by panic, I accepted the beer.

The next day I was told to go to Dr. Charles Nelson Spinks, and request from him the transfer of two of the men in his Special Activities Branch to come to work in our new branch. I spoke to Dr. Spinks, who told me that he would be happy to spare two men, Messrs. X and Y. He said that they were useless in his branch and that he hoped that I would be able to get some work out of them.

After the two new men had talked with me and Colonel Slade, it turned out that they saved our day. X was familiar with office procedures and described how to set up a "suspense file" that would help us maintain a record of the assignment and routing of documents. After several days we got this thing into operation. We were the Evaluation, Control, and Dissemination Branch of Operations Division.

Every document addressed to CIS in the Dai Ichi Building would come to us and we would in turn farm it out to the appropriate branch which would report back to us on any action that would need to be taken. Our branch would write correspondence, in the form of letters or "check sheets" to appropriate agencies.

One day, Mr. X, who was the principal architect of our famous suspense file, failed to show up for work. It seems that on the week-end he had gone sailing and his boat was becalmed. As a result, he was absent for a week.

After several weeks, the system ran so smoothly that it became virtually automatic, requiring almost no work from the half dozen or so folks in our Branch. The Branch itself then became unnecessary, and was abolished. The work of the branch would be accomplished by a major who had familiarized himself with our operation.

I was awarded a Civilian Meritorious Service Award, which included a ribbon.

SPECIAL ACTIVITIES BRANCH

Our new branch was abolished, and I was transferred to the Special Activities Branch, headed by Dr. Spinks. There the amount of one's work largely depended on how seriously he took the reports coming from the counter-intelligence corps (CIC) or elsewhere. A serious report would be forwarded to higher headquarters with a letter of transmittal which I would write. For a while, the CIC reports I was reading did not seem to require such correspondence, so I spent my spare moments reading George H. Sabine's *History of Political Theory,* a famous textbook that I had brought with me from the United States. Dr. Spinks saw me doing this and told me to work on my reports. Taking his admonition seriously I drafted a flurry of letters of transmittal which briefly occupied as many as three typists at a time.

(In 1997 when I was preparing a lecture to Japanese Diet members about the Japanese constitution, Professor Thornton Anderson told me that my study of Sabine, which included a detailed historical analysis of the contract theory of government, was much more important than my bureaucratic correspondence in SCAP headquarters.)

As was perennially the situation, MacArthur's name was being mentioned as a presidential possibility. In an uncharacteristic spell of deviltry, I posted on my desk in the Dai Ichi Building a prominent sign reading "Eisenhauer for President." Dr. Spinks came over to my desk. To my surprise, he helpfully suggest that I correct the spelling to "Eisenhower." Dr. Spinks seemed to share my sense of humor. After a day or two I removed the sign.

One day Colonel Robert McCormick, the famous editor of the *Chicago Tribune,* spoke to us in the auditorium. It was his view that the Russians were almost as bad as the British. He did not advocate MacArthur for president, much to my surprise, but strongly supported the candidacy of Senator Robert Taft.

Although some of my Army Security Agency friends moving to Tokyo knew the Japanese language much better than I, they did not have my academic credentials, and ended up working in ATIS (Allied Translator and Interpreter Section) in the NYK building, while I got a lovely job with a good civilian rank in the same building as MacArthur, where the Japanese materials crossing my desk had already been translated by someone else. On my own initiative, I continued my language studies in Tokyo with a Japanese tutor. However, because only English was used at the office and because my social life was confined almost exclusively to Americans, I had little need or opportunity to speak and improve my spoken Japanese.

In CIS my title was Research Analyst, with a rank of P-3. The base salary was $4,149.60, with an added overseas differential of $1,037.40, for a total of $5,187.00. The cost of room and board in army facilities was extremely small. (After I left Japan, it would take a number of years before I could equal that salary.)

I heard that there was a shortage of professional civilians in Seoul, Korea. One woman from Seoul visiting in Tokyo told about the difficulties that General Hodges was having with Syngman Rhee, the leading Korean politician. It appeared that if someone in my position moved to Seoul he could get a P-5, a very respectable rank indeed. Because I had gotten quite fond of my small circle of friends in Tokyo, especially John Sato, his wife, and Carol Yoder, I had no desire to move to Seoul. If I had taken a P-5 job in Korea, I would likely have continued the rest of my life as a well-heeled bureaucrat.

As the patient reader may have noticed, I have said nothing at all about the substance of the activities of the CIS directly relevant to the philosophy and purposes of the Occupation. It was inherent in the nature of intelligence that the work must be secret. I will refrain from describing the operations or cases that I was involved with because I was bound to secrecy on such matters.

However, in the 1990s I had lunch at Archives II in College Park, Maryland, with a Finnish graduate student who was engaged in doctoral research on the relations between the Americans in Tokyo and the Japan Communist Party. Many of the CIS records had been declassified, and he was in the course of studying them. Later, I consented to critique his dissertation and finally to become his "opponent" in the formal public defense. Myra and I therefore visited him and his family and major professor in Finland in 1999. As I read his dissertation, which described in detail the affairs we in CIS had been investigating, it was easy to imagine that I was once again sitting in my office in the Dai Ichi Building perusing reports from the Counter Intelligence Corps. The dissertation, by Henry Oinas-Kukkonen, was published in January, 2003, by Greenwood Press under the title *Toleration, Suspicion, and Hostility: Changing U.S. Attitudes toward the Japanese Communist Movement, 1944-1947.*

THE NEW CONSTITUTION AND WAR CRIMES TRIAL

On Sunday, November 3, 1946, the promulgation of Japan's new democratic constitution was celebrated on the plaza of the imperial palace in Tokyo. It was a cool, overcast day. A stage decorated with pine branches had been set up. Japanese dignitaries and some Americans in military uniform were sitting or standing on the stage. The proceedings were in Japanese. The emperor and empress were introduced to the audience by Prime Minister Yoshida. Yoshida led the audience in three cheers: *"Banzai! Banzai! Banzai!"* I was at the time shocked by this as I had associated the word *banzai* with the expression "banzai charges" which applied to the suicide attacks glorified by Japanese militarists. Actually, in this case it simply meant literally "Ten Thousand Years," or "Long Live the Emperor!"

One day, when things at the office did not seem unduly busy, I asked the boss if I might attend the Tokyo war crimes trial, officially, the International Military Tribunal for the Far East (IMTFE), where Tojo and his associates were on the dock. I was given the necessary permission and attended the trial, which was held in the main building of the campus of the former War Ministry, where my billet was located. I sat in a balcony reserved for observers. The darkness in the room was relieved by glaring spotlights and the atmosphere seemed heavy with gloom. The proceedings were amplified and consisted largely of discussions of the diplomacy leading to the Axis Tripartite Pact.

The aim of the prosecution was to prove, citing diplomatic documents, the aggressive and illegal nature of Japan's policies and the culpability of the defendants. It seemed to me, however, difficult to hold specific individuals criminally liable for complex policies adopted by their government. The debate over diplomatic issues was made more tedious by technical disputes over the English translations of the Japanese documents. Unimpressed by the arguments on both sides and bored by the proceedings, I decided that I did not want to see a second day of this trial, although I had the impression that my superiors would have been quite willing for me to spend several days of observation there.

American military men seemed to feel that the defendants were being tried because they had lost the war and that a precedent was being set for the possibility that American soldiers might be tried if they lost the war. The trial dragged on month after month. When the civil war in China turned in favor of the Communists, Tojo's argument that the Japanese had fought in defense of Asia against communism garnered sympathy among the Americans. When finally in 1948 all of the defendants had been found guilty in various degrees, it was decided not to try the Class A war crimes suspects that had been awaiting their turn to be tried. The Cold War had brought the trials to an end.

One day Father Edmund Walsh, head of Georgetown University School of Foreign Service, lectured in the auditorium on the final days of Karl Haushofer, the famous expert on geopolitics and advisor to Adolf Hitler. Father Walsh, who struck me as being very impressed with himself, told us that because he (Walsh) was the leading American authority on geopolitics, he was entrusted with the evaluation of the Haushofer's war responsibility. As I recall, Allied authorities had billeted Haushofer and Walsh in the same residence, and the two became very well acquainted. During this time Haushofer and his wife poisoned themselves. I was left to wonder about the possibility that Walsh's strong personality might have played some role in the tragedy. (Early in his academic career, Haushofer had established himself as an authority on Japan. In my personal library, I have a copy of his book, *Japan und die Japaner* (Leipzig, Teubner, 1923.)

EXTRACURRICULAR ACTIVITIES

The rest of this chapter has to do with my experiences in Japan outside of my official duties.

One of the first things I did after arriving in Japan was to exchange my money for Japanese yen. When I arrived at the short cue at the window of the American Express Office, there stood Mrs. Douglas MacArthur, dutifully exchanging her currency. I was amazed that the wife of the Supreme Commander for the Allied Powers (SCAP), concurrently Commander in Chief Army Forces Pacific (CINC-AFPAC), should be obliged to await in a cue like such plebeians as I. From the American Express I then bought yen at the rate of $1.00 to ¥15.00.

Later that day I was told that I could buy yen in the street at rate of around ¥40.00 to the dollar. The Japanese yen which had been trading at the rate of four to the dollar before the war had become almost valueless, and I resorted to the barter system. This system was facilitated by the massive introduction of American alcohol into the Japanese economy by the U.S. Army. In my instance, as a member of my billet I was entitled to purchase each month from the Army one crate of alcoholic beverages (20 or 30 bottles of a variety of advertised brands of whiskey, gin, cordials, etc.); at my place of employment, each month, a similar crate of alcohol; and each month at the American Civilian Club a similar crate. The price was about $12.00 a crate. However I scarcely drank any of it, as I was a teetotaler when I first arrived in Japan and, after I began drinking, bought all my drinks at the bar in my billet at $0.15 each.

I failed to take full advantage of the commercial potentialities of this system, because it was illegal (although widely tolerated) and there was little in the Japanese economy that appealed to me beyond rail travel and antiques. My room and board were strictly military at little more than nominal prices paid in dollars. I deposited most of my salary in savings and loan institutions in California, where they paid three percent interest rather than the two percent paid in the rest of the country.

After I returned to the States, I applied my savings to tuition and room and board for graduate study at Columbia University, with some money left over.

There were no laundry facilities at the War Ministry Hotel, so shortly after arriving in Tokyo one evening I decided to take my clothes to a laundry in the neighborhood outside the base. It had already gotten dark (there were no street lights) as I went into the street, and for perhaps the very first time I put my oral Japanese to a test. I asked several children, "*Sentakuya wa doko desu ka?*" (Where is a laundry?) The children seem to be intrigued with me, a Caucasian in civilian clothes who spoke Nihongo, and were more than willing to help. More and more children emerged from the side streets to see what was going on. I was swept up by the crowd into an intricate route through the darkened streets until we came to the laundry and I left my clothes there.

I was very struck by the friendliness and helpfulness of the children and from then on felt no sense of physical danger while in Japan. Samuel Chew's warning to me that the Japanese would stab me in the back seemed completely inappropriate.

To my surprise I was able to find my way unassisted to the *sentakuya* a few days later. My clothes bore the faint scent of diapers.

In October 1946, The *Mainichi Shimbun*, a major Japanese daily, consisted of only two pages—the front and back of a sheet only one half the size of a single page of an American newspaper. Train tickets are made of tissue paper. There was an acute paper shortage.

I ate my breakfasts and dinners and weekend meals in our mess hall. At my first breakfast, the Japanese maid came to me and said, "*Engoo opp oo ohbah.*" I thought I knew the Japanese language and was embarrassed by my complete inability to understand what she had said. A neighbor translated her English for me: "Egg up or over?" In Japanese, nearly every word ends with a vowel, so that when they speak English the Japanese are apt to add a vowel. Also they tended to pronounce the English L as if it were an R. Later in the little bar in our billet, I was exercising my language skills by talking Japanese with one of the waitresses. Everything went smoothly until she mentioned "*oh foory meetsoo.*" She seemed disgusted that I was unable to understand that common English expression: "Off limits."

As it was inconvenient for the residents of the War Ministry Hotel to return to Ichigaya to have their lunch, we were permitted to eat lunch in the annex of the Imperial Hotel. This hotel, an internationally famous creation of Frank Lloyd Wright, was serving as a billet for American generals. The waitresses in our dining room shuffled about in kimonos and slippers, and each day would bring us a menu printed in French. Only one entree would be listed; it was the Army fare for the day. Once the menu said "*Viandes froides et frommages,*" cold cuts and cheese.

At the end of the work day, I could return to Ichigaya either by taking the elevated railroad from Tokyo Station, a few blocks from the Dai Ichi Building, or,

more conveniently, by riding in a weapons carrier, a noisy truck serving as a bus
with steps attached to the back so that we could clamber in. As I was awaiting the
weapons carrier one evening, I briefly talked with Professor Harold S. Quigley,
who was conservatively dressed in a black suit. (Before the war, Quigley, of the
University of Minnesota, had written the best known book in English describing
the government and politics of Japan.) Like me, he was an employee of CIS, but
his office was separate from anyone else's and even while I was involved in
administration, I had had no occasion to consult him. Jim Fesperman, a missionary's
son and an old Arlington Hall friend who was now working in CIS, told me that
although Quigley was an authority on prewar Japanese politics, he was unfamiliar
with the Japanese language and knew little about contemporary Japan.

In my very brief and only conversation with Quigley, he made it clear that
he was unhappy working for MacArthur and that he was eager to return to the
campus. My view was just the opposite. It seemed much more interesting, even
more important, to participate in the democratic reconstruction of Japan, than
to talk about political theories to students on a campus. (I much later learned
that Quigley's friends in Tokyo had urged that Quigley be transferred to the
SCAP's Government Section where his talents would have been put to better
use, but evidently Quigley was not interested in this option. Back in Minnesota,
in 1956 in collaboration with a colleague, he published an excellent book about
government in postwar Japan: Harold S. Quigley and John E. Turner, *The New
Japan: Government and Politics* University of Minnesota Press, 1956). In the
preface he acknowledges the help of his American friends in Tokyo, including
Kenneth Colton, of CIS. I should mention that while I was working in CIS
headquarters, whenever someone had a question about Japanese politics, the
answer was "Ask Kenneth Colton.")

Once I dated a WAC captain who worked in our office. After I had walked her
back to her billet, I phoned the motor pool for a ride home and waited in the
lobby. There were two or three other men awaiting rides. The desk clerk would
announce, "Colonel Johnson, your sedan has arrived," or "Major Appleby, your
sedan as arrived." Finally he announced, "Mr. McNelly, your transportation has
arrived." Transportation was a jeep.

POSTWAR TOKYO

It was generally said that Tokyo was 45 percent destroyed by the war. Of course I
had arrived in Japan over a year after the war had ended, but apparently little had
changed. To test the 45 percent figure, I took a ride on the Yamanote line, an
elevated train that made a complete circle around the core of the city, taking two
or three hours to do so. Just looking at the scenery during this ride confirmed to
me that 45 per cent was just about the right estimate. In many sections of the city,

most if not all of the buildings had been made of wood and had burned to the ground. The concrete blocks on which the houses had stood were still there, along with burned-out safes and occasionally the charred carcass of an automobile. Some people had built shacks or caves in the rubble, using blackened sheets of corrugated iron for roofs. In the winter of 1946-1947 green stuff, it looked like lettuce, had been planted in the rubble. In the 1950s, when I visited Germany, the rubble there, unlike in Japan, consisted mostly of bricks.

One of the modern buildings on Avenue B had been taken over for use as a Civilian Club. (One evening at the club, I saw Prince Takamatsu, the emperor's brother, who was being entertained at a nearby table.)

A few blocks away was the famous Ginza shopping district. One department store, still intact, had been taken over for use as a PX. Beyond that stood the formidable old Tokyo Station. Its outer walls of red brick were still standing but the inside had been gutted and only partly restored. The sidewalks in downtown Tokyo were cluttered with little stands, or just piles of merchandise; this was the black market. One day, in my capacity as coordinator of the Evaluation Control and Evaluation Branch, I had run out of paperclips. There were no more available in the building. So I went out in the street and bought a supply with my own money.

In the winter, many of the men wore old army uniforms or long overcoats. They had metal cleats on the soles of their shoes, evidently to conserve leather, and when they walked on the side walk they made a crunchy clicking sound. The glass windows of many of the street cars had been blown out and replaced with unpainted plywood. Civilian automobiles were rare, and were apt to be equipped with smoking charcoal burners which supplied the combustible gas for the vehicles. (In France, these devices were known as *gazogène*.)

The women who cared for our billet, usually wore *mompei*, quilted suits that made them look dumpy and unattractive. Generally speaking, the Japanese were much shorter than the Americans. I remember taking the train to Kamakura once: I was a head taller than anyone else in the train car. Everyone, including the conductor reminded me of children. (In later years, with changes in diet, the Japanese have become taller than they used to be.)

On many of the principal trains one car was labeled for use by occupation personnel only. The other cars would be extremely crowded but there were usually plenty of seats for the car reserved for occupationaires. If a train did not have such a reserved car, occupation personnel would then be apt to ride in the front of the train with the engineer.

During the early months of my stay in Japan, I made rail trips with friends to Kamakura, Enoshima, and Nikko. Japanese restaurants and hotels were off limits, so that I ate all of my meals at military messes. (Japanese food was scarce and regarded as unsafe, because human waste was used to fertilize it. Our vegetables were grown hydroponically. Our meat was imported from the states. The only time I stayed at a Japanese-style hotel (*ryōkan*)was on a trip to Nikko sponsored by the Red Cross. (I did however spend a couple of week-ends at the wonderful Fujiya Hotel in Miyanoshita in Hakone, which was very Japanese, but was reserved exclusively for use by Occupation personnel.)

FRIENDS

Hill, one of the translators living at War Ministry Hotel, arranged for a bunch of us to go to Teidai, Tokyo Imperial University, to help with the English language club. We were on the stage with several Japanese students who were very interested in democracy and the elimination of "feudalism," a term which referred to authoritarianism in general and arranged marriages in particular. Our little group included Herschel Webb, whom I later knew at Columbia, where he ultimately became a professor of Japanese history.

A neat little bar in Japanese style was being constructed in our hotel, and about that time a government for the billet was established and I was elected to the board of governors. The War Ministry Hotel was intended as a transient billet, but I preferred to remain there rather than move to the Yaesu hotel downtown, because of the congenial company. Charles Terry, who spoke perfect Japanese, became acquainted with noble Japanese families, and managed to find fresh eggs (at mess we ate frozen eggs as a rule). Terry attended Columbia when I did in the early '50s, where he distinguished himself in the Japanese language and sometimes played the piano beautifully in the lounge at Hamilton Hall. I again stumbled in to him in Japan later in the same decade, when he was involved in language teaching for the Maryland Overseas Program. In 1981, Kodansha, the leading publisher of English books about Japan, issued Charles Terry's translation of the immensely popular novel by Yoshikawa Eiji, *Musashi,* based on the life of the famous swordsman and painter of the feudal age, Miyamoto Musashi. Charles died of cancer on July 3, 1982. (I am afraid that some of the "congenial company" I associated with at our billet in Tokyo may not have been as distinguished as Charles Terry.)

For a while in Tokyo I continued to see Arvilla Chick and Esther Wright, whom I had known on the *Wisteria.* Arvilla was stationed in Yokohama and we lost touch. Originally she had been slated to teach GIs in the education program, but later she was transferred to Government Section, where she was involved in the political purge and became acquainted with Minobe Tatsukichi, the eminent political scientist.

Gwen Fillman, whom I had known at Foundry Methodist Church, showed up in Tokyo, working in the Occupation. In the 1950s she was a secretary at the East Asian Institute at Columbia, where I was studying.

At several meetings of the Allied Jesuit Alumni Association, I met some Sophia University professors and discussed the possibilities of studying constitutional law at Sophia, but nothing came of this.

In letters to my mother I described several American girls whom I was dating, and the dinners and dances at the American Club or elsewhere where I took them. One of the girls was Mercer Roach, a Smith College graduate and a New Dealer, whom I had originally met on the *Wisteria*.

Johnny Sato, a billet mate who was working on MacArthur's military history project, introduced me to a girl who had come to Japan on the same boat as he: Carol Yoder. Carol's father had recently resigned from the presidency of the state college at Whitewater, Wisconsin. Carol, who was attractive and bright, was Major General Edward Almond's private secretary. The general normally lunched between 2 and 4 in the afternoon, so that several times I went to his office to enjoy a cup of coffee with Carol.

In February 1947, with Carol Yoder I attended a performance of the beloved *Mikado*, performed in Japanese at the Hibiya Public Hall in downtown Tokyo. As his imperial majesty appears in a comic light in this opera, it would have been lese majesty to present such a performance before the war. (The performance we saw was especially for the benefit of Occupation personnel. Of course, Gilbert and Sullivan's intent had not been to criticize Japanese institutions, about which they apparently knew little, but rather to exploit an exotic location in order to satirize English customs.)

In around April 1947, I received a letter from Father Gerard Yates, my Georgetown professor. He agreed that I might begin research for a dissertation that would be a political and legal analysis of the government of occupied Japan. This led me to spend several Saturdays studying thick reports in the SCAP Historical Section. As the Allied Occupation of Japan was deeply involved in virtually every aspect of Japanese life, social and economic as well as political, the detail was overwhelming, and I soon lost interest in the project. There were more pleasant ways to spend my weekends. I ordered a portable typewriter from Sears and Roebuck.

In the spring with some friends, including Gwen Fillman, I took train and trolley to Gora to see the cherry and plum blossoms in the country. In my letters, I complain about restrictions on travel, and the need to get special permissions and travel orders to use recreational facilities in the mountains. In August, however, I spent a long weekend at the elegant Fujiya Hotel in Miyanoshita in the Hakone mountains, with splendid side trips.

Kyoto, Japan's capital city before 1868, was famous for its ancient temples and shrines. It had been relatively untouched by American bombing. I and a Mr. Sorrell took a train to see the famous sights there. On the way I seem to have gotten something in my eye, and although it was apparently removed, when I returned to Tokyo I found that the entire right side of my face was numb and paralyzed, so that I was unable smile with the right side of my mouth. Although I did not feel ill, I was very fearful that this affliction might never end or even that it might spread to the rest of my body.

The physician in the Dai Ichi building referred me to a neurosurgeon at the 49th General Hospital. The neurosurgeon took one look at me and said, "You have Bell's palsy," which I had never before heard of. He asked if I had been sitting next to an open window in a car. I said that I had sat next to an open window in the train to Kyoto. It seems that the prolonged blast of cold on only one side of the face had affected the facial nerves, causing the paralysis on the other side of the face. He then told me of facial exercises that would hasten a recovery. In my case, after several weeks the problem disappeared. However, persistent cases may require surgery. I have never met anyone who was even aware of the existence of the disease, but was recently interested to read that Sir Anthony Blunt, the Surveyor of the Queen's Pictures and key member of the Cambridge Ring of Soviet spies, had to put up with a severe case of Bell's palsy contracted in 1953 on a train in France (Miranda Carter, *Anthony Blunt: His Lives* [New York: Farrar, Straus and Giroux, 2001, pp.397-398]).

In September I went to a little dinner party given by Leslie Bratton at her parents' house—a western-style house formerly occupied by a Mrs. Mitsui, once a golf champion, who had a small 3-hole golf course next to the house. The Mitsui house had been requisitioned by the Occupation for Colonel Bratton's use. The grand piano, I suspect, had been Mrs. Mitsui's. Mrs. Mitsui's family lived on the same grounds, I believe in the former servants quarter. Someone brought to our party a cultured pearl necklace for sale. But the purchaser would have to sign a certificate that he had obtained his yen from a legal source. This legal precaution was no doubt insisted on by Colonel Rufus Bratton, who was the effective head of the Civil Intelligence Section. (In the well-known movie about Pearl Harbor, *Tora Tora Tora*, Colonel Bratton's role was played by E. G. Marshall.)

Leslie Bratton was an attractive girl who spoke Japanese fluently. Before the war she had attended the American School in Japan, where she had known Joan Fontaine, who also attended that school.

One winter at Hibiya Hall there was a demonstration of relative speed of electric calculators and the abacus (a traditional oriental hand-operated calculating device). On one side of the stage stood an electric calculator, on the other side of the stage stood a Japanese famous for his speed with an abacus. There were four races using quite large numbers: adding, subtraction, multiplication, and division. This was before the widespread use of *electronic calculators*. The electric adding machines, as they were called, were actually mechanical devices, not electronic devices, and were powered by an electric engine. The mechanical action was slow and noisy, and the machine would go chug chug chug. The man with the abacus won three of the four contests. (He lost only division.) In actuality, I understand, much of the man's speed with the abacus was the function of his ability to do much of the calculation mentally, in his head. (The electric adding machines used in the 1940s long since have gone the way of manual and electric typewriters, in favor of electronic machines and computers.)

As a former WAVE officer, Carol Yoder was a member of a naval reserve organization that set up an excursion to Oshima Island, in the ocean, south of Tokyo Bay in February 1948. Carol kindly invited me to join the trip. Oshima Island is famous for its camellias that bloom in the winter. Some us hiked to the summit of the volcano on the island.

A MEDICAL PROBLEM

In March I had a bad cough and felt a heavy weight in my chest. I thought I just had a cold but Carol insisted that I see the doctor. On March 8, 1948, at the Dai Ichi building dispensary, the doctor rapped my chest and sent me directly to the hospital getting an x-ray on the way. At the 49th General Hospital (the former St. Luke's hospital) the doctor told me that I had pleurisy. Fluid was extracted from my chest.

I was pleasantly surprised by how many of my friends from the billet and the office came to visit me the first few days in the hospital. On March 14, I asked the doctor how much longer I would be in the hospital. He said that I was not acutely ill when I had been brought in, but that they would have to determine the cause of this thing, and this would take more than a day or two. In a very few days, I felt completely recovered and expected soon to be released, but one day an orderly came to my room and said that I was to be moved. I asked why. He said that I was being sent to the contagious ward.

On March 23, a Dr. Gibbons told me that the most common cause of pleural fusion with pleurisy is TB (tuberculosis), but that TB is not the only cause. It would take eight weeks for some laboratory tests involving guinea pigs to prove TB or not TB, the consumption devoutly to be eschewed. I might be evacuated even if it was not absolutely proven that I was tubercular. Friends of mine who came to visit had to wear masks. I felt fine and was confident that the TB test would prove negative.

On April 16, I wrote my mother that the pleurisy was apparently all gone and that I felt about 100 % perfect. "I study Japanese history and political philosophy, read novels, and play autobridge [a machine to practice the game on] .... Since today is a holiday, Carol may drop by this afternoon." A few days later I reported to my mother that I "Will be glad to get out of here [the hospital] in three or four weeks. Feel perfectly OK and have to watch myself not to walk around the room too much, as the doctor says I should stay in bed."

HOMECOMING

After a month or so had past, the test result was in: I had tuberculosis. On May 14, I was told by the Board that I would be laid up for at least a year. I was loaded on a stretcher and put on a plane that stopped at Johnston Island on the way to Hawaii. I spent a night at a hospital in Hawaii. I was flown to California, where I changed planes and flew over the Rockies (I could glimpse the snow-covered peaks) to Denver. I was put up for a night at the Fitzimmons General Hospital, a new institution notable for its facilities for curing tuberculosis. After a day or so there I flew over Chicago (where I glimpsed the planetarium, Field museum and Shore Drive) to Battle Creek, Michigan. At Battle Creek, I was assigned a bed in the Percy Jones General Hospital.

Every few days a doctor would see me to determine the nature of my illness. It seems that all of my past tests, except the guinea pig test, had proved negative for TB. I had never had a bad cough. The people at Fitzimmons administered another TB test, which would take weeks to complete. I still had some effusion in the chest, but my symptoms seemed not serious enough to give me a shot of streptomycin, which was now being used to cure TB. In any case, I suspected that it would take a month for the effusion to clear up.

As in the hospital in Tokyo, I did not feel ill. I had not the faintest notion as to how long I would be hospitalized.

My mother, either in a letter to me or in a phone conversation, mentioned something about her savings. The thought that my widowed mother would be burdened with the trouble and expense of caring for an invalid like me was very upsetting. I assured my mother that I had plenty of money (actually several thousands of dollars in California savings and loan companies). Around May 23 a doctor said he prescribes bed rest as I was not sick enough to bother with the shots of streptomycin (which have painful side effects). He would see about me getting transferred, possibly to Fitzimmons. I had the impression that I would be OK in two months.

In the middle of June I reported to my mother that I had been gaining weight and that at 161 pounds I now weighed more than ever before in my life. A doctor said that he saw no reason for isolation since I did not have a cough. He said for me not to over exercise, get plenty of rest, and a tan and that the pleuritis is clearing up.

During my time in Percy Jones hospital, I read several law books that I had my mother send to me including Oliver Wendell Holmes *The Common Law*. In connection with my proposed Georgetown doctoral thesis I ordered copies of Sir George Sansom's *Japan: A Short Cultural History*, and Hillis Lory's *Japan's Military Masters*. In my letters home, I discussed what I might do when I returned to the States. I especially favored the idea of returning to Washington and finishing my degree at Georgetown, where I needed 6 more course credits and the dissertation to complete the Ph.D. degree. Some of my friends at Arlington Hall had heard about my illness and wrote to me. On the suggestion of Jim McDowell, I might rejoin the Army Security Agency or get into the CIA, where the pay was better. Although I had heard of good paying jobs for linguists in the United Nations, I felt that I could not successfully compete with the kind of individuals whom I had known at Arlington Hall who were individually masters of numerous languages.

Carol Yoder had kindly overseen the packing and shipment of my personal effects to Madison. She had also efficiently straightened out my business with the personnel office. I wondered about the future in connection with Carol, who was on the other side of the world.

I must say that lying in bed in a ward full of invalids 24-hours a day in Percy Jones hospital with very little congenial company, I no longer found being sick very much fun. It had been different in the hospital in Tokyo, where I had a single room and a phonograph, with jolly friends of both sexes coming to see me every day, looking forward to an early release. In Percy Jones, days would pass without a word from anyone on the outside. I felt very lonely and isolated. The world was passing me by. Although I did not feel ill, the pleurisy seemed to hang on forever with no clear end in sight.

Of the existing letters that I wrote my mother from Percy Jones Hospital the last is dated June 17, 1948:

> Talked things over with the doctor yesterday . . . . He said he saw no reason for isolation since I don't have a cough. Said for me not to overexercise, get plenty of rest and a tan. The pleuritis is clearing up. I don't see any point in reorganizing the whole house on account of me or for my piddling around for a prolonged stay in a sanatorium. What I want to do is this: loaf a while and this fall move to Washington, D.C. into a bachelor's apartment and finish my degree at Georgetown. Meantime I can keep my eye pealed for a job in the State or Army Departments . . . . I can also keep in touch with my professors and government officials there better than in Madison. I might not get a job till about February, but by then I ought to have most of my schoolwork wound up and be perfectly recuperated. The winter in the D.C. is less severe than in Madison and I can get outside more. The more I think about it the less I like the idea of a sanatorium. Well, we'll see when I get home.

In the summer or fall of 1948 I was discharged from Percy Jones Hospital. I stayed at home with my mother several days, and following discussions between an army physician and state health officers, I was almost immediately put in TB sanitarium near Milwaukee sponsored by the Wisconsin state government. I felt all right, but I had to be cured of tuberculosis before I could be released into society.

Occasionally my mother, driven by John or Jimmy, would come to visit me. My being in a TB san was extremely worrisome to her. In her day, tuberculosis was regarded as a frequently fatal disease.

In those days there was no quick fix for tuberculosis except streptomycin, which was just coming into use. The only known cure was *rest*, and that was not always successful. The rest cure involved sleeping most of the time on a porch outdoors, even during the winter, which in Wisconsin was cold. The patients were assigned to grades, each of which prescribed a given number of hours each day in bed. We ate our meals in the dining hall.

Many of the patients had been there for several years, and some would likely spend the rest of their lives there. One cure involved filling an infected lung with plastic balls, or with oil. This seemed never to work. One patient was sent to the hospital to have a lung removed. The surgeon reported that there was nothing at all wrong with the lung, and she was discharged from the sanitarium. Nowadays TB can be cured with antibiotics and there is even a vaccine that can be used to prevent it. TB almost become extinct, but in the 1980s, people with HIV became vulnerable to it.

Halloween was a major celebration at the san. Long before the date patients would make plans for the costumes that they would wear that day in the dining hall. The patients were human beings. Many if not most of them were young adults, and there were love affairs. These might begin with eye contacts in the dining hall, leading to conversations afterwards. I met "Ginny" that way, and had a little crush on her. These affairs would be a favorite topic of endless discussion. One patient on my porch made it a point to constantly badger and tease another of the patients. Sometimes little cliques would develop. Some of us had a little photography club where a fellow patient would talk about how to take pictures, etc.

Occasionally some of the men would gather to smoke cigarettes, which were forbidden. One of the men in my cabin had formerly been in prison. He told us how he once forced a woman to get into his car and how he took her to a field in the country where he had sex with her. He was apparently very proud of this accomplishment.

There was an old colored man who every day studied the Bible. Every intelligent person in 1948 was convinced that Dewey was going to beat Truman in the presidential election. The old Negro, however, insisted that Truman would win. It turned out that he was right. He crowed, "Ah reads de Bible and ah knows." I had learned an unforgettable lesson in political science. Politics is very unpredictable.

One night the old man got into a violent argument with one of the best-liked doctors on the staff. As a result, the Negro was expelled from the sanitarium. I do not know whatever became of him.

A therapist instructed us how to weave leather belts and make other things. I had no interest in this and instead started the first full-length book I ever read in

Japanese. It was an introduction to the Japanese Constitution, written by Minobe Tatsukichi. It was full of hard words and I had to use the dictionary frequently. To look up a word in Japanese is not easy for a foreigner. Often one must first figure out the pronunciation of the Chinese characters in a word by consulting a Chinese-Japanese character dictionary and then look in an alphabetized Japanese-English dictionary for the definition. Sometimes the search in the Chinese-Japanese character dictionary can take quite a bit of time and even then turn out to be futile.

Occasionally a doctor or nurse would reprimand me for studying when I should be sleeping.

After perhaps six months in the state san, I was declared cured and instructed never to return to Japan. I went home to Madison.

All of my medical and hospital expenses had been paid for by either the U.S. Army or the state of Wisconsin. I had several thousand dollars saved up from my Tokyo job, and decided to finish my doctorate in political science.

CHAPTER 9

COLUMBIA UNIVERSITY

I must have spent much of the winter in the sanatorium as I clearly recall the cold days sleeping out on the porch. When probably sometime in the spring of 1949, I was released from the san, a doctor told me never again to return to Japan.

While in hospitals and the san, my thought had been to finish my doctorate at Georgetown, where I was within 6 credits of fulfilling all of the course requirements, and where I had been planning to write my dissertation under Father Gerard Yates. After leaving the san, however, my plans changed.

I had heard that Sir George Sansom would be teaching at Columbia, and because he was rightfully reputed to be the leading western authority on Japan, I decided to go there to study. Indeed, Sansom had been appointed as director of Columbia's new East Asian Institute, which would commence operations in the fall of 1949. I cannot recall the details of my applying except that the application would have been facilitated by the fact that I already had an M.A. in French from Wisconsin and had earned a fair number of credits towards a Ph.D. in political science at Georgetown, so that the application was in a sense a transfer from one reputable graduate school to another. I cannot recall that I applied for a fellowship of any kind. In any event, I had sufficient funds to pay tuition and room and board for possibly a year and a half at Columbia.

Before I made an irrevocable commitment to Columbia, however, I considered attending the University of Wisconsin and talked to some of the professors in the Departments of Political Science and History there. Professor Frederick Austin Ogg had served as president of the American Political Science Association and had been editor of the *American Political Science Review* from 1926 to 1949. (I did not, however, talk with him.) It would cost me less to attend the university in Madison than to go to New York to study; I could continue to live at home as I had before. Eugene Boardman, an expert on China, taught Asian courses in the History Department. As I recall, however, there was no course in political science devoted to Japanese or Asian government in particular, but comparative government was taught by Frederick A. Ogg, famous for his textbook on American government. At

Wisconsin, the pickings on Japan and China were pretty thin as compared with the full raft of courses in numerous disciplines then being brought together in Columbia's East Asian Institute. So I would go to Columbia.

LIFE AT COLUMBIA

In the summer of 1949 I went to New York. The East Asian Institute had taken over a town house on 117th Street, just across Amsterdam Avenue from Columbia's elegant campus, and after I had figured out the door bell system, I went upstairs to the office. Professor Hugh Borton was in his shirt sleeves moving book cases around. Sansom had come to Columbia with the understanding that Borton would assume the bulk of administrative tasks. (Actually, before the war, Sansom had taught for short periods at Columbia.) I owe much to Professor Borton. He was always most friendly and helpful to me. The East Asian Institute formally began its operations in the fall of 1949.

I started attending classes at Columbia in the summer of 1949. I was assigned a room in Livingston Hall. During my first weeks at Columbia I thought I was in heaven. After many tedious weeks in hospitals and a sanatorium, I was now cured of my disease and was embraced by the splendor of Columbia. My fondest dream had come true, and my only remaining desire was to do as well as I possibly could in my studies.

During a large part of my stay at Columbia, because of shortage of dormitory rooms on the campus I was assigned to live in an old dormitory belonging to City College. This meant a short commute via the IRT subway to 116th Street and Broadway. During my last term (fall 1950) I lived in John Jay Hall, where none of the inhabitants, all of them stressed-out graduate students, ever spoke to one another. It was depressingly quiet. The gloom was once relieved when the School of Nursing on the other side of Amsterdam Avenue extended an invitation to us for a dance, where the girls were friendly to us.

In those days, the East Asia collection was located in the rotunda of Low Library, which building included the office of the president of the University. Once I nearly collided in a revolving door with Dwight Eisenhower, in civilian clothes, who had recently become president. On another occasion, I joined a small group standing around him outside, while, clad in a light brown tweed suit, he talked about his ideas on education, which seemed innocuous. My move from Tokyo to New York had not freed me from the orbits of America's most famous generals.

Near the entrance to the East Asian collection, just about every day one might see Morton Kaplan, a student of international relations, studying the current issue of the *New York Times* spread out across the table in front of him. I could not quite understand why he used the East Asia Library just to read the *Times* every day.

Possibly it was because he was a student of Nathaniel Peffer, who taught international relations and who was interested especially in East Asia. (Kaplan later became a professor of international relations at the University of Chicago.)

I ate most of my meals in the dining room (cafeteria style) in John Jay Hall. It was a lovely place, light and airy, the food quite palatable, and the people friendly.

Several of my old Tokyo friends had shown up at the EAI. They were Herschel Webb and Charles Terry as grad students and Gwen Fillman as a secretary. Charles Terry and a friend of his who liked Franz Liszt, would take turns playing the piano beautifully in the Hamilton Hall lounge.

Paul Langer and Peter Bernstein, who had been living in the Far East before the war, were jointly writing a book about the Japan Communist Party.

Professor Arthur W. MacMahon, the famous authority on public administration, gave a party for grad students in political science at his beautiful home on the side of a mountain overlooking a bend in the Hudson River. There I met Sayuri Tada, who had once been a singer in a club in Tokyo and was now a grad student at Columbia, supported by her uncle, a prosperous farmer in the South. One day I was walking on Broadway with Sayuri, and we met Peter Bernstein. I began to make an introduction, when Sayuri said to Peter, "Didn't you play violin in the Harbin symphony orchestra?" Peter said yes. Sayuri said she remembered seeing him playing in the orchestra when she had been in Manchuria. It is a small world. (Peter later changed his last name to Burton, and recently retired as a professor from the University of Southern California.)

I saw Elizabeth Park a few times while I was in New York. She had studied piano with Mme. Nadia Boulanger and was the organist at a large church in Brooklyn. Her day job was with *Facts on File*. She was a Madison girl (but not a West High graduate). She had majored in German and English at Wisconsin, and was a member of Phi Beta Kappa.

In one of Professor Peffer's classes, there was a young man who spoke with a marked British accent and also a stunning blonde lady. The young man was Otto George. We became good friends, and we took several trips in his old car, which we had to push to start, to his family's home in elegant Westchester County. He was one of Borton's students in Japanese history and earned extra money by translating documents from Japanese to English. One day a shocking event occurred. Someone had jumped out of a window a number of stories above Otto's room, landing on a roof just outside Otto's window, and the dead body was carried from the roof through Otto's room.

Otto was a reservist, and when the Korean War broke out he was drafted to serve. With respect to the stunning blonde, mentioned above, I was not aware that Otto had been dating her when we were students, but years later, when Otto was working for the CIA, I learned that he was married to her.

Nostalgic for choir singing, I auditioned successfully to sing in the Columbia University Chapel choir in the summer of 1949, I believe. Most of the choir was made up of music majors, and we sang lots of Orlando di Lasso. We had services every week-day at 8:00 AM. The services were poorly attended; I recall one day when there was only one person in our audience. A Mr. Douglas Pike, who had retired as a lawyer to become an Episcopal priest, presided as the chaplain. I cannot recall that he gave sermons. For reasons that completely escaped me, he was lionized by the girls. From 1958 to 1966 he was the Episcopal bishop of California and became famous, or notorious, for the books he published, in which he dabbled in multiple heresies, including spiritualism. In 1968 he renounced the church, and after being lost in the Judean desert, was found dead after his wife, in a vision, had learned of his location.

I became interested in the blond organist, but I made no attempt to cultivate her acquaintance. I felt that because I was living off my savings and my clothes were beginning to show their wear, I could not afford to date girls. In the fall, she left Columbia to became a minister of music in a church in Texas. Several years later, I was told that the girls at Barnard College wanted nothing more than to be invited to dates at the Lion's Den, the smokey dive in the basement of John Jay Hall, where there were cheap beer and music for dancing and where I sometimes hung out with friends.

SOME PROFESSORS

I signed up for Nathaniel Peffer's courses on international relations in the Far East and American Foreign policy and Henry Reining's course in American political institutions. Peffer's style was not very academic. He did not have a Ph.D. but had for years been a journalist in the Far East and had first hand knowledge and strong opinions. He so passionately disliked Chiang Kai-shek that he seemed to tremble when he mentioned the name. When in China he had done some teaching and Chiang's police would arrest his students. The class discussions were interesting. When the Korean War broke out, Peffer attacked Truman's policy of sending the U.S. fleet to the Taiwan Strait to prevent a Chinese Communist invasion of Taiwan. Peffer predicted that this project would last indefinitely, with the sons of the American sailors continuing to patrol the area.

Nat Peffer was my official adviser. To prepare for the Ph.D. comprehensives in IR (international relations), the mantra of the grad students was "Bemis 'n' Bailey": i. e., the famous textbooks on American foreign relations by Samuel Flagg Bemis and Thomas A. Bailey. Professor Peffer told me that to pass the comprehensives you had to know (1) the facts, (2) the interpretation of the facts, and (3) the bibliography.

Lindsay Rogers taught the course on European political institutions that I took at Columbia. There was also a required course for all poly sci majors on the scope and method of political science, at which poly sci professors took turns lecturing. In the East Asian Institute, I took the important seminar on studies in history and government of the Far East, in which Professors Peffer, Borton, Sansom, Edwards, and C. Martin Wilbur participated.

In the fall of 1949, I took Sir George Sansom's course on the early history of Japan. Sir George was a smallish man wearing a tight fitting English-tailored black suit, carrying a battered brown leather briefcase. He would walk into the room without saying anything to anyone, take his notes from his bag, lay them on the table, and present a polished and urbane lecture, seasoned occasionally with dry wit. As I recall, there was no class discussion and he would walk out of the room, again without talking informally with anyone. I just loved him. He was so far superior to my other professors that it was pathetic.

Sir George's correspondence reflects his fondness for Columbia, as shown in a letter he wrote to Hugh Borton in 1957 during his retirement in California. First, it should be explained that Columbia's elegant buildings dating from the reign of President Nicholas ("the Miraculous") Murray Butler were in contrast to the encroaching slums near the campus. Sir George candidly describes the scene where I occasionally glimpsed him:

> I still have a nostalgia for the dingy purlieus of Amsterdam Avenue . . . . I often think of it all—the dirty streets never properly cleaned, and the wind which blows rubbish through them. And the shops down the road on Amsterdam Avenue. You know, it's a sort of dirty village. Oh. I know you are improving it all, and I'm sure it will be spoiled. It had to happen of course; but I liked it as it was. (Katherine Sansom, *Sir George Sansom and Japan: A Memoir* [Tallahassee, Florida: The Diplomatic Press, 1972], pp. 164-165.)

In the spring term (1950) I took Hugh Borton's course on modern Japan. Borton's approach was quite the opposite of Sir George's. He began his lectures with comments about the source materials that he had brought with him and put on the table. (Sir George had never talked about bibliography; his famous cultural history of Japan had no bibliography and is relatively unencumbered with footnotes.) Borton was very much the teacher. His speaking style lacked elegance, but he would get his main points across. During the war he had been a principal formulator of American postwar policy towards Japan, and his lectures on current policy were down to earth and to the point.

Hugh Borton invited some of us students to his farm in Pennsylvania to celebrate Thanksgiving Day. A professional farmer living in a second house on the land did the actual farming I understand. The farm was part of a Quaker community. Mrs. Borton played the piano and we sang Thanksgiving songs. (This event may be the one described in Hugh Borton's autobiography, *Spanning Japan's Modern Century* [Lanham, MD: Lexington Books, 2002], p. 225.)

J. Dixon Edwards, a former Foreign Service Officer who had worked in the embassy in Tokyo before the war and who spoke Japanese, taught the course on Political Institutions of China and Japan. There were about fifteen students in the class, mostly political scientists, some of them Nisei. After class meetings, there was a tendency of the students to band together to evaluate, sometimes unkindly, Mr. Edwards' lectures. Key Kobayashi, whom I later met in Washington in the 1960s when he was in the State Department, was one of the students.

It was in this crowd that I first met John Thomson. John Thomson was the son of a missionary in China and a student of Nathaniel Peffer. He was teaching in Barnard College. One day John said that Peffer had gotten him a teaching job at the University of Wisconsin. Thomson seemed unenthusiastic about the idea, but I envied him. I had a high regard for Wisconsin and to teach in Madison would have been a dream come true for me. Later Thomson said that he had accepted the Wisconsin position with the understanding that he would finish his dissertation that summer before going there. However, his father had invited him to vacation in Switzerland, so he was not sure that he would actually work on the dissertation that summer. I was shocked by his cavalier attitude towards his academic commitments.(Ironically, although John Thomson got the political science job at Wisconsin in 1950, I received my Columbia Ph.D. in 1952, a year before he got his.)

A few years later, I visited him in Madison. He had written a letter to the newspaper in which he strongly commended the views of Nathaniel Peffer concerning our China policy, without simply writing on his own authority. In 1957 Thomson left the University of Wisconsin to join the CIA and for a while taught at the Foreign Service Institute in Washington. (His brother, James Thomson, was a China specialist at Harvard University.)

John Thomson was an avid canoeist, and became famous for canoeing on the Potomac River to his work at the CIA. In July 1998 while canoeing on a whitewater stretch of the Potomac John suffered a fatal heart attack. His obituary in the *New York Times* details his varied career.

In connection with teaching at Wisconsin, sometime in the early 1950s, I received a letter from Wisconsin offering me a temporary or part-time position there to teach a course on Asia. Because of prior commitments, I reluctantly declined, but the idea was intriguing as conceivably it could have led to a regular position at Wisconsin. In retrospect, given my difficult situation at Washington University in the spring of 1953, I suppose I should have handled the Wisconsin offer with greater finesse.

THE INSTITUTE OF PACIFIC RELATIONS

Senator Joseph McCarthy, with his exaggerated charges of Communists in the U.S. government, was enjoying the beginning of his prominence at the time I was taking Borton's course. Some of McCarthy's principal targets were State Department personnel associated with American policy towards Asia. In class, Borton expressed his deep concern that such challenges of the loyalty of these employees could impair their ability to provide their informed advice on policy.

In connection with my research on the Japanese Constitution, Borton suggested that I might wish to consult the files of the Institute of Pacific Relations (IPR) in downtown New York. The people of the IPR were very helpful. One day Miriam Farley, an expert on Japanese labor and former analyst in SCAP's Government Section, called my attention to the two massive volumes just published by the Government Section: *Political Reorientation of Japan: September 1945 to September 1948.* I was flattered when she asked me to write a review article on the books for the *Far Eastern Survey*, a well-known publication of the Institute. The books reported on the elimination of ultra nationalists, and the reforms of the national executive, the Diet, the legal system, the civil service, local government, and electoral system in Japan. Most notable was a remarkably candid account of how personnel in the Government Section had drafted a new constitution for Japan and persuaded the Japanese cabinet and parliament to adopt its principles. My review of the books focused especially on the constitutional reform, as I regarded the constitution as fundamental to just about everything else.

This "review article" (it was longer than the usual book review) would be my first professional scholarly publication. I mentioned this project to my Japanese language teacher, Osamu Shimizu. Shimizu seemed alarmed, and cautioned me that the IPR had a pro-Communist image. From my experience in intelligence in Tokyo, I knew that he was right, but Borton had encouraged me to visit the IPR for my research, and I thought that the prestige I might acquire by the publication of the article would outweigh any disadvantages. I eagerly waited to see my review article in print.

I spent the summer of 1950 at home in Madison. On June 25, 1950, North Korean forces invaded South Korea, and very soon the United States was at war in Korea. I attended a meeting of left-wing students at the University of Wisconsin where it was charged that the United States had started the war and was the aggressor. Outraged by what I regarded as a gross distortion of the facts, I wrote a very long letter to the Madison *Wisconsin State Journal* itemizing point by point facts and arguments in support of the United States and United Nations actions in Korea. On August 1, 1950, the *State Journal* published the letter unaltered. It occupied almost all of one entire column of the newspaper.

The outbreak of the Korean War took priority over my review of *Political Reorientation,* which finally appeared in the *Far Eastern Survey,* September 13, 1950 (Vol. xix, No. 15, pp.161-164.)

ACADEMIC PROGRESS

A requirement for the Columbia Ph.D. in political science was the passage of a written examination in political theory. I signed up to take the exam, but at the last minute decided that I was not ready for it. I went to the examination room, and before I could indicate that I would not be taking the exam, the proctor, who stood at the door, handed me a copy, face up, of the questions. So I had to take the exam anyway. A week or so later, I asked Miss Black, the departmental secretary, what had been my grade in the exam. She said C+. As course grades below B were considered failures in the graduate school, I assumed that I would have to retake the exam. But no, in this case C+ was passing, so that the political theory requirement was satisfied.

(For many years, I wondered how I had been able to pass this exam, for which I had made inadequate preparation. However, I had taken four semesters of political theory during my wartime night studies at Georgetown University, about five years before taking the exam at Columbia. Moreover, I had taken the famous textbook, Sabine's *History of Political Theory*, with me to Japan and had read parts of it during dull days in the Civil Intelligence Section.)

Through most of Japanese history, serious books were all written in Chinese, not in Japanese, so that students of medieval Japanese history had to be able to read Chinese. Thus my course in advanced Japanese involved the reading of Chinese classics, Japanese style. A Confucian selection in Chinese characters in their original sequence would be cluttered with diacritical marks added by the Japanese indicating how the characters would have to be rearranged in order to make grammatical sense in Japanese. The task of the American student was to read the passage in Japanese, not Chinese, and provide an English translation. I managed to outshine one or two other students more competent and conscientious in Japanese than I. Because Chinese word order is very similar to word order in English, I just translated the Chinese directly into English, before attempting the Japanese translation.

In the fall of 1950 I took my comprehensive Ph.D. examination, majoring in comparative government and minoring in Asian studies. Present were Professors Nathaniel Peffer (international relations and Far East), Hugh Borton (Japanese history), Lindsay Rogers (comparative politics), L. Carrington Goodrich, C. Martin Wilbur, and Franklin Ho. (The last three mentioned individuals were sinologists.). My performance in the comparative government section, focusing largely on British and European politics, was satisfactory, but in Asian studies I was unable, even with the help of Professor Goodrich's leading questions, to describe the boundaries of the Han empire. The examiners decided that at the time of the defense of my dissertation I would be re-examined on Chinese history.

In effect, I had passed the comprehensive examination, which had not been easy. A friend who had been a Foreign Service officer, had failed his comprehensive examination a week before I took mine. He took a week off to recuperate from the shock, and came to the conclusion that his Ph.D. effort had come to an end. He had already been promised a good new post in the State Department and did not need the Ph.D. for his career. (In those days, it was possible for someone who had failed to pass the Ph.D. comprehensive examination to be re-examined only if the initial examiners chose to extend such a privilege.)

I was able to get the Department of Government to approve my dissertation topic. This involved their approval of the Table of Contents of my dissertation, "Domestic and International Influences on Constitutional Reform in Japan, 1945-1946."

AT HOME IN MADISON

I had spent at least part of the summer of 1950 in Madison. I could not find any of my old friends from West or the university; they had all dispersed. In search of a social life, I attended a few events at the Pres House (the Presbyterian Student Center). One day a Pres House bunch gathered in the ballroom of the Student Union. It was there that I first met Myra Koehler. I was immediately much taken with Myra. She had gone to West High and was an accomplished violinist. Her father was a professor of electrical engineering at the university. (I had previously known Myra's brother, Karl. It also developed that before Myra's mother had married she had been employed as a teacher in Lancaster by my father.)

Myra gave a slide party at her house that my brother John and his girl friend and I attended.

My original intent in studying at Columbia was to earn the Ph.D. in political science and in addition earn the certificate of the newly established East Asian Institute. However, by Christmas vacation 1950, I had second thoughts. I had essentially passed the Ph.D. comprehensive examination, had more than enough academic credits for the Ph.D., and the dissertation was the only thing that remained to be accomplished for the doctorate. The certificate was a minor matter, frosting on the cake, so to speak; the principal credential for a college teacher was the doctorate. I was by now utterly fed up with college courses. To get the certificate I would have to finish Professor Orchard's course on the economic geography of Asia and meet other requirements. In the process of changing from music to French as an undergraduate major, shifting from French to political science as my graduate major at Georgetown, and transferring from Georgetown University to Columbia, I had taken more college courses than anybody else I knew and I had had enough.

In the meantime, my sister had her fourth child, Jane ("Zany") in November 1950, and my brother Jim married Pat Colligan on December 30, 1950. (My mother's shocking comment: "You know, isn't Pat almost too nice a girl for Jimmy?") I enjoyed seeing my sister's children in Madison, and I wanted to take time out to enjoy life a little. So after Christmas, I did not return to New York to complete professor Orchard's course and decided to wind up the dissertation at home in Madison. (The period of my actual residence at Columbia University was perhaps shorter than usual, consisting of one summer term, one fall term, one spring term, and part of a fall term.)

By 1951, of course, the house was pretty quiet. Lucille and Charles and their children lived in the Adam Street house, which mother rented to them, and I would see them occasionally. John had graduated from the university in 1946 and was working for United Press in Milwaukee. Gramma Taylor, a widow for nine years, was ailing, but living at home. I think there were just three of us in the house: my mother, my grandmother, and I. Occasionally a student came to take music lessons from my mother. We may have had a student roomer, or two. I blush to say that I cannot recall making any contributions to the household budget at that time. At least I should have been helping with the shopping and other chores. My mother spoiled me. I think she was still thankful that I had survived TB.

I had in effect already completed several chapters of my dissertation. In the course of writing course term papers, I had chosen topics directly related to the dissertation, and two or three of these would serve as dissertation chapters. I wrote to a book dealer in Tokyo and purchased thirty or forty very recently published Japanese books related to my the dissertation—books not available in the University of Wisconsin Library, and, for that matter, probably not yet available even in the Columbia Library. In the University of Wisconsin Library were documents relating to America's postwar policies and the Far Eastern Commission. Satō Isao's book, *Kenpō kaisei no keika* (Tokyo, 1947), which was a detailed and authoritative account of the Japanese side's involvement in constitutional revision, was of tremendous help. (I became personally acquainted with Professor Satō in later years.)

As I wrote finished chapters I would mail them to Professors Borton, Sansom, and Peffer. From January through August, a period of eight months, I worked in the large upstairs bedroom in the front of the house on my dissertation. There were few serious distractions and I stuck close to my original outline. By essentially completing both the research and the writing of one chapter at a time, I avoided the trap of spending all of my time on research without giving myself the time to write up my discoveries. My dissertation may have been at least two-thirds finished by the end of August.

During my 1951 eight-month stint in Madison, I tried to resuscitate my social life. Scarcely anyone that I had known so well during my years at West and the University of Wisconsin seemed to be available. I rejoined the choir at Westminster Presbyterian Church, which was now led by Mrs. Laura Klein. Jane Bundy, daughter of Professor Bundy of the University French Department, had an unusually fine voice and was singing in the choir then. Around Easter, I sang a solo in church. I attended the annual dinner of the Société des Amis de la Maison Française, at Professor Julian Harris's house, riding my red bicycle several miles to get there. I dated a girl at the French House. I went to a concert by the University of Wisconsin symphony orchestra, of which Richard Church, formerly at West High, was now conductor. I took driving lessons at the vocational school.

On April 11, 1951, President Truman "fired" General MacArthur, i. e., removed him from all of his commands. This drastic action provoked demands for Truman's impeachment. MacArthur made a moving address to Congress attacking the president's policies in the Far East. The general then made a tour of the country. I went to see him when he visited Milwaukee. MacArthur was sitting or standing majestically in an open car, smiling and waving at the crowds on the sidewalk. I could swear that he beamed directly at me for a moment, but I suppose he gave a similar impression to other onlookers. My brother, John, then a journalist in Milwaukee, was covering the event while riding in a press vehicle in the MacArthur caravan. He said that at the end of a very long day in Milwaukee, MacArthur showed no sign of fatigue whatever, but the journalists who were covering the same events were completely exhausted.

In the summer, Myra returned to Madison from Dearborn, Michigan, where she had been teaching. She knew how to sail, and we rented a little boat and sailed on Lake Mendota. She had a *soirée musicale* at her house. She and her sister Della were accomplished violinist and pianist respectively and people took turns performing. Della accompanied my rendition of "Be My Love," a piece favored by Mario Lanza. I took Myra to one or two movies and to the Student Union to see the play *The Heiress,* in which Charles Crosby's sister played the leading role.

Elliot Sweet and his wife (the former Marion Blum) had Myra and me for dinner at their place in Verona. Myra was getting ready to go to Japan to teach in the dependents' school there, and was thinking of either selling her Ford or taking it to Japan with her. I was at the Koehler's house the night before Myra and her sister-in-law, Anita Koehler, drove together to San Francisco to put the Ford on the ship.

Sometime in the summer, I received a telephone call from Professor Stuart Queen, head of the Sociology and Anthropology Department of Washington University (St. Louis), offering me a position to teach Asian courses interdepartmentally for one year at that institution. The instructor, Lucian Pye, had been offered a fellowship to study in China, and he could not accept it without someone to substitute teach for him. I was at first reluctant as I was completely unfamiliar with the school and wanted to finish the dissertation. A few days later, Pye himself called me up. If I wished I need only teach 6 credits a semester at full pay, giving me time to work on the dissertation. I learned that Washington University had a fine reputation and in the fall of 1951, I moved to University City, Missouri. (I later learned that Pye's Yale professor, David Nelson Rowe, had asked Hugh Borton if he knew of someone with an interdisciplinary background that could stand in for Pye, and that Borton had recommended me.) I would teach courses in Asian sociology, Asian politics, and Asian history in the three relevant departments. I would also teach an interdisciplinary course on American society.

MY COLUMBIA DOCTORATE

While at Washington University, I continued writing my dissertation, all the time forwarding chapters to my Columbia professors. I hired a professional typist to type the final copy (with carbon copies), and an English graduate student to proof read the document. The dissertation was 444 pages long in pica double-spaced. Nathaniel Peffer was my adviser, and Sir George Sansom and Hugh Borton, director and assistant director of the East Asian institute, also critiqued my work in the course of its writing. Because Sansom had been the chief British representative in the Far Eastern Commission and Hugh Borton had been a principal formulator of American occupation policy in Japan, a reader of the dissertation might feel assured of the essential accuracy of my writing.

I successfully defended the dissertation and at the same time was reexamined on Chinese history, in the spring of 1952. To meet the publication requirement, the dissertation was published on microfilm by the Xerox Corporation in Ann Arbor, Michigan. The 1952 copyright is in my name.

Dissertations as a rule are not commercially marketable as books unless they have been very substantially rewritten. Although the Columbia University Press showed interest in such a project, over the years I made efforts to recast the dissertation into the form of a readable book. In 2000, ten years after my retirement, the University Press of America published my *The Origins of Japan's Democratic Constitution*. In the meantime I had published articles related to aspects of the constitution. Until 1991, my dissertation was the only book-length treatment in English of the origins of the present Japanese Constitution, and scholars on the topic found it expedient to refer to my dissertation.

My Ph.D. degree was to be awarded to me in May 1952. However, the ceremony occurred at the very moment that I was required to turn in final semester grades at Washington University, at a time when I seemed overwhelmed with other problems as well. I failed to show up at the ceremony and later learned that a Chinese luncheon had been set up by the East Asian Institute, attended by my professors, following the ceremony.

It is a source eternal regret to me that I did not take part in what for me would have been a most gratifying occasion. In retrospect, I am sure I could have made some special arrangement with Washington University respecting the final examination and grading schedule that would have permitted me to go to New York. I could have taken my mother with me and the whole event would have been, I am sure, just as exciting for her as it would have been for me. My diploma was mailed to me in Madison, Wisconsin. It is dated May 6, 1952.

My relations with Sir George Sansom did not end with my graduation from Columbia. When in the spring of the following year as I was making critical decisions concerning my future career, I was in New York and got some friendly counsel from that eminent authority. Sir George expressed greater confidence in the viability of Asian studies than in the discipline of political science, which was becoming embroiled in methodological controversies.

In 1959, while I was connected with the Far Eastern Program of the University of Maryland overseas program, I was asked by the program administrators to make indirect inquiries as to the possibility of the conferment of an honorary doctorate to Sir George at our forthcoming graduation ceremony in Tokyo. I wrote Douglas Overton, whom I had known at Arlington Hall and was now the director of the Japan Society of New York. Sir George was then in retirement in sunny California, busily writing his magnum opus, a three volume history of Japan. Overton answered that Sir George was not in sufficiently good health to make the trip to Tokyo to accept a degree. The university officials were unwilling to award the degree *in absentia.* So the project was dropped. Besides, Sir George Sansom, G.B.E., K.C.M.G., already had a number of honorary doctorates, and was a member of the Japan Academy.

In the summer of 1963, I accepted the invitation of Professor James Morley, the director of the East Asian Institute, to teach a course in Japanese politics at Columbia University. A day or so before classes started as I was walking down Amsterdam Avenue I noticed a boy carrying a copy of the plum-colored textbook for the class: Theodore McNelly, *The Contemporary Government of Japan* (Houghton Mifflin, 1963).

(The relationship of my family to East Asian studies at Columbia may be traced to Edwin Hurd Conger, U.S. minister to China during and after the Boxer Rebellion. He was a first cousin of my grandmother, Mrs. Clara Hurd Taylor, the wife of a missionary to Japan in the early 1890s. Seth Low, president of Columbia University, wrote to Mr. Conger asking for help to build a Chinese library and museum. Li Hung-chang, regarded as prime minister to the Empress Dowager of China, wrote to Conger on November 3, 1901, four days before Li's death. On behalf of the Empress Dowager, Columbia University was given the 5,044-volume encyclopedia, *Tu shu ji cheng,* which was received early in 1902, forming the foundation of the Chinese collection at Columbia. *[http://www.columbia.edu/cu/lweb/indiv/eastasian/about.html])*

CHAPTER 10

ST. LOUIS

From 1951 to 1953 I was an instructor at Washington University in St. Louis. Although I would be teaching courses sponsored by each of three departments (Political Science, History, and Sociology-Anthropology) at Washington University, the interdepartmental Far East Program was, for all intents and purposes, mostly under the direction of Stuart Queen, head of the Sociology-Anthropology Department. My first contacts with him in St. Louis were very cordial; we talked together frequently and he was very helpful to me. Together, for example, we went to a talk given by a Jewish member of the faculty who spoke in glowing terms about the future of Israel. Professor Queen expressed concern that, given the extreme tension between the newly founded Israel and the Arab states, Israel might in the future become dependent on the United States for defense against the Arabs.

I rented a room in a private home in University City within fair walking distance of the university, although I usually drove back and forth to school. I ate most of my meals, including breakfast, at the cafeteria at the university, although often I had lunch in the faculty dining room, especially with colleagues in the Sociology-Anthropology Department. I made friends with Professor David Carpenter of that department. He was a friend of Esther Wright, whom I had known on the *Wisteria*, and he had a Japanese wife and little boy, whom he would take to cowboy movies.

I was assigned office space in a large room assigned to the Sociology-Anthropology Department. The room also accommodated desks for several graduate assistants, with whom I became well acquainted, as well as computers that processed the punch cards produced by student researchers. I became involved in the Sociology-Anthropology Club, which had social as well as scholarly activities involving both graduate students and faculty. I was in the custom of going to faculty meetings of the Sociology-Anthropology Department, and for better or worse, my relations with History and Political Science Departments were not close.

My initial teaching load at Washington University was unusually light—only six credit hours per semester, i.e., six 50-minute hours of lecturing per week. The light load was intended to permit me to complete my dissertation, which I successfully defended at Columbia on April 2, 1952, during the second semester of my teaching at Washington University.

The teaching at Washington University represented a substantial challenge. I would teach one course on Asia sponsored by one or another of the three relevant disciplinary departments per semester and one course on contemporary society in the basic college curriculum per semester. It will be recalled that my Wisconsin high school teaching certificate qualified me to teach French, music, and English. I had never had any training or experience in teaching courses in political science, history, or sociology. I had never served as a graduate assistant, as had many if not most new Ph.D.s. However, I had had experience teaching French and English at West High and Kemper, and was not bothered with stage fright. Organizing my courses, selecting textbooks, preparing syllabi, making lesson plans, preparing lectures (6 hours of new lectures per week),and devising examinations. took a great deal of thought and of time. Sometimes the best I could do was to stay a chapter ahead of the students.

I had a habit of driving to a park near the university, and while sitting in my car with my textbooks at hand, preparing my lectures. To avoid the impression that my lectures merely reiterated the student's textbook, I often based my lecture on a rival textbook, providing students with factual material and interpretations that would be fresh for them and suggest that I knew more about the topic than just what was in their textbook. In the early stages of my teaching, I was fearful that students might ask me questions that I would not be able to answer intelligently. I met this problem by making sure that my eleven pages of notes would take up the full fifty-minute period to present, so that when the bell rang and students began rushing to the restroom or to meet their friends, I would ask if there were any questions. Usually there weren't any.

In addition to my regular 6-hour teaching load, I took on a night course. In theory night courses are thought not to be very demanding for the instructor, as they usually involved repeating the same lectures one has been giving in the day program. In practice, unfortunately, it may be more complicated than that because of administrative problems, the day and evening classes may be out of phase with each other, the notes have to be rearranged, and new examinations must be prepared. Besides, if nothing else, the time taken to teach the night class must be subtracted from time otherwise available for the research and writing necessary for promotion or even to keep one's job in a major university. For night and summer courses, the instructor is usually paid a flat sum for each course that he teaches, and this flat sum is far less than the instructor is paid if calculated on a per course basis in the regular day program. Also, teaching in the summer and night courses usually earns no extra credit towards the retirement system. Because the beginning instructor's salary is quite modest and regular pay checks are not issued during the summer months, the economic pressure on the instructor to teach at night and during summer may seem compelling.

The system was stressful. Usually by Wednesday afternoon I was completely exhausted and would return to my room to take a nap before I would go out for a late dinner.

ME AND MY CHEVROLET

In the summer of 1951, I had attended a driving class at the Madison Vocational School. We learned the rules of the road and how to change tires (from time to time in later years I would myself exchange a flat for a spare). The scary part of the course was having to drive around the capitol square in downtown Madison. The teacher was a retired policeman. At the end of the course, we were scheduled to be tested for our driver's license. For those of us who did not own a car for the test, I chose the option of using the teacher's personal car for a fee of $5.00. The teacher himself administered the driving test. Very much as I expected, the test did not involve backing the teacher's car into a parking space or any other of the more difficult feats that we had been learning in the class.

From a private individual, I bought a three-year old Chevrolet sedan, which John Schumann, a family friend, helped me to choose, and drove it to St. Louis. During the Thanksgiving week-end, I drove to Madison. On the way back to St. Louis, I decided to drive by Galesburg, Illinois, a city that had been founded by my great great grandfather George Washington Gale. After looking at the court house and the campus of Knox College, also founded by my ancestor, I drove on. It became night and was raining. As I drove onto a bridge crossing the Mississippi River, the right side of my car scraped along the side rail of the bridge making a terrible racket and shooting sparks. I got out of the car and for a moment it looked as if a wheel were missing. I noticed that at the very point were the land touches the bridge the roadway narrows about a foot, and I had struck the protruding curb, which I would probably have seen in the daytime. A garage at the far end of the bridge sent a tow truck. I left the car at the garage in Louisiana, Missouri, took the bus to St. Louis, and two weeks later returned to Louisiana to retrieve my car. I had only been driving two or three months, and I was afraid that my mother, who tended to be a worrier, would hear about my accident from the officers of our local bank, whom she knew and who had a lien on my car. From then on I have been chary of driving fast at night in the rain, and have never since had such a bad accident.

THE CHANNING CLUB

It was said that socially prominent families in St. Louis sent their children to private universities in the East, but during one academic year, the child would be enrolled at Washington University so that he or she could participate in the Veiled Prophet's Ball. The festivity included a parade, led by the Veiled Prophet (a young socialite), and an elegant ball where people danced or from a balcony watched the dancing, and so on. I was too busy with my work and my own social life to become involved in the activities connected with the Veiled Prophet's Ball.

I began attending the Unitarian Church in St. Louis, singing in the choir and joining in the activities of the Channing Club, which was made up of mostly unmarried young people, but also a few young married couples. The Channing Club activities tended to be loosely structured, the participants seemed to rotate in and out, and occasionally people would pair up. On our trips to Camp Solidarity, for example, who went depended pretty much on who had cars and who happened to be dating whom. Camp Solidarity was a public park about an hour and a half drive from St. Louis, near Pacific, Missouri. Camp Solidarity was also favored by Washington University's Sociology-Anthropology Club. The Camp's principal feature was a muddy little river that ran through it, which could be used for bathing, but not serious swimming. There was also a fair expanse of woods. Being from Wisconsin, where we had lots of lakes and other beautiful scenery, I was surprised that St. Louisans made so much of Camp Solidarity.

Some of the Channing clubbers would visit a wonderful tavern in East St. Louis, across the Mississippi River in Illinois. The pianist was an old queer who openly flirted with the male customers as they entered the establishment. He played the piano by ear with great expression, but seemed quite unconcerned that he was using the wrong chords. One night he accompanied a not unattractive old lady with blond hair who sang "You Made Me Love You." She was a trooper who had seen better days, and her seductive style made it eminently clear that the kind of love she was celebrating was of the worldly sort.

One Halloween, the Channing Club held a beer party in the back room of a downtown tavern, where we had our own keg of the beverage. I took as a date one of the secretaries at the university. She covered herself completely, including her face, in a cat costume, which was very cute. During our party, she was completely anonymous so far as everybody but me was concerned, so that no one ever knew who my date that evening was.

One young married couple in our group had separated. The young husband invited me and a girl I knew over to his place for dinner, where his estranged wife would be present. (Apparently he was making an attempt at reconciliation.) The four of us seemed to get along all right at the dinner. However, apparently a reconciliation failed to take place, and a few weeks later I learned that the young husband had committed suicide.

The Unitarian Church sponsored a retreat at a bible camp at Lake Geneva, Wisconsin, and I attended that. The facilities at the camp were surprisingly

Spartan. We resided in tents, not in cabins. I was assigned to a bed to be shared with another male camper whom I had not previously met. The program of speakers on serious subjects was fine. There was considerable social interaction among the campers and some gossip was generated. I happened to favor a certain red head—although several ladies reminded me that the woman's hair was only dyed red. I did not concern myself with the gossip. However, after we had returned to St. Louis, an attractive lady who had not been accompanied by her husband at the camp asked me not to mention to her husband what she had been doing at the camp. Actually I had no idea what she had been doing but I began to wonder.

TROUBLE WITH THE LAW

I was once a passenger in a car driven by a friend who was an aggressive driver. When we found ourselves at the end of long backup of cars, he drove some distance along the shoulder and thus managed to squeeze in near the front of the line. I assumed that this was illegal, but thought that perhaps I should myself be less of a milque-toast when driving.

A few days later I was driving at faster than my usual speed in St. Louis, congratulating myself on how I managed to reform my approach to driving, when a motorcycle policemen caught up with me and ordered me to stop. I was arrested on the spot and told to drive to the police station. I was charged with speeding and with passing a streetcar stop on the wrong side. The policeman showed me the little jail consisting of two or three cells connected to the station. Each cell was equipped with a bare cement floor, a toilet (without a seat) in one corner, a wash basin, a narrow bunk, and a heavy barred door that clanked convincingly when slammed shut. It reminded me of the bear cages in the Madison zoo. I would be incarcerated in one of these cages until my trial unless I could post a bond. A property owner in St. Louis could vouch for me. I gave the name of a professor at a local teachers college whom I scarcely knew at the Unitarian Church. He reluctantly agreed to guarantee my court appearance, placing some two thousand dollars at the mercy of my showing up for my trial.

On the day of the trial I drove to the court house and was briefly panicked by the inability to find a legal place to park. In the courtroom, which was the size of a small auditorium and was full of people, I was one of the two civilians dressed in a suit. Everyone else was either a uniformed police officer or more casually dressed, except that the judge wore a brown suit. (I had expected to see him in a robe.) He was expeditiously handling one case after another, and mine appeared to be only one of many cases that session. A policeman described my transgressions. I knew that I was completely wrong and admitted my guilt. I was fined a total 35 dollars for my multiple offenses.

The sight of that horrid jail had a lasting and salutary effect on me. Perhaps if more people were shown the inside of a jail they would show a more wholesome respect for the law.

SOCIAL LIFE

Both at the university and at my church, I led an active social life and knew a number of girls. Audrey Rosenbaum was a brilliant young sociology major who beautifully played excerpts of a Rachmaninoff concerto on the piano in the auditorium. Although I played golf poorly I went golfing with two or three of the girls I met in Channing Club.

The summer of 1952 was divided between Madison and St. Louis. I taught two courses in the 5-week summer session at Washington University, when I occupied the house of a friend of Professor Carpenter. The early and later parts of the summer I spent in Madison. Myra Koehler was in Japan and therefore unavailable. I took voice lessons at the Wisconsin School of Music (not affiliated with the University of Wisconsin) and sang in the choir at the Westminster Presbyterian Church. I took a girl from the French House canoeing. I visited the Rices. I met a girl at the Presbyterian Student Center, and later visited her in Ann Arbor.

Back at Washington University in the fall of 1952, there was much support for Adlai Stevenson among the faculty, and I went to a "Volunteers for Stevenson" meeting downtown. (It had been explained to me that this "volunteers" meeting was intended to round up the support of the professional classes for Stevenson, people who might be uncomfortable among the union workers in the Stevenson camp.) In November I voted for Eisenhower, as did my brother John, who had been a Democrat. On October 23, I heard John Foster Dulles, who would become Eisenhower's secretary of state, speak at the university's gothic chapel. He advocated a hard line against the Soviet Union, emphasizing that the Soviets were atheistic.

During 1951-1952 Gerald Heard, the eminent English essayist, was guest lecturer at Washington University. His lectures were elegantly delivered, well attended, and provoked much comment. However, his speech was replete with mystical generalities, and because he seemed to be taking flying saucers more seriously than they deserved, I found it difficult to take him seriously.

One spring, Professor Edward ("Ted") Kidder and I drove in Kidder's car to Cleveland to attend the annual meeting of the Association for Asian Studies. Kidder, an archeologist specializing in Japan, taught in the Art Department at Washington University. I particularly recall hearing a talk at the convention by George Blakeslee, who had been involved in making Occupation policy for Japan in the State Department. We made the mistake of parking Kidder's car in the wrong place, so that it was towed away and had to be retrieved from the police department with the payment of a hefty fee. One morning we had breakfast at a popular cafeteria, where among the clientele, we recognized, from her regal bearing and eye-catching attire, the queen of the burlesque show that we had seen the night before.

A CAREER DECISION

My original appointment at Washington University was as a one-year replacement of Lucian Pye, who was on leave for research. However, when Mr. Pye asked for an extra year of leave, it was decided that I would remain at Washington University for another year. During my second semester of my second year, it appeared that Lucian Pye would not be returning to Washington University after all. I was asked if I wished to remain at the university for a third year, with hints that I might be in line for some kind of promotion and tenure. I asked for a week or so to think about the matter. In the meantime, Rutgers University was looking for a one-year replacement for its Japan specialist, Ardath Burks. I made a trip to New York and was interviewed at Rutgers and discussed the situation with my professors at Columbia, especially Sir George Sansom. Sir George seemed to think that Asian studies was a more promising field than political science. On my way back to St. Louis, I felt that my best prospect would be to remain at Washington University.

However, during the two or so weeks while I was pondering my reply to St. Louis, Stuart Queen, impatient to settle things, began looking at other candidates besides me and hired someone who suited him—a sociologist. The fact that the *Political Science Quarterly*, a leading scholarly journal, had just published, in December 1952, my article on "American Influence and Japan's No-War Constitution" seemed to count for nothing. My hesitancy about agreeing to remain at Washington had cost me my job. My potential future at Washington University had evaporated into thin air.

An underlying problem with Asian studies, or any area studies program, is that at most but not all universities area studies are *interdepartmental*. That is to say that there is no department of Asian studies. The disciplinary departments, not the area studies programs, hire, promote, and fire professors. Professors in the area studies programs are beholden to their respective departments for their positions. At Washington University, the Asian studies program had been in effect ruled by a sociologist, Stuart Queen. During my two years at Washington University I had failed to identify myself firmly as a political scientist in the Department of Political Science. I had become embraced by the Sociology-Anthropology department, a department which, as may be expected, gave priority to its own disciplinary preferences. Thus my replacement by a sociologist. (It should also be noted that within this department there was tension between the sociologists and the anthropologists. At the same time, in the 1950s with the contraction of veteran students subsidized by the GI bill of rights, Washington University, like other universities across the country, was faced with a shrinking budget.)

During my first year at Washington University, the chairman of the political science department was Arnold J. Lien. During the second year, the chairman was Thomas Eliot, brother of Mrs. Rice, a family friend. But I was given to understand that my position at Washington University was entirely dependent on Professor Queen, and I do not recall that I ever discussed the matter of my future at Washington University with Professor Eliot. Nor did I discuss the matter with Professor Gerhard, the chairman of History Department.

When Professor Queen told me that my contract at Washington University would not be renewed, I immediately began searching for another job. One obvious idea was to check out the possibilities at St. Louis University, a Catholic institution. I had a pleasant talk with Professor Paul Steinbicker, who headed the political science department there. He asked me what my specialty was. I said comparative politics. He said he already had someone on his staff teaching that subject. It was Kurt Schuschnigg, whose name I instantly recognized. Schuschnigg had been chancellor of Austria in 1938 when Hitler invaded that country. He was arrested by the Germans until freed by American troops in 1945. In 1947 he settled in the United States and found himself a job in St. Louis. I had not previously known that he was living in St. Louis, and I had never met him.

I thought after my talk with Steinbicker that in a sense I had been a victim of Hitler's aggression, because one of his refugees had taken a job that otherwise might have been open to me.

I hired a young lady part-time to type application letters. It would not be easy to find a job as good as the one I had been holding at Washington University. I would have to find a department of political science in a research university that had an opening for an East Asia specialist. My applications at UCLA and Indiana University seem to have been taken seriously but were ultimately not successful. I learned of an opening at Oklahoma State University in Stillwater and wrote them a letter. Their reply was that my specializations did not correspond to what they were seeking. I wrote them a second letter that emphasized my qualifications in comparative politics and Asian studies. They replied that they were interested and would reimburse me $50.00 for travel costs for an interview in Stillwater. I therefore drove my Chevrolet to Stillwater, passing through much semi-desert country and, in one area, many oil wells. Around 9:00 PM, I had a flat tire. Fortunately I was close to a little town where I found a mechanic who helped me out.

On a Saturday morning I drove into Stillwater. The green of the university campus, most notably a pond graced by the presence of white swans, was in pleasant contrast to the drought of the surrounding country. There was a new library with pink marble walls. The chairman of the political science department was very friendly and introduced me to several deans, making a big point of my being a Presbyterian. He then showed me an apartment that he owned and which I might be interested in renting. I mentioned that I was thinking of getting married and that if I was married before I came to Stillwater, I would indeed be interested in the apartment, but that if not married I might settle for just renting a room as had been my custom in St. Louis. When I was about to leave, the chairman said that, it being Saturday, his secretary was not present but on Monday he would have her write me a letter offering me the job. I felt pretty pleased by the trend of events; I had a job.

About Wednesday I got a telephone call from the department chairman in Stillwater. He asked whether or not I was planning to get married, I said no. A few days later, he informed me that he had not been authorized to offer me the position at Oklahoma State.

Time was passing, and I needed a job for the fall. I registered with a commercial teachers agency. They found an opening at a Northwest Missouri State College in Maryville, 277 miles as the crow flies from St. Louis. I drove to the college, which was at the edge of a small town and adjoined some thriving corn fields. The nearest large cities were Omaha, Kansas City, and Des Moines, each about a two-hour drive from Maryville. The coeds were healthy-looking and attractive. A couple of deans showed me around, and because I had shown little enthusiasm and not said much, they took the initiative and asked me if I was applying for the job. I said yes, and signed a contract. I was then committed to pay a substantial commission to the teachers agency.

Back at Washington University, I discussed my situation with a young acquaintance in the economics department. He said that if I took the job at the state college, I would be unable to get a job at any better place and would be stuck in that kind of school for the rest of my life. He said it would be better to get a temporary job in industry and try to get a better teaching job. I discussed this with my mother, who saw nothing wrong with teaching at a state college and said that her childhood friend, Myrtle Barker, who had a Columbia doctorate, taught at St. Cloud state college in Minnesota.

At a faculty meeting some months previously, Professor Queen had mentioned openings in the European Program of the University of Maryland, a night extension program for American servicemen in Europe. This would involve teaching at military bases in several different European countries. It sounded much more interesting than the job I had accepted in Maryville. I immediately applied for the Maryland job and was accepted. I then wrote a letter to the Missouri college resigning the job that I had just accepted at that institution.

The teacher's agency of course insisted that I owed them a commission for finding the Missouri job, even though I had resigned it. They had a point and I paid up. The agency also tried to get a commission for the Maryland job, but I truthfully pointed out that I had learned about the Maryland job before the agency had ever sent me a notice of the Maryland opening. The agency then desisted from charging me a commission on the Maryland position.

In all of this confusion, I failed to note that the relevant dean of Northwest Missouri State College did not reply to my resignation letter. Then late in August, I received word from him that when he had returned to his college *at the end of the summer* he found my letter. He was incensed about the inconvenience this had caused him as he had to find at the last minute someone to fill in for me. But evidently he was not going to take action against me.

I don't blame him for being upset. However I felt that an administrator at Oklahoma State had pulled a fast one on me and that, given the unequal relation that usually obtains between young instructors and college administrators, someone should allow me a little slack. There were many drawbacks to the Maryland job— for example there was no tenure track involved, and I could have a difficult time moving from the Maryland overseas program to a state-side position. But I am not at all sure that I would have been happier or better off to have stuck with the state college job. (The college at Maryville is today known as Northwest Missouri State University.)

CHAPTER 11

EUROPE

I taught in the European Program of the University of Maryland from the fall of 1953 till the fall of 1958, when I moved to the Far East Program.

I had to report to the University of Maryland at College Park on my way to Europe. The university is in a suburb of Washington, D. C., and for several days I stayed at the home of my uncle Edwin Taylor and Aunt Lois, who lived on a farm near Rockville, Maryland. My uncle drove me to the university once or twice, and I managed to find my way around Washington and Maryland using the bus system.

I stopped to see a Mr. Coolidge in the State Department. We had been corresponding about the possibility of my working in the Department concerning Japanese questions. Perhaps I should explain my preference for work in the State Department over college teaching. (1) During the war and immediate postwar period, as an employee of the War Department I had been actively employed in "making history." This activity seemed much more interesting to me than the thought of merely talking about such things to college students. (2) The hours for a bureaucrat were less demanding than those for a teacher. As a civilian intelligence analyst for five years in Arlington, Virginia, and Tokyo, I had worked five days a week from 9 to 5. My week-ends and evenings were free. However, in college teaching my work seemed never to end. I was always having to prepare lectures, grade papers, and engage in publishable research in order to earn a promotion or even, for the that matter, to keep my job. The work was open-ended and there was always something more that had to be done. (3) The pay in college teaching, especially for beginning instructors, was relatively poor. Normally the pay is for only 9 or 10 months rather than 12 months. If one wants to earn additional money in the evenings or summer, he might, or he might not, depending on extension or summer school schedules, be able to teach for extra pay. However, pay for extension and summer courses is much smaller than pay during the regular academic year, and such teaching does not count for credit in the retirement system. Normally only administrative personnel in a university are paid on a 12-month basis. (4) There seemed to be more employment security in government work. One cannot earn academic tenure until serving a number of years in untenured positions. Even after one thinks that he has legitimately earned a promotion and/or tenure because of his excellence in teaching and publications, departmental politics may result in a denial of tenure and promotion. Most major institutions have "up or out" policies, meaning that tenure is denied and one loses his job, unless he is promoted. The competition for jobs and promotion, especially while the GI programs on campuses were phasing out, could be very fierce. (5) In my particular case, the Maryland overseas program, an ocean away from the United States, would seem to be a very inconvenient location for moving ahead in the American academic world.

When Eisenhower took over the presidency in 1953 and John Foster Dulles became secretary of state, as an economy measure the State Department had frozen hiring and I was not offered a position there. I had not completely given up on the State Department, however, so in the course of reporting to College Park, I stopped at the State Department to see Mr. Coolidge and remind him of my continuing interest. After talking with him and telling him that I was joining the Maryland overseas program, he referred me to another person in the department who, he said, would like to talk to me. I thought great, maybe after I have finished working for Maryland, I will be hired by the Department.

It turned out that the man to whom Coolidge had referred me was in the course of leaving the Department and was interested in the possibility of a teaching job with Maryland overseas program.

The failure of my effort to join the State Department was the cause of my first complaint against the policies of Mr. Dulles. The second disappointment in my relations with him occurred in 1955, when Dulles engineered a thaw in the U.S.-Soviet Cold War. I had been teaching at a series of unattractive military bases in the rural areas of France, England, and Germany and was slated for assignment at Salzburg, Austria. There the university had a lease on quarters in the Osterreichischer Hof Hotel. The university's room overlooked a picturesque stream and commanded an unobstructed view of the mountainous scenery later made famous in 1965 film, *The Sound of Music*. Salzburg is a beautiful city, famous for its architecture and music, and it was now my turn to reside there. Mr. Dulles, however, negotiated a treaty with the Soviets that ended the Allied occupation of Austria, so that terminated the Maryland program there. That was the genesis of my second grudge against Dulles.

In the 1960s I got my revenge. The international airport being built outside of Washington D.C. was named after Mr. Dulles. There was a difficult engineering problem involved in the construction of the airport's sewer system. Day after day, banner headlines in the *Washington Post* would refer to the "Dulles Sewer."

THE OVERSEAS PROGRAM

I reported to Franklin L. Burdette, the prominent political scientist then head of the Department of Government and Politics in the College of Business and Public Administration in the University of Maryland's main campus in College Park. He greeted me cordially. I also made it a point to visit Professor Wesley Gewehr, head of the history department, at his home in Washington D.C. as I would be teaching courses in history as well as in political science. I was of course very aware that my new job did not carry tenure, and that the sooner I found a permanent teaching position in the United States the better. By maintaining constant contact with those in authority at College Park conceivably I might transfer from the overseas program to the main campus. (Actually no one at that time hinted that there might be such a possibility, and the ties between the College Park campus and the overseas program were tenuous.)

Dean Stanley Drazek of the College of Special and Continuing Studies (CSPS), a very sympathetic individual, and one of his assistants, escorted several of us new overseas faculty members around the campus and to the Pentagon to fill in forms and get identification cards and military travel orders, in preparation for our work with the military in Europe.

We then had to go to Massachusetts to catch a military flight to Europe. Seated next to me on the plane was Leonard Lutwack, a College Park English professor who would serve for a year in the European Program. The plane stopped in the Azores Islands, where we had an elegant dinner (for which the university reluctantly reimbursed me $10.00) and overnight stay. When the plane reached France, I looked down and saw the Normandy peninsula, which I immediately recognized from my memory of the map of France that I had drawn with coordinates in Miss Young's French class at West High. We flew almost directly over the Eiffel Tower and landed at an airport outside of Frankfurt. (We are talking here about Frankfurt am Main, in what was then called West Germany. Frankfurt an der Oder, a much smaller city, was in East Germany, which was occupied by the Soviet Union.)

The overseas program was sponsored by the College of Special and Continuation Studies of the University of Maryland, which administered night college-level courses at the Pentagon and American military bases in the vicinity of Washington D.C. as well as at the College Park campus. The full-time instructors in the overseas program were hired on a year-by-year basis, with no provision for tenure, although the university might rehire instructors for subsequent assignments. Most of the instruction, however, was actually done by part-time instructors hired on a per-course basis. The part-timers might be either Americans or non-Americans whose appointments—like those of the full-timers—were cleared by the disciplinary departments in College Park.

Because the cost of the instruction was borne by the Defense Department and because the overseas stationing of the troops, who were the students, was contingent on changing budgetary and strategic considerations, it was understandable that the program found it inexpedient to provide for academic tenure. At the same time, it was much cheaper to hire part-time instructors than it was to hire full-timers, whose pay would be comparable to that of full-time instructors stateside. Also, the part-timers did not as rule require the extent of logistical support such as post exchanges (PXs) and bachelor officer quarters (BOQs) that the full-timers needed.

As a rule in this program, each term lasted eight weeks. A three-credit course would involve two three-hour class meetings at night twice a week. The normal teaching schedule for a full-time instructor consisted of teaching two courses per term. That is to say, he would teach a total of four three-hour evening classes each week during the eight-week term. The full-timer would reside on or near the military base where he was currently teaching, in a BOQ if available, on the local economy otherwise. In order to minimize the instructor's having to make frequent moves, he was apt to be assigned to a given base for two consecutive terms.

Much of the instruction at large bases with large educational programs close to major cities, such as London or Paris, was conducted by part-timers. Full-time instructors were often assigned to smaller remote bases which might offer as few as only one or two courses per term. Needless to say, some full-timers were very disappointed with their assignments, although in my case, I fully understood the system before I signed on. (Having served in the occupation of Japan, I had some notion of what military bases were like, and before being hired pictured myself on trains or buses moving from one base to another.)

The Heidelberg office liked the full-time instructors to own automobiles, which would facilitate their transportation. We were cautioned, however, to drive very carefully, as there was a distressingly high rate of fatal accidents. The story was told of one deceased professor. In order to avoid payment of a fee of $6,000.00 to a steamship company for the return to America of his body according to the relevant regulations, his ashes were mailed from an army post office (APO). I once had dinner with the widows of two faculty members who had been killed. I was taken aback by their desperate flirtatiousness and brassiness.

The full-timers, most were Ph.D.s, were expected to teach a variety of courses. Those with Ph.D.s in history or political science might be expected to teach courses in both of those disciplines. As I was as often as not teaching at least one course that I had not previously taught, much of my time was devoted to the preparation of notes for new lectures. Quite naturally, I made it a point to save all of my lecture notes.

For me, who had never before been in Europe, the opportunity to travel there was extremely attractive. As I normally taught only four nights a week, with an automobile I was able to see a great deal of Europe.

For me, the most difficult course to teach was American history. One might think that anyone with a Ph.D. ought to have no problem with that. However, I had never taken a college course in American history. When I met my first class in Wiesbaden, I was faced with military officers whose lifetime hobby had been the Civil War. For example, I was asked questions like "If general so and so, who was a Union officer, had fought on the Confederate side with his brother major so and so, wouldn't the South have won the Battle of such and such place?" Professor Walter Posey (on leave from Agnes Scott College) would have been delighted to exchange his course in European history for my course in American history, which would have suited me just fine, but we were unable to arrange the switch. Actually, because of my M.A. in French I was much better at European history, which never gave me a problem. In the Maryland program I taught American history, European history, American government, comparative government, American foreign policy, international relations, East Asian history, and Russian history. I once graded a make-up exam in international law.

I liked to tell jokes that would help make my points. One instructor told me in envious tones that he could hear my students laughing in the next room, and he wished that he could hold his students' attention as well as I. In one of my classes, I began to tell a joke and then said that I better not tell it because it was so old. One lovely student said, "Please tell it to us Dr. McNelly; you never let that stop you before." (That pretty blond was nice to me. I had just purchased a beautiful made-to-measure sports jacket that she liked and she asked to take my picture after class.)

I felt obliged to do more than merely regurgitate the textbook and made it a point to give them information and analysis above and beyond what was in the text. I also liked to encourage class discussion.

One of my students praised a professor who took exactly the opposite approach. The student said that while the professor was lecturing, the students could simply underline the points in the text as the professor recited them. This greatly simplified note keeping by the student and he thought that this was great.

From time to time I liked to open up the session to a class discussion. Some students objected to this as a waste of time. They felt that we should concentrate on getting ready for the questions that might appear in the final examination. While I appreciated the seriousness that the students showed towards their studies, it disturbed me to think that political science was so completely cut and dried that all it required was memorization. Class discussions encourage students to do some thinking for themselves and to see the relationships among ideas.

I enjoyed teaching in the overseas program. The students took an adult attitude towards their classes and worked hard. I especially liked to teach international relations. There was no problem at all about arousing the interest of the students in this topic; they were American soldiers serving their country overseas, and the course was obviously relevant to their mission.

Chester Easum, a professor of history at the University of Wisconsin, was a Madison neighbor temporarily assigned as cultural attache to the West German government. He was familiar with the Maryland overseas program and in a discussion with me spoke highly of its academic quality.

WIESBADEN

A bunch of us newly-arrived Marylanders were temporarily stationed in a spa hotel in Bad Homburg, near Frankfurt, for several days. There we learned that the Germans preferred door handles over door knobs and liked showers with elaborate controls for the temperature, direction, and force of the water. A faculty meeting (there must have been twenty or thirty of us) was held in the venerable Rose Hotel in nearby Wiesbaden. After the meeting we dispersed to our respective assignments in Germany, France, and England. One professor was sent to the American base in Sidi Slimane, Morocco, another to Tripoli. I would be stationed in Wiesbaden for my first term of teaching. As a full-time Maryland professor I had the assimilated rank of a major or lieutenant-colonel and could live in bachelor officers quarters (BOQ).

One of my priorities was to pick up my car in Heidelberg. Before going to Europe, in Madison I had traded in my Chevrolet for a Hillman Minx that was to be delivered to me in Europe. In those days in the United States before the advent of Japanese imports if you wanted a small compact car you would buy a British-made Morris Minor, but the little British Hillman Minx was beginning to make inroads into the American market. My theory had been that the Hillman was a European car, but once in Europe, I realized that it was not a European car; it was an English car, and the Americans in Europe favored American cars. Gasoline was ten cents a gallon at the PX.

A dealer in Heidelberg was scheduled to have my Hillman ready for me. On a week-end I boarded a train at Wiesbaden, and I would change trains in Mainz. I had heard that there was a French bookstore in Mainz, which was in the French zone of occupation, and between trains I managed to visit the bookstore. I hustled back to the railroad station and boarded what I thought was the train to Heidelberg. After a bit I found out that I was on an express train to Stuttgart, which was the first stop, and I was required to pay full fare from Mainz to Stuttgart and then from Stuttgart to Heidelberg, where I put up at a hotel. The following day I picked up the new car (in which no heater had yet been installed) and drove it back to Wiesbaden.

With my Hillman Minx, I made short trips, often with my new friends, to see much of the surrounding countryside. From the towers in the cathedral in Mainz we saw a beautiful view of the Rhine and less beautiful view of the city, which was still very largely rubble. The reconstruction of Mainz was said to be inhibited by the political uncertainties stemming from the occupation of that corner of Germany by French forces. We saw the Bone Cellar in Oppenheim where the remains of 15,000 people were stacked like cord wood. The remains of these victims of the Thirty Years War and a subsequent plague had been removed to make more room in the cemetery.

One cold Sunday, I drove Professor and Mrs. Lutwack and a girl friend to hear Bach's *St. Matthew's Passion* performed in a magnificent, but unheated, Romanesque church in Bad Homburg. I made the acquaintance of Professor and Mrs Walter Posey, Professor Ed Sampson, a handsome bachelor, and Lee Schadle, a cute fourth-grade teacher in the American dependents school.

The Poseys and Ed Sansom signed up for a bus tour of Italy during the one-week break between terms. I would have loved to join them, but because I was making payments on my Hillman, did not have the necessary funds.

Life in Wiesbaden with my new but congenial friends was very pleasant. But it came to a sudden end after two months, when my friends felt sorry for me for being assigned Chateauroux, France, for term II. Although the base there was reputed to be the best American base in France, it was said (accurately, I later learned) to be a mud hole.

FRANCE

I had looked forward to the possibility of a post in France that would give me a chance to exercise my skill in speaking French and to become directly acquainted with the culture I had been taught to admire at the University of Wisconsin. Chateauroux was a city of modest size about 150 miles south of Paris. Driving there proved difficult. The roads in France were not nearly as good as those in Germany, where the famous autobahn made distant driving simple. The autobahn strongly resembled the Interstate highways that we now have in the United States. However a number of the bridges on the autobahn had been destroyed by Allied bombing, so that from time to time the driver had to make a winding detour through a valley.

In France I persisted in misreading the highway signs. In France, the arrow showing you to go straight ahead *does not point up*. The driver is directed to go straight ahead by two signs, one sign on each side of the road. The arrow on the right-hand sign points left and the arrow on the left-hand sign points right. Thus the two signs point to the road straight ahead. Not noticing the sign on the left side of the road, more than once I interpreted the sign on the right side to mean that I should make a left turn. I became lost in the foggy hills of Champagne for hours before I finally figured out where I had gone wrong. Also, as there was no heater in the car, I had to leave the windows open in the cold damp weather to keep the windshield from fogging up.

Arriving in Chateauroux, in French I asked a policeman how to get to the American base (*la base américaine*). It took a while to realize that the local people insisted on using the expression *la Martinerie* to refer to the American Base. I lived in the BOQ on the base, and being busy with preparing lectures, seldom left. For some reason everything on the base seemed to be covered with mud, including the pants and shoes of its inhabitants. Here and there were drainage ditches crossed by little pedestrian bridges. I explained to my class that in case of a surprise attack by the Russkies, our strategy would be to destroy these bridges. One day the education adviser and I drove into Chateauroux, the capital of the department of Indre, and were pleasantly surprised at how clean and pretty the city looked.

In Chateauroux a local auto dealer installed a heater in my car, all the more necessary as it was mid-November and I needed protection from the cold and dampness and a frosty windshield.

A young Frenchman on the base urged me to learn more French slang expressions, such as are often used in informal conversations and in the movies. I would have loved to do this, but I had to spend most of my time preparing lectures, as I was nearly always faced with teaching at least one course that I had never before taught. I visited Paris at least once during my posting at Chateauroux, and I spent two or three Sundays in Bourges, which has a lovely cathedral surrounded by a low moss-covered wall.

I had heard that George Sand's chateau was near Chateauroux, and inquired at a filling station about how to get there. As a student of French literature, I was shocked that the first person I asked seemed not to know what I was talking about. Actually the chateau turned out to be little more impressive than a large, rambling Victorian farmhouse. (It is depicted, I do not know how accurately, in the 1991 movie *Impromptu*, in which Judy Davis played the role of George Sand and Hugh Grant represented Frederic Chopin, one of the authoress's lovers.)

Although the declared policy of the university administration was to attempt to avoid moving the professors more often than every two terms, I had been at Chateauroux only eight weeks when it was decided that my next term would be Verdun and Metz. Thus in January 1954 I drove to Verdun. I would teach Monday and Wednesday evenings in Verdun and Tuesday and Thursday evenings in Metz. I would drive back and forth between the two cities. When I asked the education adviser at Verdun the location of the local BOQ the answer was that there was none. He showed me the classroom and pointed to a spot behind the blackboard where the last Maryland professor had slept on a cot. This arrangement did not appeal to me so I checked into a small hotel in Verdun. After a week or so the management of the hotel asked me to stop residing at the hotel. I asked why I had to move. It was because I did not eat my meals in the hotel. (The food in the hotel was fine, but expensive, and I ate most of my meals in the PX.)

I then checked into a hotel in Metz that was located on the same large square as the railroad station. I kept my Hillman, which was heavily loaded with my personal effects, parked overnight directly underneath a streetlight in this large square, and no one molested it. The hotel manager seemed to have no objection to my staying at his establishment. One morning in the hotel, I saw a pair of lovers in the corridor bidding a most fond farewell.

I should explain about the education advisers. At each base there was a civilian civil service employee, usually American, who oversaw the education of the men on the base. I found the education advisers to be very cooperative and congenial.

The education adviser at Verdun was married to a French woman, and in addition to his job on the base he sold automobiles to servicemen. He told me that life in Verdun was depressing because it was so full of widows from the first World War. I frequently saw on the streets crippled World War II veterans riding in wheel chairs which they propelled by winding with their hands a device similar to the pedals of a bicycle. Where there was no sidewalk, they would use the highway, so that motorists had to take care not to hit them. Just about every day I drove between Verdun and Metz, passing the famous Verdun battlefields. I am sorry to say that I never found time for a closer view of the trenches and tunnels where so many lives had been lost in World War I.

The education adviser at Metz was a sophisticated gentleman with a recent Ph.D. who much objected to the shabbiness of his office, which was heated by a sooty old-fashioned stove in the middle of the room. I once visited him on a weekend at the fashionable Paris apartment which he rented from Helena Rubinstein, the cosmetician. At his urging I saw a performance, in Paris in English, of Samuel Beckett's *Waiting for Godot*. Although the play's symbolism did not completely escape me, I found it extremely tedious to watch and would not recommend it to anyone for its value as entertainment. (While writing this memoir, I learned that Beckett had written the original version of the play in French and later translated it into English. It premiered in Paris in January 1953 at the Theatre of Babylon, and I saw it performed in English in Paris only a year later. I am now impressed by the thought that I saw one of the earliest performances of this famous existentialist play, which is regarded as an archetype of the theater of the absurd.)

My assignment in Verdun and Metz ended after only eight weeks, when I was scheduled to teach in London. I wrote my mother, "I had a difficult time saying goodbye at Metz." I had become acquainted with Colette Bir, who was teaching French in the Troop Information and Education Program there. Although she was only 22 years old, she had studied at the Sorbonne and Cambridge University and had mature tastes. When I first knew her we spoke only in French, but later I found that her English was very fluent, although heavily accented. I fully intended to meet her in Paris sometime during my London assignment, and I requested an assignment in western Germany so that I would not be too far from her. While I was teaching in London, she became ill and my intentions to see more of her were never realized.

During my Verdun-Metz assignment I drove to Nuremberg to visit Myra Koehler, who was teaching crafts in the Army Special Services program. Nuremberg was covered with snow when I met Myra, who looked very neat in her blue uniform. I cannot remember what we did in Nuremberg, but my drive back to Metz was marred by a minor auto accident. The road was covered with hardened snow and as I was coming down a hill the car in front of me suddenly turned to the left side of the road. Then the driver made a right turn in front of me. Because of the ice I was unable to evade him and I hit his vehicle. Unwrapped baguettes flew out of his car (he was a baker making deliveries). There ensued correspondence between me and his insurance company, and some minor repairs had to be made on my Hillman.

LONDON

The great attractions of the London assignment were the city itself and the flat that was owned or leased by the University of Maryland. The flat was in the center of the city, near Marble Arch. I drove from Metz to the English channel, where my car was loaded by a crane into the hold of a ship, and then unloaded on the English side of the channel. For the first time in my life, I had to drive on the left side of the road although my English Hillman Minx, built for Americans, had the steering wheel on the left side. It seemed that the entire distance between the channel and London had been urbanized, so the traffic was dense the entire way.

I did not have a map of London, and I constantly had to ask people for directions. People would refer to the "top of the road" where I would have to make a right turn, and I never quite understood what the top of the road was. I must have driven around Trafalgar square a dozen times, thinking that the arrows at street intersections meant that I could not exit the square; actually the arrows were indicating the one-way traffic for the square itself. When I finally found the Maryland flat, I was thankful that I had made it in one piece and was completely exhausted. I parked my car in the street and did not move it for two weeks. I wrote my mother that I had completely lost interest in sight seeing and that I knew scarcely a person in London. For the first time in my life, I prepared my own meals, buying groceries from the American military commissary.

The flat had two bedrooms, and on one week-end one of the bedrooms was occupied by a German girl who worked at the Maryland office in Heidelberg. We became acquainted and made an automobile tour to Salisbury, famous for its cathedral, and the Stonehenge. The London Ballet's stunning performance of *Swan Lake* under the direction of Herbert von Karajan was a highlight of my stay in London. I visited Westminster Abbey, Hampton Court Palace, famous for its maze, and Windsor Castle, where each section of the toilet paper bore the imprint "Property of Her Majesty's Government,"

My class in international relations in London had 45 students, the largest Maryland class in the UK. It was the largest class I ever had in the overseas program.

The Maryland people in London set up a spring ball. I tried to get Colette to come to London for this but she was under observation for appendicitis. (Besides it would have been quite a trip.) While I was discussing matters in the London office, an attractive girl dropped in. It seemed that no one had asked her to the dance and she didn't want to go alone. Her father was a colonel and wouldn't let her go out with enlisted men, and all the officers she knew were married. She was as pretty as could be and I asked her if she would go with me—this being negotiated in public. She said yes and then we introduced ourselves. I met Lannie's father and her step-mother (who was not much older than Lannie), and half-brother, and they were all very nice and we had a lovely time at the dance. She had just finished high school and was attending an art school in London during the day and attending Maryland classes twice a week. Billie Eckstein was at the party and sang for us. After the ball we went to a little party at Bob Daley's place. (Daley was the director of the program for the UK.) I am afraid that I did not get Lannie home until 3:30 and I hoped that her father would not be upset. But my London assignment was over and I had to move to Germany.

THE PALATINATE

I was assigned to teach at the large American Air Force base near Ramstein, a village in West Germany not far from Kaiserslautern. Across the road from the air base was an American Army base which had informally assumed the name of the nearby town of Landstuhl. While assigned to the Ramstein base, I became well acquainted with Ulrich Groenke, a German scholar who taught and helped to administer the Maryland foreign languages program, and Sidney Gelfand, the educational adviser at the base. According to Groenke, this corner of Germany, the Palatinate (Pfalz), which was very hilly and covered with forests, had been economically undeveloped for many years. It had been under foreign military occupation after both of the World Wars, and the military occupations provided employment for the local population. Many of the famous Pennsylvania Dutch, early settlers of William Penn's colony, were Germans from the Palatinate.

ALSACE

In June, 1954, between terms, Myra Koehler and I spent a week touring picturesque villages in Alsace. The famous Michelin guide for the area featured the storks that lived in the area, and indicated the locations of buildings on which storks maintained their nests. It seems that the storks made a point of returning to the same nests year after year. We were pleasantly surprised to find that the storks were indeed established on the specific buildings listed in the guide and Myra took pictures of the nests, sometimes including their inhabitants. The weather was lovely that June, and Myra got excellent photographs of local churches and castles.

ITALY

There were no classes scheduled for August, and I made an automobile trip alone to northern Italy. I was so dazzled by the alpine scenery and the towns I visited that I was unafflicted by loneliness. I stayed overnight at an inn where the bed sheets reeked of a previous guest's perspiration. The television was completely dominated by retrospectives of the life of Alcide de Gasperi, Italy's famous postwar premier who had just died (August 19, 1954). I saw Pisa, Florence, and Venice. My guidebook described the imposing stillness in the cathedral at Venice. Actually, the place was so overrun with noisy sight-seers that I felt as if I were in Grand Central Station in New York. While the famous sights in Italy lived up to their reputations, I found the most charm in Ravenna, whose more modest attractions had been less hyped. There I enjoyed seeing the ancient Romanesque basilica, with its fine mosaics, and the tombs of Dante and of the Roman Empress Galla Placidia. The church in the middle of the town had a tower that leaned badly. The church bell was reputed to have a sad tone, caused by the tears of the bell-maker's daughter, who had been forced to separate from her lover.

DUBROVNIK

Sid Gelfand, the education adviser at Ramstein, had heard that Dubrovnik, in Yugoslavia, was the place to go, and he persuaded me to drive with him to that exotic destination. Our plan was to drive to Dubrovnik, on the Adriatic Sea in the southern part of the country, and after spending several days there, put my car on a ship to the northern part of the country, while we would be passengers on the ship, viewing at our leisure the Adriatic Sea as we sailed northward.

We were determined to cover as much ground as possible on the first day of our journey. We drove all day and all night without stopping through the mountains of southern Germany and Austria and early on the following morning, on a mountain road overlooking Zagreb, Yugoslavia, a tire blew out. Fortunately we were able to find a tire that would fit my car. We stayed overnight at a hotel in Zagreb, and during supper in the dining room I ordered mineral water. The waiter brought a glass, which he held with one thumb on the inside of the glass, and a bottle of water. I poured the water into the glass and saw little black dots floating in it. I asked the waiter what the dots were. He said they were the minerals.

We proceeded to Sarajevo. The stores in Sarajevo were labeled in both Croatian (with Roman letters) and Serbian (with Cyrillic letters). We visited the little museum near the bridge close to the site of the famous assassination of the Archduke Ferdinand, which had provoked the outbreak of the first World War. We also visited the Turkish museum, where we discussed the exhibits with the guide in French, although German seemed to be the lingua franca in Yugoslavia.

The roads in Yugoslavia, and here I am referring to the principal highways, were mountainous and unpaved. Except for a few dilapidated trucks, we saw extremely few automobiles as we drove south from Sarajevo. In one instance, a horse pulling a wagon on a side road started to buck wildly, apparently frightened by my car. Coming around a turn in the highway, we saw a group of girls dressed in what looked like harem costumes. Their task was evidently to level out the gravel that would be displaced as vehicles rounded the turn. When the girls looked up at us they drew their veils over their faces. We encountered several wagon loads of peasants in colorful costumes apparently headed towards a festival. We also saw, from time to time, women in peasant costumes carrying distaffs, from which they were spinning thread as they walked along the road. At the edge of one village, market was being held. The field was covered with horse-drawn wagons loaded with produce. In the centers of villages, would be large piles of watermelons, which evidently were being sold in lieu of soft drinks, which were apparently unknown in this part of the world. Towards the end of our drive, we were struck by the beauty of the city of Mostar, with its mosques and famous Turkish bridge.

Dubrovnik is a walled city on the shore of the Adriatic Sea. At one time known as Ragusa, it had been a major trading rival of Venice. The city walls are white, as are the buildings in the city. Sid and I stayed at a beautiful small hotel on the side of the hill overlooking the city, which extends some distance into the sea. Room and board—the food was excellent—was less than $5.00 a day. Most of the tourists were English, who were in those days permitted to take only a limited amount of money out of England, and Germans. American tourists were not at that time interested in Yugoslavia. Not far from our hotel was a villa owned by Mr. Tito.

The Dubrovnik Summer Festival presented plays in Serbo-Croatian nearly every night by the best actors. We saw a splendid performance of *Midsummer Night's Dream* in Dubrovnik. It was presented in a park among the trees, a slope, and small pool of water. Lights, hidden in bushes or behind trees, provided the lighting. The costumes, acting, music, ballet, and comedy were excellent, and I thoroughly enjoyed the performance without understanding a word of the language. The play must have been pretty much as Shakespeare had imagined it—a night in the forest near Athens.

In my life, I have traveled widely and I can say that Dubrovnik is certainly one of the world's most beautiful cities.

The return trip to Germany proved to be more eventful than we had anticipated. Our original plan had been to load the Hillman and ourselves onto a ship at Dubrovnik and to ride the ship back to Rijeka (Fiume). Thus we could enjoy viewing the Adriatic and avoid the tedium of driving the car. However, there was no room on the ship for automobiles, so we hired a man to drive my Hillman to Rijeka for us while we took the boat. We registered the car and driver with the local police. When the driver saw a stack of empty coke bottles in the back of the car, he asked, "What are those?" The lowly coke bottle, the icon of modern civilization, was unknown in Yugoslavia.

The cruise on the Adriatic along the Dalmatian coast was at first lovely, but later became very tedious as no cabins were available and, since the trip was 24 hours long, we had to sleep on deck chairs. There were not enough chairs for everybody, and if one left his chair even for a moment it would be seized by someone else. A pair of German tourists helped us to reserve our chairs while we used the stinking restroom. From the ship we saw Split and from the harbor at Split, the Emperor Diocletian's summer palace

At Rijeka we received a telegraph from our driver that he had had car trouble, so we went to Opatia, a resort on the Yugoslav Riviera, to wait for him. After two days, which we spent sunbathing and swimming at Opatia, my car and driver finally showed up. However, someone had stolen Sidney's suit and other items from the car.

We resumed our trip home via Trieste. In Italy my car refused to go up a mountain. After more attempts to make the grade and consultations with mechanics, we learned that the compression in the cylinders was inadequate for mountain climbing and that the valves needed grinding. Sidney took the train back to Germany. After I left the car in Udine, Italy, for repairs, I took trains to Heidelberg and was able to report promptly at the fall faculty meeting.

The following day, I got a ride back to Munich with Professor Bouvier, and from there I took the train across Austria to Italy. I then began the drive back to Ramstein.

As I was driving up the Brenner pass on a two-lane highway, the engine in my car stopped running. Fortunately there was no traffic, and I was able to coast the car backwards down the road and into the parking lot of a *Gasthaus*. By now it had become dark, so I rented a room for the night and ate supper in the dining room.

Next to the dining room was a bar, and there the guests were yodeling and making a lot of noise. I thought this was just great; as a tourist, that was exactly what I had been hoping to experience. But my fellow diners, respectable bourgeois that they were, were clearly disgusted with the vulgar proceedings in the next room.

The next day I telephoned a mechanic who arrived on a bicycle, on the handlebars of which was mounted a small gasoline engine. He looked at my car and reported that there was water in the gas lines. Before going to Yugoslavia I had stored several jerry cans full of gasoline in the trunk of the car, together with one jerry can of water. I had completely forgotten about the water and had mistakenly poured it into the gas tank.

The car needed a new tire or so and a new spare wheel, but otherwise ran OK. Thinking back over the Yugoslavia adventure, I was indeed fortunate that my car had not been deserted or stolen in some remote mountains. I resolved that on my next big trip I would take the train.

FRANKFURT

After checking out of Ramstein (September 12, 1954), I moved to Frankfurt, where I would be teaching international relations, Far Eastern politics, and modern European history. Classes were held in the I.G. Farbin Building and Rhine-Main Air Base, near Frankfurt. I was assigned an apartment in Frankfort all to myself. I paid $13.00 rent per month, including gas and electricity, and paid a lady 10 marks a week ($2.50) to spend 10 hours a week washing my dishes and underwear and keeping the place clean. With PX and commissary privileges, I would fix many of my own meals. According to my cleaning lady, Germany's contemporary politicians were less concerned with the well-being of the common people than Hitler had been.

Myra Koehler came up to Frankfurt, and we saw Rossini's *Barber of Seville* performed in German by the Frankfurt opera, which was excellent. I also dated Lee Schadle, whom I had known when living in Wiesbaden, and Evelyn Palmer, an attractive blonde who taught American dependents in Heidelberg and advocated the phonic method for the teaching of reading. During my four terms at Frankfurt. I gave two large parties at my apartment, where I invited American and German friends. At one of the parties, I set up a radio phonograph combination and we danced. The party broke up at 3:30 AM.

One Sunday I drove Miss Willmow, a bright German girl who worked in the office of the education adviser, and Donald Kyte, an economics professor, to Bonn and Cologne. At Bonn we saw some gliders, and Miss Willmow, much to my alarm, chose to ride in one. The glider was towed by a tractor until it rose to about 500 meters, then it would glide down. We saw the parliament building in Bonn and ate at the parliament restaurant, which faces the Rhine River. Of course, since the unification of West Germany (Federal Republic of Germany) with East Germany (German Democratic Republic) in 1990, Bonn is no longer a capital of Germany; Berlin is the capital.

One week-end I drove to Kaiserslautern to visit Ulrich Groenke. I took Miss Willmow along, as she planned to spend the weekend with friends in a village near

Kaiserlautern. The Groenkes and I made a strenuous trip to Luxembourg. To get there we drove through the Saarland, including Saarbrücken, where the industrial cities were dirty and sooty from the heavy industry. The Saarland, whose population was German, was at that time under French economic domination and used French francs. In 1957, the Saar became part of West Germany.

Luxembourg had fine roads and lovely rugged hills and forests, a beautiful place to see. Driving home we came by way of Trier. North of Kaiserslautern we temporarily got lost in the mountains, where the roads were narrow and winding and full of holes. Groenke and I were map buffs, but our maps were not much help. One of Ulrich's hobbies was the collection of Celtic place names, and no matter where we went he seemed able to find a few.

SPAIN AND PORTUGAL

Late in December on a Friday night after meeting my last class in 1954, I drove some 90 miles from Frankfurt to Karlsruhe to meet the tour that would take me to Spain and Portugal. I parked my car in a garage in Karlsruhe. The three busloads of tour participants were mostly women who taught in American dependents schools.

The bus drove all night Friday night. The seats did not recline and it was impossible to sleep in the bus. We had breakfast at a hotel in Dijon and later a good lunch at a dirty restaurant in Lyon. We stayed overnight in a crumby ("first class," they had said) hotel in Montpellier, in the south of France.

We saw the impressive walled city of Carcassonne. It had been the home of the Albigensian heretics, who were the target of a crusade led by Simon de Montfort in 1209. Our guide, a lady with an electric bull horn, described the fighting and the suffering of the people. At a shop in the town I bought a book in French that addressed the question, "Was Simon of Montfort a War Criminal?" One had the impression that there are still some folks in Carcassonne, like American Southerners still agonizing over the War Between the States, who have yet to reconcile themselves to defeat.

It was winter in Spain and just about everything was brown, the fields, the trees, and the villages. For some of our meals in Spain we stopped at government-sponsored cafeterias, not unlike American cafeterias. These places were clean and the food decent. The alternative in some cases would have been to eat in village bars that had dirt floors and looked filthy. There were no restrooms in our bus, and for long stretches there were no forests or trees. (The only trees would be those in olive groves, which provided inadequate cover. So sometimes we had to stop at the village bars, where the facilities were off-putting.)

We were impressed by the elegant buildings and fine parks of Barcelona. As I wrote my mother, "We also saw the Cathedral of the Sacred Family, a monstrous thing under construction. Just the façade is partly finished. At the top of the façade is, among other things, a huge Christmas tree carved from stone—this gives you an idea."

From there we drove to Montserrat, where the mountains were strange and rugged. We saw the monastery near the top of the mountain and the basilica with the Black Virgin, said to have been made by St. Luke and brought to Spain by St. John. It was quite small, black from candle smoke, and covered with jewels, in a glass case and in a niche above the high altar.

We could spend only one day in Madrid. Given the choice of seeing either the famous Prado Museum or the Escorial, I chose the latter. The Escorial, located at some distance from Madrid, was the huge sprawling building from which the ascetic Philip II administered the Spanish empire. Its appearance and function brought to mind the Pentagon. We saw the king's Spartan living quarters. At a nightclub in Madrid we enjoyed superb guitar music and flamenco dancing. The music seemed to still ring in my ears after I returned to Germany, and I half seriously considered taking castanet lessons.

In Granada we stayed at the Alhambra Palace Hotel, very plush, in Moorish architecture. We saw the Alhambra, a beautiful rambling Moorish palace on a bluff overlooking Granada, romantic courts and pools and lovely gardens. We saw where Washington Irving lived while he wrote his book on the Alhambra.

We spent Christmas in Seville, where our hotel, once a Moorish palace, served a tremendous dinner, each place provided with five glasses for various drinks. Our celebration became frenzied and we made a conga line. We saw Columbus's tomb in the cathedral in Seville. The cathedral tower, converted from a minaret, was impressive. Some of the streets in Seville were lined with trees bearing ripe oranges. I asked why the oranges were not being eaten and was told that they were bitter and exported to England for the manufacture of marmalade.

In Portugal, after our tour of Lisbon, we were given the choice between seeing Estoril, the resort on the Atlantic Ocean, or visiting Fatima. I chose the latter. Our bus wound its laborious way up barren mountains. At one point the tour guide suggested that the passengers begin to recite the Stations of the Cross.

In 1917 the Virgin appeared numerous times to three peasant children near Fatima, sometime after Gabriel told them she would appear. We saw the well where Gabriel spoke to the children. The Virgin said everyone should love God and say their rosaries. If they did Russia would be converted. If the people did not say their rosaries Russia would not be converted and there would be wars and countries would be conquered. We also visited the little village nearby and saw, sitting near a miserable peasant house in a wheel chair the mother, very aged, of two of the children who had seen the apparitions. Also we saw the father, who was a jolly little old peasant in black clothes with the long black stocking cap the Portuguese peasants wear. I took pictures of these people.

The guide did not insist on the literal truth of the apparitions at Fatima, but he was a staunch Catholic conservative and monarchist who regarded the apparitions as important ideological barriers to Communism and Free Masonry. In my brief discussions with him I deliberately tried to draw him out on these political issues. He said that the Free Masons, who were political gangsters, were a bigger threat than the Communists. There was no question of where Portugal stood on the Spanish Civil War; 14,000 Portuguese died on Franco's side. Some later joined the Blue Legion (of Franco) to fight the Russians. Portugal was neutral in World War II, because Portugal's tie with Britain was a *defensive* alliance; Britain had declared war on Germany, not Germany on Britain.

On the return trip to Germany, we passed through Biarritz, saw the Bay of Biscay (the Atlantic Ocean), and stopped at Lourdes. The town was junky, full of souvenir shops selling cheap rosaries and bottles to carry home the famous water. Most of the hotels were named after saints. One cheap inn was called "L''Immaculée Conception." The grotto, which was near the river, was a large hole in the side of a stony bluff, black inside from candle smoke. In front of the grotto, chairs were lined up for worshiper. On the left side is a row of faucets where you could turn on the water from the miraculous spring, and visitors could fill up their bottles there. Nearby were some big wooden boxes containing candles of various lengths, some several inches in diameter and about five feet long. At the right just inside the grotto was a life-size statue of the Virgin. Around her head are the words, in French, "I am the Immaculate Conception." People entering the grotto kiss the blackened stone under the statue. Not far from the grotto were public latrines (French, and therefore primitive). I would hesitate to drink the water from the miraculous spring. I bought a pious book of 500 pages by an "eyewitness" of the ecstasies of the Soubirous girl (Saint Bernadette) and I was even less impressed after reading the book.

New Years Day we spent at Avignon, where we visited the palace where the popes had lived in the fourteenth century.

Several of the people in the tour were unable to endure the excessively long periods of riding in the uncomfortable buses, and had to fly home before the end of the tour. I calculated that the round trip journey had covered about 4000 miles, and I suffered from indigestion and a severe cold when I got back to Germany.

SCANDINAVIA

Leonard Lutwack, the College Park professor of English whom I had gotten to know in 1953 in Wiesbaden, won a Fulbright grant to do research in Oslo and he and his wife invited me and Ed Sampson to visit them in Norway. So between terms in the spring of 1955, Ed and I made the trip in my car. While driving through Denmark we stopped to say hello to the parents of one of Ed's former students. Their place was near the German border and as was often the case in that area, the husband and wife were of different nationalities. They served us lunch, beginning by opening little cans of delicious fish. Thinking this fish was the hors d'oeuvre I ate very little of it and repeatedly turned down second helpings. It turned out that the fish were actually the main course, so I was still very hungry after the meal.

At Frederikshaven, near the northern tip of Denmark, we and the Hillman boarded a ferry that took us to Göteborg, Sweden. From there we drove to Oslo. The Lutwacks resided in the same apartment building as Trygvie Lie, the former first secretary-general of the United Nations. At their place we met some Norwegian graduate students, including a couple that included an American Negro. (The term "African-American" was not yet in general use.)

CAMBRIDGE

Each spring it was the custom of the Overseas Program in Europe to hold a graduation ceremony at which the university awarded diplomas to the students who had completed all of the requirements of the bachelors degree. Faculty attendance was mandatary. The ceremony in Heidelberg in 1955 was honored by the presence of the governor of Maryland, Theodore R. McKeldin, the president of the university, Wilson Elkins, and the supreme commander of NATO, General Alfred Gruenther. Visiting VIPs from College Park paid annual visits to Heidelberg and Munich. (Some years later, when I taught at the College Park campus of the university, I had the impression that I had seen the university president more frequently in Europe than I would see him in College Park.)

I would teach the summer term (term 5, June and July, 1955) in England. I would not be living on a military base with BOQ privileges or at the University's London flat but would live on the local economy. My car was loaded on a ship and taken across the English channel. I drove to Cambridge, which seemed like the most logical place to live, given that I would be teaching at bases in Mildenhall and Chicksands.

I briefly stayed at a hotel in Cambridge, where I was initiated to the delight of warmed herring for breakfast (a pleasure which I later in life indulged to the disgust of my wife, who disliked the smell of fish in the kitchen). A lady American school teacher was also in the hotel. Although I did not cultivate her acquaintance, she seemed like a decent enough person. I overheard one of the waiters, however, referring to her as "very common," and wondered what his opinion of me, another American cousin, might have been.

Through a real estate agency, I arranged a two-month rental of a furnished flat at 1 Silver Street, near the center of the city. The first floor of the building was occupied by a tailor shop. I had a view of the Cam River and the Mathematical

Bridge. During the school year, the flat was occupied by a Cambridge professor, whose Irish wife and child would be living in Ireland during the summer while he taught and resided in university quarters. I got to know him personally, and one day he invited me to sit at the "high table" in the college dining hall. One of the professors there described the generous treatment he had received while teaching during the past year at Indiana University.

Moving around constantly, it was not always easy for me to find women that I would like to date. When an assistant director in the London office married, I knew that he had a done a lot of dating, so I asked him if he could give me some names and telephone numbers of his former girl friends. One of these was Ellie (to protect the innocent or the guilty as the case may be, this is not her real name.)

After telephoning Ellie, I drove to her address in London. Her mother said that Ellie was at her own house nearby. I went to Ellie's house. A man answered the door and invited me in. He said that Ellie would shortly be back from an errand and invited me to have a drink. He was very much at home in Ellie's kitchen. When Ellie returned, I was struck by her beautiful pale skin and features. She was Eurasian; her father was Chinese and mother English. Also she spoke with what I thought was an elegant upper class English accent. I was very impressed by her.

I asked Ellie's boyfriend what he did (for a living). He said that he was interested in horse racing, which led me to believe that he did not have a job in the usual sense. Ellie seemed to like parties and introduced me to some of her crowd. One night it was decided that we would go to a famous Mexican restaurant in London. The meal was exotic, including octopus. At the end of the dinner, the waiter brought me the bill and no one else offered to share in the payment. So I paid the bill for the whole crowd. I didn't like this, but in 1954 I was a rich American and the English economy had not yet recovered from the war. I accepted this situation as a way in which we Americans could in a measure compensate the British for the disproportionate burden that they had suffered from the war.

It was then time to drive Ellie back to her house. Once there, she found that we were locked out and that her doggy was barking, wanting to get out. She did not have a key, so she told the lady across the street that her "husband" (actually Ellie's boyfriend) had locked her out. Ellie borrowed a ladder from the neighbor so that she could get into the bathroom window upstairs. We put the step ladder on top of my Hillman Minx. The gap between the upstairs window and the top of the ladder was substantial. I warned Ellie that she could kill herself trying to climb into the window. She said, "It's all right, I used to be in a circus." However she did not try to get into the house. The problem then was where Ellie would sleep that night.

We drove over to the flat of one of her friends. This lady had rented out several rooms in her spacious flat and Ellie slept in one of the rooms, and I slept on the sofa in the living room. Around 2 AM I was awakened by a noisy argument. One of the lady's tenants, an Irishman, had brought in a female acquaintance with whom he planned to share his room. The landlady vehemently objected and the tenant accused her of an insulting attitude towards his friend.

The next morning I drove Ellie back to her house. She and her boyfriend invited me to join them for breakfast. We had a leisurely and copious meal. I noticed that they had tabloid newspapers with headlines about sex scandals. I felt somewhat out of place because I had been out all night with Ellie, but this did not seem to bother her "husband" at all. I asked Ellie if I could visit her the following week. She said no, a man was coming from Scotland to visit her and "he might marry" her.

Ellie's unstructured lifestyle must have turned me off because I almost instantly lost all interest in her.

I became acquainted with Ralph Lombardi, an American formerly connected with the Maryland program, who was a graduate student at Oxford University. He invited me for an overnight at his place, which was a small house he shared with his lovely wife on the embankment of the Thames River. The ocean tide reaches far up the river, and when the tide is out, junk that has been hidden by the high tide becomes exposed. Although the sight was not especially inspiring, the air was pleasant and one was free from the congestion of the city.

Ralph showed me around Oxford University, and I was impressed by the fact that the professors and the students all had to wear gowns. These black but often dusty garments were short, scarcely reaching the knees, loosely thrown over civilian clothes. Ralph was a skillful pianist and was a member of little jazz orchestra that frequently performed for other students. I went to one of their performances where ten or so students listened, tapping there feet to the music. All of the performers were playing from memory, and I saw no evidence of printed music. Ralph seemed completely at ease and relaxed.

I also became acquainted with Hal Orel and his wife. Hal was teaching in the Maryland program and the couple rented quarters in a house occupied by an English student at Cambridge University. Hal said that his landlord said he was delighted to know such nice Americans as Mr. and Mrs. Orel. The Americans at the nearby airbase had given the impression that all Americans were "like that" (referring to the disgusting types at the air base).

I recall seeing at the entrance of an American base several men who were seeking rides to the nearby city (Oxford). They were already drunk. In downtown Oxford, I saw American soldiers talking loudly and picking up prostitutes on the streets. In Germany, I heard of American soldiers robbing and beating up (or murdering) taxi-drivers. I would say that the soldiers taking Maryland courses all seemed to be decent responsible people. The problem is of course complicated by elements in the local population that seek to profit by catering to the worst elements in the bases.

In August 1955 I made a trip to Ilfracombe, Devon, famous for its Atlantic beach, together with two Maryland couples. We took two cars, and I drove one of them. The roads were narrow two-lane affairs the whole long distance. It was not a pleasant drive. I was nostalgic for the German autobahn that made distant travel easy. The beach consisted of gray sand interrupted with huge odd-shaped rocks.

ROME

The International Congress of Historical Sciences was held in Rome in early September, 1955. I wrote to Dr. Mason Daly, Associate Director of the Overseas Program, asking for permission to be absent from the fall faculty meeting in Heidelberg in order to attend the congress as a representative of the University of Maryland. In return for such permission, I would write reports for the Departments of History and of Government and Politics. Daly granted the permission and also provided orders for military air transportation from London to Rome and return. I had never been to Rome before.

When I arrived at the Rhine-Main airport, I found that I could get to Italy quicker by flying that same evening to Naples rather than wait for a flight to Rome. During several free days in Naples, I toured Pompeii and took a bus tour of the Amalfi coast, which was beautiful except for the bus driver's repetitive and unnecessary commentary in three languages. As the Isle of Capri, famous for its Blue Grotto, was temporarily inaccessible because of rough seas, I stayed overnight at an elegant villa overlooking the sea. Bougainvillea in full bloom were everywhere.

I took the train to Rome, where I arrived in time to join an afternoon bus tour of the Castelli Romani (towns around Rome). We stopped at Castel Gandolfo, the pope's summer palace. The pope emerged onto a balcony overlooking the crowd in the courtyard. He addressed the crowd in various languages. The crowd was made up largely of organized bands of pilgrims from various places in the world: each with its distinctive banners and cheers of "Long Live the Pope," "Vive le Pape," "Viva il Papa," etc. As he was being cheered the pope lifted his arms and waved them towards himself, encouraging the cheering. This gesture struck me as egotistical. But it may be that he just enjoyed being the pope. (Pius XII died at Castel Gandolfo in 1958).

In Rome I stayed at a small tourist hotel full of French students close to the Pantheon, and ate most of my dinners, which were drenched in olive oil, on the terrace in front of the hotel. I was on the constant but futile alert for signs advertising pizza.

The meetings of the congress were all held at the Palazzo di Congressi of the Esposizione Universale Roma. The Esposizione was an enormous fairground, the construction of which had been begun by Mussolini for a world's fair that had been called off on account of the war. The buildings were all in classical style, monumental in design and proportions, and built of white marble. Half of them were still incomplete. I was unaware that special busses were carrying the delegates from their hotels in the city to the Esposizione, and every day I took a city bus from my hotel to the Rome railway terminal, where I took the Metropolitana (Mussolini's subway) to the Esposizione. The heat of the city and the full schedule of the Congress discouraged me from sightseeing and photographing in Rome, but constant travel to and fro meant that I glimpsed the most famous sights.

The predominant language at the conference was French. If a paper was presented in a language other than French, somebody would provide a French translation. There were many priests in black robes in attendance and I struck up a conversation in French with one of them, He answered in French with an American accent, and it turned out that he was Canadian.

At the conference, I became acquainted with Fred Harvey Harrington, professor of history at University of Wisconsin. Also in Rome I met Professor Chester Easum, history professor at Wisconsin who was a neighbor of our family on Jefferson Street in Madison and was serving as American cultural attache in Bonn, and Professor Dietrich Gerhard, chairman of the History Department in which I had taught Far Eastern history at Washington University and who was currently serving as director of the America Institute, University of Cologne.

The most interesting aspect of the conference was the Russian participation. At the start of the conference, all the participants were provided with thick booklets containing the papers to be presented. At the last moment it was decided by the Soviet Union that the Soviets would participate, and they brought their papers in multiple copies for distribution. One Russian speaking in English expressed his delight, which I am sure was genuine, with the opportunity to participate in the international meeting. This was the year of the Austrian Peace Treaty and the "Thaw" in the Cold War.

I attended a panel chaired by Arnold J. Toynbee. After papers had been presented a prominent German professor who had been permitted to comment said that he felt that it might be more worthwhile if he yielded his time so that we could hear more of what Joseph Needham might say. (Needham was the famous British authority on the history of science in China.) Toynbee said, "No, no, no. You were granted time and we want to hear what you have to say." Possibly because I myself was not a Needham enthusiast, I have a soft place in my heart for Toynbee because of the way he chaired that meeting.

One evening Pius XII granted an audience to the Congress in the Hall of Benedictions. He was carried seated on a litter the full length of the hall to his throne at the far end. He gave a long address in French, which was difficult to understand because of the poor public address system. He conferred an honor on Oscar Halecki, a Fordham University professor who had written a highly regarded book on the *Borderlands of Western Civilizations: A History of East Central Europe*, presumably Poland, the historian's homeland.

Because of the unavailability of military transportation back to London September 10, I took the BOAC the entire distance from Rome to London at my own expense in order to report promptly for my fall assignment

When I returned to England I sent a report which summarized the proceedings of all of the congress panels that I had attended to the Overseas director's office and to the chairmen of the Departments of History and of Government and Politics in College Park. The large set of printed conference papers I later donated to the University of Maryland library.

In the fall of 1955 I had to move out of 1 Silver Street, because the Cambridge don's family would be returning to occupy it. For a brief spell I lived in a large boarding house, and later rented a rambling house in the country outside of London. It had various electrical circuits stapled to the floor and walls and gas heaters operated by dropping in shillings, and I was afraid, during the winter, that I might set the house on fire. Before taking possession of the place, I had signed a multi-page inventory of the contents of the house (furniture, brooms, dishes, etc.) and when I moved out several months later someone came to check that inventory against what he actually found in the house, and I was charged with damage to a number of items that I could not recall ever using.

SWITZERLAND

In the winter of 1955-1956, I spent the Christmas and New Year holidays with one of my friends' former girlfriends in Switzerland at a ski resort. I took skiing lessons, which ended when I failed to keep up with the rest of my class. The class moved elsewhere while I was trying to negotiate the ski lift. I fell on my face, bent my glasses, and with a bleeding cheek I went back to the hotel alone in a bus. Later two people whom we had met one evening lost their lives on the following day in an avalanche while on an expedition with their skiing instructor.

I and the woman who accompanied me were relatively unacquainted before we went to Switzerland, and it developed that our personalities were not at all compatible. She behaved so capriciously and meanly towards two lovely German couples with whom I had expected we would celebrate that we became isolated from them. Christmas eve was a disaster. I have no memory at all of the return trip to England nor of how my involvement with the lady ended, which is probably just as well.

RUSSIA

In April 2, 1956, I was back at the "Ramstein Campus," teaching Far Eastern history. With the "Thaw" in the Cold War, exemplified by the Austrian Peace Treaty of 1955 and the Soviet participation in the International Congress of

Historical Sciences of the same year, the Soviet Union was opening up to tourism, and I decided to make an auto or rail trip to that country. I visited a Soviet diplomatic office in outskirts of Bonn in order to obtain a visa, but the office was closed. After a futile quest for a visa, I saw an advertisement of a Baltic cruise from Le Havre to Leningrad sponsored by the French Line. The French Line would obtain the necessary visas for its passengers. I signed up for the cruise. I took Russian lessons from Ulrich Groenke, learning the Cyrillic alphabet and how to say a few greetings in Russian.

I looked all over for a guide book to Russia, but the only one seemed to be published in Switzerland by Nagel, *Moscou et Léningrad,* 258 pages long in French and copyrighted in 1956. In late summer 1956, I drove my Ford sedan (I had recently bought a fairly new used Ford and sold my Minx) to Le Havre, where I parked it, and boarded our ship.

The passengers were a mixture of English, French, and Americans. My regular dining partners were a French couple, a French lady from Algeria who was worried about developments there, and myself. Our conversations of course were in French, although I had difficulty in understanding the lady from Algeria. The passage in the Baltic Sea was very rough, windy, and cold. The small swimming pool on the deck was not much used. The ship's five- or six-member orchestra was versatile, playing classical music for dinner and popular music for dancing.

As the ship approached Leningrad, we passed the Soviet naval base at Kronstadt, famous for a naval mutiny during the 1917 revolution. From my porthole I saw several naval vessels at anchor there, and took a picture of them. We took a bus tour of Leningrad, and whenever we stopped, Russians crowded around taking a friendly interest in us; for many of them we were the only foreigners from the Free World that they had ever seen. On the streets, we noted a number of drunkards wandering around.

We saw the famous palace grounds outside of Leningrad. I saw one or two ice-cream peddlers with their little carts. Because under pure communism, everyone would presumably be paid equally, I wondered what would impel a peddler to aggressively sell his wares rather than push his cart under a tree and nap. I asked the guide if the peddlers were compensated on the basis of how much ice cream they sold. The guide looked at me as if I were stupid and said of course. Then I recalled reading that this system was known as "socialist incentive" in the Soviet Union.

While in Leningrad, we resided on the ship, to which we returned every evening. We took an overnight train with bunks for sleeping to and from Moscow, where we spent two nights. I was assigned to the Peking Hotel, where the dining room was under reconstruction, so that I had to take a bus to a nearby hotel for meals, including breakfast. At Red Square, we were permitted to enter the famous tomb of Lenin and Stalin, whose very natural-looking bodies were on display in glass caskets. (We foreign tourists did not have to wait in the long line with the Russians who had come to see this attraction). Inside the Kremlin walls, the onion domes and spires of churches had been very recently gilded and the interiors restored. The Soviets were evidently gearing up for tourism. We visited the famous Gum (Goom) Department Store on Red Square, but were unimpressed by the merchandise.

In Leningrad, we visited the famous Winter Palace, which had been converted into one of the world's greatest art museums, the Hermitage. Everything was neat and clean and very impressive. The only shortcoming was the poor quality of the postcards and booklets for sale at the museum shop.

While in Leningrad, the passengers were divided into groups, each of which would visit a particular attraction. I chose to see a steel rolling mill. I have no expertise in manufacturing methods, but it seemed to me that the workers were very lackadaisical, and the assembly line was not operating efficiently, with work piling up here and there. After our tour the manager of the facility talked with us. I was impressed by the fact that rather than praise his factory, he was very modest about it and asked us for our views as to how its operation could be improved. During our return voyage, the passengers met together, and each of the groups reported on what it had found. One group had seen an area near Leningrad where farmers were permitted to build houses that they would own and cultivate the land on the family basis rather than collectively. Officials had explained that the soil in that area had been unsuitable for collective farms.

We had some free time in Leningrad. I became acquainted with a Swiss lady on our tour who had done a better job of learning Russian than I. She would occasionally stop to talk with Russians in the street. At a restaurant we bought coffee, which was self serve from a large tank. The coffee already had sugar and milk in it; that was the only way coffee was served there. We talked with a woman who was vacationing in Leningrad; she was an employee of a factory in a distant city in Siberia.

I had heard that there was a museum of religion and atheism in Leningrad. I took a taxi to the address of the museum, but after I got out of the cab and wandered about I saw no evidence of the place, there were just shabby shops of one sort or another there. Discouraged, I decided to visit the large domed cathedral in classical architecture across the street. The interior of the imposing church had been converted into the museum of religion and atheism. The exhibits of pious frauds included religious icons that had been rigged by the priests to weep. A large photograph depicted the 1905 Bloody Sunday demonstration led by Father Gapon, during which Tsarist troops fired on the workers, killing 70 people and wounding many others.

As we tourists were boarding the ship upon leaving Leningrad, the orchestra was on the deck playing "Arrivederci Roma."

Several weeks after our return to Le Havre, the middle-aged French couple with whom I had been dining invited me to their apartment in a fashionable ward of Paris for dinner, and following the dinner we drove in my Ford to Versailles, where we saw a splendid sound and light show. Also, I dated once or twice a pretty American office girl whom I got to know during the Russia trip.

I described my Russia trip to one of my classes in Germany and later got a phone call from some U.S. Army intelligence people. It seems they had heard about my photos of the Kronstadt naval base and wanted to see them.

Professor McNelly, lecturing to his class in Germany, indicates the route he had recently taken to reach Leningrad.

MUNICH

At the fall faculty meeting in Heidelberg in 1956, I was introduced to a Colonel Lewis Perry, Ph.D., an educator who was taking charge of the Munich Branch of the University. This was a two-year college for children of American military people, located in McGraw Kaserne in Munich. The young people were lodged on the base, and classes were held in that same compound. Classes ran daytime on the semester system, with 16-week rather than 8-week terms. This set-up would involve less travel for me and I would be able to enjoy the cultural advantages of an attractive European city. I was delighted to accept Colonel Perry's invitation to join him in Munich.

The next day I learned that the University of Maryland had taken over the University of California's Far East Program, headquartered in Tokyo. In view of my professional interest in Japan, I would have much preferred going to Tokyo over Munich. Having committed myself to Colonel Perry, I was reluctant to ask for a transfer to the Far East Program. Two years later, however, I did transfer to the Far East, where I served for two years in Japan, Korea, and Okinawa.

The Munich Branch faculty members were assigned a large room as their office, an arrangement that facilitated the kind of collegial interchange among faculty that had been impossible when, as was often the case, I was the sole professor on a military base. I found my coworkers to be both highly intelligent and congenial. At the same time, I found the students, all of them "army brats," respectful and well motivated, and usually above average in intelligence for their age. The school was relatively small, with only about 200 students. The boys and girls were assigned to separate dormitories under adult supervision. Just about everyone knew everybody else. In 1957 and 1958, the Munich Branch students published yearbooks that contained pictures of students and faculty and student organizations. The close-knit faculty was conscious of the academic and personal problems of the students and could cooperate to be of help. We would sometimes celebrate Fasching (Bavarian Mardi Gras events) and Oktoberfest together.

I went to concerts downtown, including performances by Andrés Segovia and Dame Myra Hess. I got to know Russell Crosby, the Munich Branch chorus director, and his wife. Having heard, while a student at the University of Wisconsin, a splendid harpsichord performance by Ralph Kirkpatrick, I had become interested in that instrument. With the Crosbys, I visited two harpsichord factories in Bavaria. I had a harpsichord made to order by Wittmeyer, whose small factory was near Garmisch. The instrument is seven feet long, has a single keyboard with black naturals and white sharps, can play octave stops, and has a lute stop. My teacher was very strict about rhythm, and frequently criticized my *rubato*. When I struck a wrong key she would rap me sharply on my knuckles with a pencil. I learned to play some simple pieces by Scarlatti and Bach. A principal disadvantage of the instrument is that it requires retuning almost every time one plays it.

I sang with the college chorus when they presented a rousing performance of the Handel's *Messiah*, accompanied by a local youth orchestra. Betty Jackson, an attractive lady whom I had once seen in a play sponsored by the Special Services and was involved with the supervision of the girl's dormitory, was a versatile musician with whom I shared interests, and we frequently socialized with the Crosbys. James Lester, who taught psychology, was a jazz pianist, popular with the students, with whom he sometimes fraternized at a nearby bar. He once played popular music on my harpsichord.

Ann Demaitre was a lovely lady who taught French, and some years later, Myra and I visited her in Washington. Her daughter was in the Munich Branch women's football team and seems not to have been adequately trained to cushion the violence. I saw the game where she was knocked unconscious and I feared that she might be killed. Ann's husband was a Hungarian employed by the Voice of America in Munich.

In 1956, at the time of the Hungarian uprising, while sitting in the faculty office with her colleagues, Ann received a telephone call from her father in Hungary whom she had not seen for years. The subsequent treacherous suppression of the freedom movement in Hungary was a great shock to everyone.

Marion Waggoner, who taught sociology, had previously been a congressman. Others on the faculty were equally interesting. Dick Srb, with whom I shared an apartment, was the coach. He had been a Rhodes scholar, and was a brilliant basketball player. He played with the Munich Branch team, which competed with U.S. Army teams.

An English professor in the Munich Branch told me the story of how, while teaching in College Park, he had obtained his promotion to assistant professor. Dr. Harry Clifton "Curley" Byrd, at that time the gallant president of the University of Maryland, asked the chairman of the English Department to promote an instructress who was particular friend of Dr. Byrd. The chairman said that if he promoted this lady, out of fairness to two male professors who were equally qualified, it would be necessary to promote them as well. All three instructors were then promoted.

The December 1956 issue of the *American Political Science Review* contained an article by Professor Robert E. Ward of the University of Michigan on "The Origins of the Japanese Constitution." I noted the frequent footnote references in the article to my doctoral dissertation. I began an effort to update and revise the text of the dissertation so that I might propose it to a publisher as a book.

The Munich Branch did not operate in the summer. During June and July 1957, I resided in Frankfurt to teach at Frankfurt and the nearby Rhine-Main air base. For my advanced course in comparative politics at Frankfurt, I arranged an elaborate field trip in cooperation with U.S. embassy officers in Bonn. At 6:30 AM on a beautiful June day my class and I boarded a bus, and between 10:30 and 12:00 in Bonn we witnessed the Bundestag (the lower house of the West German parliament) in session. Chancellor Konrad Adenauer and his cabinet were seated as a group in the Bundestag during the session. After lunch in the U.S. embassy, embassy officials briefed us in detail on German politics and American diplomacy.

At a concert in Munich I became acquainted with Peter H. Lee, a brilliant Korean student of comparative literature. (He later became a professor at the University of Hawaii and published numerous books.) When the International Congress of Orientalists met in Munich in August 1957, Peter and I took Professor and Mrs. Leland Goodrich of Columbia to an Indian restaurant overlooking the Isar River and later to my apartment to see the slides of my Russian trip. Professor Goodrich seemed unhappy with my professional situation. (He was a historian of China and had served on my Ph.D. comprehensive examination.)

Colonel Perry left the Munich Branch in the spring of 1957 and was replaced by Colonel Paul Dickson, Ph.D. Dickson did not enjoy the same high regard in which the faculty had held Colonel Perry. As a gesture at the Christmas Party hosted by Dickson, the faculty, I blush to say, deliberately drank all of his wine, including wine in storage not intended for the party. I forbear burdening the reader with the details of the controversial Dickson regime.

Betty Jackson and several of the students served as actors in the making a German motion picture. The producer appealed for contributions of American cereal boxes and canned goods as props in a store scene. In 1959 in Japan I saw the picture, *The Trapp Family Singers in America*. The sound track was in German; there were subtitles in Japanese. This cinematic effort anteceded by about seven years the *Sound of Music* (1965).

(In 1960, Jeff Poland, a professor specializing on German history and very well liked by everyone when I had taught at Munich Branch, was killed in a senseless automobile accident. The residential campus, which had been located in Munich since 1951, was moved to Augsburg in 1992 and then to Mannheim in 1994.)

CZECHOSLOVAKIA

For the Thanksgiving Day week-end of 1956, I joined a bus tour to Prague, which was then behind the Iron Curtain (i.e., in the Soviet sphere of influence). Our tour group consisted almost entirely of two busloads of Americans who taught in U.S. dependent schools. Before the tour we had to submit our passports to the Munich tour company which forwarded them to Czech officials for visas. We had to leave Munich without our passports, which would be picked up when our bus crossed into Czechoslovakia. At night, as we neared the border, the bus ran low on fuel, and drove around a bit in search of a filling station. This was during the Suez War crisis, when there was an international shortage of oil.

At the Czech border, guards examined our reading materials (mostly magazines) for subversive material, and let us by. We did not stay overnight at Prague, as had originally been planned, but were quartered in a hotel in Karlsbad (or Karlovy Vary), a famous international spa. The Czechs justified the change in plan on the ground that facilities in Prague had been taken over for some kind of conference. We suspected that the uprising in neighboring Hungary the month before had made the Czech officials nervous about the presence of American tourists in the Czech capital. After an overnight in Karlsbad, we were taken to Prague for a tour of that interesting city, and were then returned to Karlsbad. Most of our group remained in Karlsbad that evening, but some of us wanted to see more of Prague, so I and one of the girls who spoke German better than I hired a taxi to go to Prague.

I engaged the taxi driver in a conversation in bad German and was surprised by his frank comments. I asked why it was that he was driving such an old vehicle when Czechoslovakia was exporting attractive automobiles, Skodas, to Germany. (One of our Munich faculty had one of these Czech-built cars.) The taxi driver said that only government officials could buy Skodas in Czechoslovakia. For some reason the matter of uranium came up, and the taxi driver said that the Russians were exploiting Czech deposits, paying less than the prevailing global price for the ore. I was a complete stranger to the taxi driver, and if I had been a Communist spy, I suppose I could have reported him to authorities who might not be gentle with him.

It was night and there were almost no streetlights Prague. However, we found a lively nightclub and became acquainted with a very sociable Czech couple who wanted to show us their home, which seemed impractical that night. The couple was very outspoken against the Communist regime so I pointed to a guard standing at the door and asked if it was not dangerous to say such things. Their answer was that just about everybody felt the way they did, and no danger was involved. (Our conversation in German was rather loud because my German was terrible and I had the notion that by yelling I could make myself better understood.) It was the consensus in those days that although the Czechs did not like the Communist regime any more than the Hungarians did, the Czechs, being less emotional, would not rashly challenge their communist dictators the way the Hungarians had recently done.

Back at the hotel, a Hungarian band had been performing for our group, and we learned that the band members had been in tears when they described how the Russian troops had treacherously reimposed Soviet control of their country. (In 1968 the Czechs sought to end Soviet domination, but the liberalization movement was suppressed by an invasion by Warsaw Pact forces.)

We later learned that our tour group had spent vastly more money in Czechoslovakia than had any of the tour groups from the Soviet bloc.

As our bus drove back into Germany I was impressed by how brightly Munich was lit up as compared with the nocturnal gloom of Prague. About a week later someone from the German tour company called up and asked if I was missing a camera. I said no, but he described the camera involved, and it was indeed mine; I had left it in the bus or the hotel and forgotten all about it. Then the tour operator told me that at the hotel in Karlsbad one of the workers had accused another one of asking a member of our tour group for a cigarette. The accused worker, in danger of losing his job, was asking if someone could certify that he had not been cadging cigarettes from the Americans. Evidently it was not uncommon for some Czechs to inform on others in order to get jobs for themselves.

THE ORIENT EXPRESS

During the Christmas break in 1957-1958, I made a rail trip to Greece. I would take the Orient Express, which had long since lost its prewar reputation of elegance. To an employee of the travel agency in Munich, I pointed to a blank area in the time table, which failed to show any stops for a twenty-four hour period, and insisted that this involved overnight travel and that the total travel time would amount to 40 or 50 hours. She challenged my reading of the table and we appealed to her supervisor, who confirmed my view. There was nothing said about a sleeper on the train. It would be a long trip. I loaded my baggage with small cans of fruit juice and took a train from Munich to Vienna, where I checked into a hotel and boarded the Orient Express the next day.

The venerable Orient Express had been rendered obsolete by air travel. When I boarded it in the 1950s, physically it consisted only of several old dingy coaches, on the sides of which was the intriguing label: "London-Paris-Constantinople." (Before World War II, ferries had taken trains across the English channel.) Every time we crossed an international border, the Orient Express cars were pushed onto a siding, and we were joined by a different steam locomotive accompanied by coaches with local destinations. The international traveler had to make sure that he was in the right coach when the train left the station, or he would be left behind. At one point a sleeping car, for which I did not have a ticket, was attached to the train. (History records that when the original Orient-Express made its final run in May 1977, it consisted of just one shabby sleeping compartment and three day cars.)

On the train I became acquainted with two Greek college boys, brothers who had been attending university in Paris. One spoke English, the other spoke French. I remarked about the mosques we saw as we were passing through Yugoslavia. The Greeks boys were proud of the fact that the Greeks had remained loyal to Christianity, unlike other nationalities that had also fallen under Turkish rule. At Thessaloniki (Salonika), we left the Orient Express and boarded a modern train that whisked us to Athens. After I had arrived in Athens, the boys took me sight-seeing. When they spoke of going back to Paris, they would refer to that as going to Europe; apparently they did not regard Greece as part of Europe.

I checked into a respectable hotel in downtown Athens and signed up for several archeological tours. The tours were led by a not unattractive Greek lady in her mid-thirties who spoke English, French, and German fluently. She had studied archeology at university and was very knowledgeable. I went on several of the tours that she conducted. The most notable was an overnight excursion to Delphi, famous for its ancient oracles, very high in the mountains. In the evening we went to a taverna, where the tourists mixed with the locals, singing and dancing together. My roommate in the inn where we lodged was a good-looking American travel agent enjoying a complementary tour. He asked me to sleep in a different room because of an understanding that he had with one of the American girls in our group. I respectfully declined because I had paid for my accommodation and did not appreciate having to move just to please him. He left our room and I did not see him until the next day.

When our group picture was being taken in front of the Parthenon, I felt very much like an aging, lonely bachelor, as I was nearly thirty-eight years old and was traveling alone. I was quite surprised one night when the guide paid me an unannounced visit at my hotel. We went to a coffee shop where she told me that her mother had died only one or two days previously. Communists had killed her husband several years before. She seemed bereft. She told me the number of the local bus to take and I visited her at her house in the country one evening. My original plan had been to continue my journey to Istanbul, but my extended archeological interests in Athens made that impossible. My Kodacolor slides of the Acropolis depict the Parthenon bathed in the gold of the setting sun.

THE FIFTH REPUBLIC

Late in January 1958, I was transferred from Munich Branch to the American base at Chaumont, France. It was not practical to move my harpsichord with me to France, so it was stored in the Munich Branch until it could later be shipped to the United States. In Chaumont I hired the education adviser's secretary as a part-time typist to help with the revision of my dissertation. Chaumont was near the German border, and I spent some of my week-ends in Germany. While in Germany, my practice was to buy French francs at a much lower price in dollars than was possible in France. The profit from the exchange transaction paid for my German week-ends.

The fighting and negotiations in Algeria had thoroughly disrupted French politics by the spring of 1958. Rebellious elements had already seized power in Corsica. There were demonstrations in Paris. Chaumont is not far from the beautiful city of Nancy. On one warm February Sunday, I sat in front of a hotel in Nancy, basking in the sun, sipping a drink and admiring the baroque elegance of the edifices surrounding Place Stanislas. On a wall of the hotel a sign had been pasted warning the population that there was a national emergency. But the square was virtually devoid of people, everything was silent, and nothing seemed to be in motion. My strong impression was that the political excitement in France was mostly concentrated in Paris and Algeria, and that much of the rest of the population was politically indifferent to the fate of the Fourth Republic.

There were reports that the French air force supported a take-over by General deGaulle. One day, I picked up a young French airman who was hitch-hiking and I tried unsuccessfully to extract his opinions. (DeGaulle was named premier on May 31, 1958, and the Fifth Republic came into existence the following October.)

NEW YORK

I was invited by the program committee of the Association for Asian Studies to present a paper on my research on the Japanese Constitution at its convention in New York in March 1958. This represented a splendid opportunity to reintroduce myself to the academic community in the United States and could conceivably lead to a state-side position at an American university. The European program did not obtain military orders for me to fly to New York (as it had done in the case of the historical conference in Rome), so I paid for a round trip air ticket from Paris to New York, with a side trips to Madison, Wisconsin, and Washington, D.C. Before the AAS meeting, in Madison I saw my mother and family for the first time in nearly five years. In College Park, Maryland (a suburb of the District of Columbia), I had lunch with Professor Elmer Plischke, then head of the University of Maryland department of government and politics, and several other members of the College Park faculty. (I had met Plischke previously in Germany when he had made an inspection tour of the European program.)

I presented my paper to a small audience at the convention. I felt gratified that the AAS had formally recognized my existence as a research scholar. After a frantic week in the United States I flew back to Europe. I spent part of the summer in Munich, and attended a performance of *Madame Butterfly*, with the Crosbys.

During my five years in Europe, I made a number of trips in addition to those chronicled above. One winter, an economics professor who was a friend of Dudley Dillard (chairman of the economics department at College Park) and I spent a week visiting the famous chateaux along the Loire River. Once the two of us took an overnight ferry to Corsica to visit Napoleon's birthplace. At a popular bar we met an English teacher who regaled us with tales of the feuds for which the island is famous. Only a month before in that very bar one patron shot another dead in the presence of dozens of witnesses but no one was arrested.

George Callcott, a College Park history professor, and I drove to Vienna, where for a week each of us pursued his particular interests. (I saw museums.) We heard a performance by a girls' chorus from Czechoslovakia, and after the concert we entertained a couple of them at a cabaret.

One spring break, I toured Vienna and northern Italy with a German friend.

Ulrich Groenke and I drove to Paris for a week-end. During a trip to Strasbourg, devout pedants that we were, we stopped in Lunéville and watched a historical sound and light show in a driving rainstorm.

Although the German autobahn greatly facilitated my frequent travels in Germany, sometimes I used them in bad weather when the road was dangerous. One rainy windy night I was driving alone on the autobahn, which was very slippery. The road was on the side of a steep hill. On the right side of the road a cliff arose; on the left side I could see nothing but a black void. In front of me was a trailer truck. The rear of the huge trailer was swinging back and forth between the right and the left sides of the slippery road. If a car was on the left side of the road at the wrong time it would have been struck by the swinging trailer, pushed off the road, and possibly rolled down the hill.

I was tired at that time and eager to get home as soon as possible. Only half thinking, I took a terrible risk. Just as the trailer had swung back to the right side of the road, I sped past the trailer truck. I had barely gotten in front of the truck when the trailer swung back to the left side of the road, Fortunately my maneuver was successful, but I was so shocked at the risk I had taken that I felt that I could go no farther that night.

I could think of nowhere to stop except at the house of my dear friends the Groenkes in nearby Kaiserslautern. So I invited myself to show up at their place in the middle of the night and they kindly gave me a place to sleep. The next day, the storm had let up, and I drove safely home.

I saw several plays at Stratford-on-Avon, including *Othello*, in which the tragic hero spoke with the authentic accent of an African-American. I saw Sir Laurence Olivier brilliantly perform the title role in *Titus Andronicus,* the bloodiest of Shakespeare's tragedies. (There are doubts that Shakespeare was actually the author of this gruesome melodrama.)

By 1956 I had worn out my Hillman Minx, which I persuaded an unsuspecting enlisted man to buy, and I bought a fairly new Ford sedan that could negotiate the Bavarian Alps without constantly downshifting. (Just before I left Europe, because of time restraints and confusion about the car's registration, I had to sell the Ford at a much lower price than it was probably worth.)

During my five years in Europe, I had spent cumulatively three years in West Germany (mostly in Munich and Frankfurt), one year in England, and one year in France.

The following two academic years (1958-1960) would be spent in the Maryland Far East Program, which accorded with my professional commitment to Asian Studies and the Japanese language.

CHAPTER 12

ASIA

As previously mentioned, the University of Maryland took over the Far East Program from the University of California in 1956. At that time, I had already committed myself to teach in the Munich Branch and did not pursue the possibility of teaching in the Far East. In 1958 I was delighted at the prospect of returning to Japan again after an absence of ten years, when I had left the country as an invalid. I had been instructed when I left the state sanitarium in 1949 that I should never go back to Japan again, but in 1958, committed to Asian studies, feeling in perfect health, and believing the situation in Japan had improved, I made the return journey.

On my way from Europe to Japan I was able to spend almost all of July at home in Madison. I did not have many friends around but I did see Charles Crosby and had lunch with Carl Schuler, whom I had known at West High, and was now a professor of history. I needed a cholera shot before going to Japan and went to the nearest neighborhood physician, who turned out to be a fellow West High alumnus, Arvin Weinstein, M.D. I went canoeing with Myra Koehler, who was home in Madison for the summer. Although I was happy to see Madison and my family again and to be going to the Far East, I was depressed by the separation from some of my friends in Europe.

The flight from Madison to Tokyo was not easy. Leaving Madison at 7:25 AM on July 31, I changed planes in Chicago and arrived in San Francisco at 3:30 PM, where I checked in at a hotel. The following day I took a Greyhound Bus to the Travis Air Force Base, near San Francisco. We left Travis at 6:00 PM. At 3:00 AM our plane left Hawaii. We crossed the international date line and arrived at Wake Island at 10:00 AM on August 3, and arrived in Tokyo at 4:30 PM. It had taken half a week to fly from Madison to Tokyo.

August was spent on faculty meetings and orientation in Tokyo. I was one of about a fifteen full-time faculty members in the Far East Program, including several individuals who had been connected with the former University of California Far East program. I took a taxi-full of fellow faculty members new to Japan to a *soba* (buckwheat noodles) shop and to a concert of popular American music played at the bandstand in Hibiya Park. I got acquainted with Professor James Dee and his German bride (a lady he had met in Korea). I was happy to meet David Earl, now a Maryland professor, who had received his Ph.D. in Japanese history at Columbia and who had a talented wife. Harold J. ("Hal") Vetter was a psychology professor who had an amazing knowledge of American military aircraft and the lyrics of popular songs. Tim Hallinan was an American with an Oxford doctorate and strong British accent. He was accompanied by his attractive wife, who taught piano. David Lewis was a Ph.D. candidate accompanied by his wife Helenan. Bob Daly, formerly in charge of the London headquarters, was now in Tokyo as the director of the Far East Program.

One of the assistant directors, Janus Poppe, was a former Dutch naval officer who had just arrived in Japan with his Canadian wife, who had a German background. He had recently joined the Maryland program with the expectation of being assigned to Europe, and was very disappointed to be sent to Japan rather than to Europe, as he had expected. I tried my best to arouse his interest in Japanese things. He and his wife were popular among the faculty, and we had good times together. Some of the faculty were hold-overs from the University of California program and knew where the best Chinese restaurants were and also where to pick up girls.

The International House of Japan had only recently been built and I chose to live there briefly rather than in the billet that I had been assigned.

I had barely been in Tokyo for a day or two when I was contacted by the staff of the Commission on the Constitution, which was a Japanese government agency investigating the origins and possible revision of the democratic constitution which had come into effect in 1947.

KOREA

After a month in Tokyo I was required to report to my first teaching post: the headquarters of the First Cavalry Division in Korea. I and one other Maryland professor were the only passengers aboard an Air Force plane carrying mail to Korea. By the time we were over the Japan Sea, night had come and a terrible wind storm raged. When we arrived at the air base in Korea, we went to the officer's club where we met the people who had set up a welcoming dinner for us. However, because of the storm, we had not arrived on time, and folks assumed that our flight had been canceled and had eaten the dinner without us. It occurred to us that if we had been downed over the Japan Sea, perhaps no one would have tried to rescue us, thinking that our flight had been canceled. Later in my lectures I would cite this incident to illustrate the contrast between the English Channel, which barely separated England from the rest of Europe, and the much wider

Korea Strait, which separated Japan from the rest of Asia. Travel between Japan and the continent has always been difficult because of the distance and the severe weather.

My first post was the headquarters of the First Cavalry Division. Although classes would be held in a wooden building, I would reside in a tent. The Korean War had ended in a military truce only five years previously, and there had been no peace treaty. I was disturbed by the thought that fighting might break out again at any time and that, if captured, I might have difficulty explaining my status as a civilian to the enemy. One of my classes was held at the base hosting the Eighth Cavalry, to which I was taken in a jeep. Once the driver got lost, and we unknowingly entered the demilitarized zone (DMZ) between the UN forces (predominantly American) and the Communist forces (North Korean and Chinese). We could have been fired at by one side or the other. There was a bridge known as the "bridge of no return." It was understood that if hostilities broke out this bridge would be destroyed and it would be impossible to return to a friendly base. I was so physically shaken up by one of my jeep trips that I could scarcely gather my wits together well enough to begin my lecture.

I was told that there were Korean "slicky boys," lurking around our camp, trying to steal things. They would slit open the side of a tent to get their loot, such as portable radios. The Turkish troops among the United Nations contingents were reportedly unforgiving to the slicky boys they apprehended. It was said that severed heads mounted on posts at Turkish camps served as cautionary reminders to would-be thieves.

Occasionally while residing at First Cavalry, by hitching jeep rides with the education adviser, I was able to spend week-ends in Seoul. The aging Japanese-built Chosen Hotel, a baroque edifice managed by the American military, made it possible to take a tub bath and sleep in clean sheets. The dining room was a genteel place to dine. In the ballroom a large band played popular music for dancing. Korean women would gather around the entrance to the hotel grounds and manage to walk into the building alongside the American patrons. These ladies became dancing partners and/or mistresses for the Americans. (I knew two education advisers who had Korean girlfriends.) It was said that the South Korean government was tolerant of this kind of activity as it brought in much needed foreign exchange.

It was cheaper to buy one's Korean won (money) from one of the old Korean ladies stationed on a back street near the Bank of Korea in Seoul than from a bank. These women must have been under the protection of sympathetic police, or possibly gangsters. I was told to get won from an American working in army headquarters, whose Korean wife resold PX merchandise for Korean money. I simply called him up at his office on the telephone indicating how many won I needed and later visited his office to pick up the money. I assumed that his operation was illegal but that everybody knew about it and nobody cared.

In November I was assigned to teach modern Far Eastern politics at the Seoul Education Center and American history at ASCOM City, an American base near Seoul. I was delighted to move from a tent near the demilitarized zone to the Chosen Hotel.

In the 1950s the venerable hotel ("the frozen Chosen") already showed its advanced age, and it has long since been replaced by a large thoroughly modern edifice, but the old name Chosen Hotel has been preserved. The pretty tile-roofed Buddhist temple that stood behind the old hotel is said to be still there.

The high points of my Korean residence were two tours sponsored by the Royal Asiatic Society, Korea Branch, in cooperation with the Korean government. It was said that the purpose of these events was to revitalize the tourist industry in Korea, which is blessed with beautiful scenery and impressive monuments. In early October I was among the 75 people who left Seoul at midnight in Pullman cars on a special train. We spent a day and night at Hae-insa Monastery, near Taegu. There, stored on the shelves of a rambling library, are over 80,000 wooden blocks (carved on both sides) used for printing the pages of the *Tripitaka* (the "Three Baskets" of Buddhist scripture). When the Mongols occupied Korea in the fourteenth century, the Korean court was in exile on Kangwha Island, at the mouth of the Han River. The king ordered the publication of the *Tripitaka* as a pious act to get the help of the Buddha in the expulsion of the Mongols. It took 16 years to do the editing, the cutting of the blocks, and the printing. The result was one of the best Chinese editions of the *Tripitaka* in existence. This happened over a century before Gutenberg printed the Bible in Germany. (Koreans also invented moveable type before such type was used in Europe.)

In primitive boats we visited a scenic stretch of the upper Han River. It was similar to the Lorelei of the Rhine River, but more formidable. As our boats constantly required bailing out, we decided that it would be better to walk back. Many of us had difficulty climbing over boulders and had to be ferried once or twice where the vertical rock cliffs came to the water's edge. At villages that our bus drove through people gathered to wave at us (I think many of them had never seen Occidentals) and misspelled signs greeting the Royal Asiatic Society were hung over the roads.

Many Korean farmers allowed their pigs to eat human waste, and we sometimes would sight a toilet located directly over a corner of a pig pen. At one inn, while seated in the primitive sanitary facility, I heard the snorting of a porker directly under me and was afraid of being bitten where I was most vulnerable.

In November, as a participant in another Asiatic Society tour, I boarded a Korean naval vessel, which took us to Cheju Island, in the East China Sea. Cheju Island constitutes the South Korean province of Chejudo and is famous for its women pearl divers. The leader of our group was the American cultural attaché, Gregory Henderson, who spoke Korean fluently. The people on the island, especially because of the shape of their eyes, seemed to be of a race separate from either Koreans or Japanese. People had put large rocks on the tops of their houses to prevent the roofs from being blown off by winds from the ocean. At various towns we would be greeted by local officials, and sometimes pretty little girls would present flowers to our leader.

On our tours, we were fed gourmet meals by a kitchen staff working under Spartan conditions. One difficulty encountered in several places was inadequate toilet facilities. Our large group, which traveled in trains and busses, occasionally overwhelmed the primitive sanitary facilities that we encountered.

In December 1958 I joined a contingent of journalists who took buses to Panmunjom to witness the truce talks there. At this international city, the North Korean and Chinese officers were in more or less continuous discussions with the United Nations officers to settle day-to-day problems involved in the enforcement of the truce terms. (The fighting of the Korean War had ended with an armistice in 1953. The South Korean government abstained from the negotiations, which were carried out by the North Korean and Chinese officers on one side and United Nations officers on the other.) With the journalists I was able to view the proceedings through one of the small windows of the building where the talks were being held. The terminology of the negotiators on both sides made eminently clear the irreconcilable ideological division between them, and there seemed to be very little prospect for a definitive peace settlement.

I wrote my mother that the North Korean guards were the saddest looking lot I ever saw. They wore ill-fitting, tattered uniforms. "They are always in pairs, *guarding each other*. Some of them are political officers but are in privates' uniforms. They have no recreation at all. A month ago one pair decided to escape South. At the last minute the political officer reneged, and his partner shot him and requested asylum at the nearest UN post. (He was given asylum and told all about his fellow guards—there are only 30 guards on each side at Panmunjom.)"

A Major Gibbens, who headed the small UN guard unit at Panmunjom, was a former student of my course in Far Eastern politics that I had conducted in Europe.

In Korea I became acquainted with William Henthorn, a young American scholar connected with the Asia Foundation, and with whom I shared academic interests. (In 1972 the Free Press published his *History of Korea*.) I also got to know the congenial Melvin McGovern, an education officer and old Japan hand who collected antiques. He had become interested in pre-Gutenberg printing. Through him I became acquainted with Korean dealers and I purchased a few items. Shortly before I moved from Korea to Japan, one of the Korean dealers told me that Japanese dealers were more honest than Korean dealers.

In a letter to my mother I said, "I seem to be having much more enjoyment from my Korean experience than I had originally expected."

I spent the Christmas holidays in Korea, and after final exams were finished I moved to Tokyo late in January 1959.

TOKYO

In Tokyo, where there was a large Maryland program, I was privileged to reside at the Sanno Hotel, which in prewar days had been one of Tokyo's three leading hotels (i. e., the Imperial, the Dai Iti, and the Sanno). It was now a BOQ and served largely as a residence for officers on leave for rest and rehabilitation (R and R). Several other Maryland professors also lived in the Sanno, and I could renew my acquaintance with those whom I had met in Tokyo in the preceding August.

The Sanno had a fine dining room and was especially convenient as it was close to the center of the city, was an easy place to find a taxi, and was close to a subway station. At that time, because the exchange rate made Japanese yen quite cheap, taxis were inexpensive. I would be teaching comparative politics at Tachikawa and international relations at Zama. These bases were a fair distance from downtown Tokyo, and although they could be reached by public transportation, the relevant two or three Maryland professors were driven there in an army sedan. All of the Maryland classes of course met at night, and the professors were usually picked up at the Sanno Hotel in mid afternoon.

One of my fellow passengers was Ayusawa Iwao, a famous Japanese economist. He would engage in long conversations with the driver. It seems that cutbacks in the American base which employed the driver threatened the possibility that he would lose his job and therefore have to revert to farming in order to make a living. It was eminently clear that he was repelled by the thought that he might have to become a farmer.

Now that I was living in Tokyo, the time and place were ideal for pursuing my research and writing on the Japanese Constitution. Mr. Horii Etsuro, who was recommended to me as a language tutor by the International House of Japan, had a perfect mastery of English as well as of Japanese and proved most helpful in the translation and analysis of critical documents and the conduct of two important interviews.

The Japanese Government Commission on the Constitution was greatly interested in my doctoral dissertation. I was invited to a meeting of the commission's subcommittee on the enactment of the constitution in the elegant Fujiya Hotel in Miyanoshita. Members of the committee, who were parliamentarians and legal scholars, were seated around a table. A number of copies of my dissertation had been distributed, and I was questioned about many points. Not being accustomed to the use of Japanese legal terms in speech, I promptly gave up trying to communicate in that language, and Sakanishi Shihō, a woman member of the Upper House who had once worked in the American Library of Congress, graciously came to my aid to serve as an interpreter.

The chairman of the Commission wanted to publish a Japanese translation of my dissertation. I was reluctant to publish it without first making substantial revisions, but I did suggest the translation and publication of substantial parts of the book, namely chapters 1, 2, 3, part of 6, 7, and 11. Professor Kobayashi Shōzō of Waseda University translated these parts and the product was published in June 1959 as part of the proceedings of the commission. I recommended and obtained a number of relevant documents and books in English for the commission. I read and commented on the report of the Subcommittee on the Enactment before it was finally printed. During its existence, the Commission kept me informed of its activities and sent me copies of its proceedings.

I had been living in the Sanno for barely two months when I suffered a rude shock. On March 30, 1959, the Tokyo district court ruled in the Sunakawa case that the stationing of American troops in Japan was in violation of Article 9 of the new Japanese Constitution, which forbad the maintenance of military forces. *Unless this court ruling was overturned, American forces, including the University of Maryland, no doubt, would have to leave Japan and my stay at the Sanno Hotel would come to an end.* Of course, I was an academic authority on this constitution, but it came as a rude surprise that my life could be so directly impacted by a court interpretation of the document.

On that same fateful day, in the lobby of the Sanno Hotel for the first time I became acquainted with Alfred Oppler, who had been a member of the Government Section when that group of Americans wrote the original draft of the Japanese Constitution. He was now one of the principal legal advisers to the commanding American general in Tokyo, and discussed with me the dramatic implications of the decision. Actually, the Japanese government appealed the decision to the Supreme Court, which in December of the same year overruled the decision of the lower court, so that for the time being I need not be removed from the Sanno Hotel.

The Sunakawa case, however, augured for more problems ahead for the American—Japanese security relationship, as we shall see.

I find no evidence in my pocket diary that I taught during the summer term (June and July, 1959), and I am quite certain that during those months and also in August, when no Maryland classes are held, I continued to reside in the Sanno Hotel. I worked with Horii on my research, visited and/or dined with other Maryland professors and their wives, including Jim and Mrs. Dee, David and Helenan Lewis, Phil Wheaton, Hal Vetter, Tom Smuck, and Chuck Borsuk, a Wisconsin Ph.D. in economics who had been a student in the French class I had taught at West High and was younger brother of Jerry Borsuk, an outstanding pianist and fellow student at West and later in the University of Wisconsin Music School.

Mme. Kohya, the widow of a Japanese professor, taught French in the Maryland program. I sometimes practiced my French and Japanese on her. She showed me some interesting places to eat and to shop. Once I accompanied her to a play in which a Japanese actor depicted Charles L. Kades, the architect of the postwar Japanese constitution. The Kades in the play depicted the real life affair that Kades had enjoyed with a Japanese lady. (The chauffeur in the play courted the lady's maid.) Once in the early spring Mme. Kohya and I made an extended bus tour of the Bōsō peninsula (on the eastern side of Tokyo Bay, opposite Tokyo) to see the very first cherry blossoms.

One interesting acquaintance was Frau Mecklenburg, the proprietress of an arts and book shop catering to foreigners in an arcade in downtown Tokyo. It may have been our common interest in German culture that accounts for our becoming friends. Before the war this German lady had owned an elegant home in Tokyo that, according to her, with its fine furnishings and objets d'art had burned to the ground owing to the carelessness of an incompetent servant. This disaster seems to have left her embittered. It developed that she had been acquainted with the eminent harpsichordist, Eta Harich-Schneider, the author of the textbook, *Kleine Schule des Cembalo-Spiels* (Kassel: Bärenreiter-Verlag, 1952), which my harpsichord teacher in Munich had prescribed for me.

It was a matter of some wonder that Frau Mecklenburg, a denizen of Tokyo, would have become acquainted with Eta Harich-Schneider. I have since learned that Harich-Schneider, while in Tokyo in 1941, had been lionized by the German community and had for a while resided in the German Embassy. She became a lover of Richard Sorge, the dashing *Frankfurter Zeitung* reporter who unbeknownst to her was the head of a Soviet spy ring. After the two had known each other only a few weeks, Sorge disappeared. He had been secretly arrested by the Japanese police and after a trial and three years of incarceration was finally hanged in 1944. (See Robert Whymant, *Stalin's Spy: Richard Sorge and the Tokyo Espionage Ring* (New York: St. Martin's Press, 1996.)

Frau Mecklenburg was a connoisseur of Japaneserie and we did some antiquing together. She kindly invited me to visit her at her cottage near Zushi, close to the ocean, where I met some of her friends who were into yachting.

Over a period of time, especially in the summers of 1959 and 1960, I became acquainted with Yoshi Takahashi. Yoshi had studied music in the United States before the war and taught piano. She was highly regarded as an effective Japanese language teacher in the Maryland program. Her sister, Tane, was the librarian at the International Christian University, and her uncle was the eminent historian, Tsuda Sōkichi (1873-1961). I never met Professor Tsuda, but sometimes he sent me catalogs of scholarly books.

Edward Kidder, a professor whom I had known at Washington University, was now teaching at International Christian University in the western part of Tokyo. When I went to visit him there, he was temporarily detained somewhere. An archeologist, he had been excavating part of the campus. Mrs. Kidder was very excited about his discoveries and, while carrying her baby, would jump in and out of the ditches, pointing to things that were invisible to me.

Kidder gained an international reputation with his articles and books on the archeology of Japan. (In later years, the Kidders were very helpful to my family when we lived in Japan during my stints of research there. Ted Kidder and his family remained at ICU until his retirement, when he moved back to the United States.)

I got to know David Sissons, a Japan specialist at the Australian National University. We were discussing the famous Japanese book *Kukutai no Hongi*, (Cardinal Principles of the National Entity of Japan), published by the Ministry of Education in 1937. This volume, which exalted Japanese nationalism, had been banned by the Allied Occupation authorities. Although I owned an English translation of the book, I mentioned that I wished I had a copy of the Japanese original; I thought that all of the copies had been destroyed. David said he had a copy and he kindly gave it to me as a present.

In April 1959, Crown Prince Akihito broke precedents and married a commoner. The newly married couple was scheduled to pass through the main streets of Tokyo in an open carriage. Wanting to view the public reaction at first hand, I opted not to watch the proceedings on television in the Sanno. I went to the nearest viewing spot. Onlookers were forbidden to stand up but were required to remain seated on the straw mats spread on each side of the street. I sat ready with my camera. When the royal couple passed by, people began standing up to catch a better view. In the evening at the hotel, people reported that on television they had witnessed the incident in which an apparently deranged youth had thrown a rock at the carriage carrying the royal couple.

HOKKAIDO

In all of my travels in Japan I had never been to Hokkaido, the northernmost of Japan's four major islands. I especially wanted to see the Ainu, the Caucasoid aboriginal race of prehistoric Japan. I knew of no package tour, so I negotiated with the local office of the Japan Travel Bureau for an eight-day individual tour, which included rail and bus transportation and stays at major tourist hotels. I left Tokyo by an overnight train to Aomori (the principal city on the northern tip of Honshu) on August 26, 1959. In the dining car, one could choose between the Japanese-style breakfast and the Western style. I and one or two Japanese chose the Japanese menu (I like *misoshiru*, salty miso soup) and the rest of the passengers, all of them Japanese, chose the Western-style, but it looked as if they were unused to eating ham and eggs with knives and forks. To get from Honshu Island to Hokkaido, one had to take the ferry from Aomori.

In a hotel dining room in Sapporo, I encountered two Americans who invited me to join them for dinner. One seemed to be enjoying Japan, especially the giant crabs for which Hokkaido is famous. His partner was openly homesick for America. The two were engineers involved in the planning for a railroad tunnel which would someday link Hokkaido to Honshu, making obsolete the use of the ferry. (In 1985, the Seikan Tunnel, 33.5 miles long, was completed, and was the world's longest tunnel, a rank which it still retained in 1994, when the English Channel tunnel, 31.04 miles long, was finished.)

Almost from the beginning it became evident that my tour involved too much travel with little time in particular places to see and enjoy them. One evening my bus stopped at a hotel on the shore of a beautiful lake, but the bus left early the next morning so that I had no time to enjoy the lake and the surrounding forest of magnificent pine trees. I managed to visit a model Ainu village, with its primitive dwellings and assembly house. An Ainu chieftain described in Japanese, the clothes, accouterments, and customs of the Ainu people to the amusement of tour groups. In a nearby town, shops displayed Ainu souvenirs, including dishes crudely carved from wood, wooden bears, and picture books. I was reminded of the Indians at Wisconsin Dells, Wisconsin, who made their living by catering to tourists.

I was unacquainted with the fine points of public bathing in Japan, about which I had heard rumors. At one tourist hotel, in a corridor on my way to the bath I was startled to see walking towards me, completely naked, a girl about thirteen years old.

By the end of the week I was exhausted by my rigorous schedule and opted to fly back to Tokyo rather than take the ferry and overnight train. The Japan airline had only recently begun its postwar operation, and it seemed that some of the passengers, whose knuckles were white from their tight grip on their armrests, were nervous about flying. At the end of the journey, the stewardess recited her farewell in Japanese and added in English, "I hope you enjoyed your fright."

OKINAWA

The fall faculty meeting and faculty reception for the Far East Program were held in elegant rooms in the Sanno Hotel in early September 1959, and on the following day the professors proceeded to their new posts. I was sent to Okinawa, the principal island of the Ryukyu archipelago extending southward from Kyushu. Although the Japanese peace treaty had restored sovereignty to Japan in 1952, Okinawa was still under American military government. I was the only full-time Maryland professor on the island and was granted the use of the university's aging Chevrolet, which after considerable repairs proved very useful. The house that served as my living quarters stood on a bluff commanding an unobstructed view of the East China Sea. In my front yard stood a small tree bearing a disproportionately large bunch of green bananas that managed to disappear just as they had finished ripening.

I served two eight-week terms in Okinawa in the fall and early winter of 1959, teaching courses in international relations, U.S. diplomacy, Far Eastern politics, and American history.

I had some embarrassment in my class in American diplomacy. In an experiment to improve my grading system for essay exams, I shifted from the use of letter grades to numerical grades. I explained carefully to the students that my particular numerical grades did not mean that less than 75 was failing, but rather that I was rating answers on the basis of 0 to 100, with 50 indicating that the answer was half right. In spite of my best efforts, I could not convince some of the students that I was not giving them failing grades and they became indignant. In any event, at the end of the semester, everyone was assigned a letter grade in the course, as required by the university, and I don't think anyone failed the course. After that experience, I avoided the use of numerical grades. I liked the courses I taught and I enjoyed getting to know my students.

While in Okinawa, I stumbled onto John Miller, who had worked at a desk beside me in CIS during the Occupation. He had a Japanese wife, with whom he was not living, and we had some interesting adventures. We became acquainted with Luyu Kiang and his beautiful wife. Luyu, a civilian employee of the U.S. military, had attended Columbia University and taught part-time for the Maryland program. The Kiangs were generous with their hospitality, and I have ever since kept touch with them.

In December I gave a series of four lectures in English on American history at Ryukyu University as a volunteer without compensation. Between terms in November and again during the Christmas week I was in Tokyo visiting Yoshi Takahashi, Mme. Kohya, and other friends.

TAIWAN

I had never been to China. While working for MacArthur I had planned to visit China during a vacation, but I was sent back to the States before I could accomplish this. Then after 1949, when the Communists completed their conquest of mainland China, that country was not open for American tourists. The island of Taiwan, however, remained under Chinese Nationalist rule and, given Okinawa's propinquity to Taiwan, I was tempted to visit the Chinese island on a weekend.

On a Friday morning (October 30, 1959) I left Naha airport for Taiwan, and on the following Monday I left Taipei for Okinawa. Saturday was Chiang K'ai-shek's birthday, and flags flew on all of the main streets. He spent the day in the country. I heard him speak on some loudspeakers downtown. On the whole, Taipei looked cluttered and dilapidated and there was a lot of construction going on, something like the Tokyo of the Occupation days. Not being familiar with the city I took an evening tour, which included a meal at a Mongolian restaurant. I found a book store that sold English language books. At this time, the Nationalist government did not subscribe to international rules concerning copyrights, and there were bargains to be had in pirated books. The books were printed on very cheap paper and flimsily bound, but otherwise they were photographic copies of the originals. The biggest bargain was the pirated *Encyclopedia Britannica* in many volumes. I bought a pirated copy of the unabridged Merriam-Webster dictionary, Second Edition in two volumes, copyrighted 1959; a second edition of the *Columbia Encyclopedia;* and *The Shorter Oxford Dictionary* (2515 pages). (These pirated books are still in my library at home.)

In Japanese I asked a clerk in the store to give me some cord to bundle up my purchases. He laughed and gave me some cord. Taiwan had been under Japanese rule between 1895 and 1945, and the Japanese language was still being used as well as Chinese.

When I got back to the Naha airport, I was detained because my papers were out of order. Although I was carrying a U.S. passport and other IDs and a military travel order (this was the travel order I had used to fly from Tokyo to Okinawa), these were technically not enough to allow me to re-enter Okinawa. But the American in charge of things probably did not want the hassle of interning or deporting me, and I was able to meet my class that evening.

MISAWA

In Japan, as in Germany, American bases sometimes adopted the names of obscure nearby towns so that some of the most important bases may be difficult to locate on maps. For some time I had known that I might be teaching at the Misawa air base but had no idea where that was. One day, when I was looking at used books in Kanda (the bookstore district in Tokyo), I picked up a pamphlet published by the Japan Communist Party. In it was a map clearly showing all of the American bases. It was from this map that I first learned that Misawa is located in Aomori prefecture in the northern tip of Honshu Island.

I left Okinawa at 2:30 AM on a Saturday morning and arrived in Tokyo about 8:00 AM the same day. Rather than go the Sanno Hotel I checked in at the new International House of Japan, which had a stunning Japanese garden. Professor Merle Curti, the University of Wisconsin historian, was residing there at that time. On Sunday morning at the Tokyo Unity Church I gave a talk in English on "The Individual in America Today," which was largely based on William White's *The Organization Man* (New York: Doubleday, 1956). The pastor, Imaoka Shin-ichiro, served as my interpreter. Among the score of listeners was a Waseda professor who was writing a book about individualism in Japan.

In late January 1960, a week after returning to Tokyo from semitropical Okinawa, where it seemed to be summer all year long, I took off for Misawa.

When my plane got there, the airfield was covered with snow and the plane had to cruise about for over an hour while our runway was cleared off. By moving from Okinawa to Misawa I had completely missed out on autumn, which is the best part of the year in Japan. (The winter is too damp, the spring is too rainy, and the summer is too hot.)

It seemed forever before spring definitively arrived in Misawa. In late February or March, the sun would come out and there would be a big thaw one day, but a great storm would come the next day, replenishing the knee-deep snow drifts. Most of the streets were unpaved, so that people were wading in mud when they were not picking their way through the snow. The big issue in local politics was the possible paving of one of the downtown streets. A week-end trip to Aomori, the prefectural capital, provided no relief from the snow, the slush, and the mud.

The commencement ceremony at the Kudan Kaikan in Tokyo on March 27 provided a welcome relief from the snow country. The president of the university, Wilson Elkins, attended, and the faculty and graduates wore robes. An honorary degree was conferred on Tanaka Kōtarō, chief justice of the Japanese Supreme Court. He seemed to thoroughly enjoy the ceremony and the reception afterwards. The full-time faculty members had been widely dispersed throughout the Far East, and annual faculty meetings and commencements provided us with rare chances to renew acquaintances. I had asked that invitations be sent on my behalf to various Tokyo friends including David Sissons, Professor James Morley of Columbia University and his wife, Professor Ukai Nobushige of Tokyo University, Horii Etsuro, my Japanese tutor, and Imaoka Shin-ichiro, pastor of the Tokyo Unity Church.

After a week of excitement in Tokyo with old friends I had to return to Misawa for term IV. On May 8, I mailed to Professor Eugene Boardman of Wisconsin my greetings from Aomori prefecture, where "the cherry trees here are now in full bloom after a long and very snowy winter." (Years later I observed that the cherry trees in Washington, D.C. bloom in March, not in May as in Misawa.)

During term V, i.e., June and July, I did not teach but made the still elegant Sanno Hotel the base for my research and social activities. (In 1983 the Sanno Hotel, the maintenance of which had been sorely neglected, was closed and shortly razed, and a replacement, the beautiful "New Sanno Hotel" was opened in a different part of Tokyo for the use of U.S.-connected personnel.)

THE SECURITY TREATY CRISIS

During my Okinawa and Misawa assignments, a great debate had been brewing in Tokyo concerning the revised U.S.-Japan security treaty that had been negotiated with America by Prime Minister Kishi's government. Massive student demonstrations protesting the substance of the treaty, which was allegedly unconstitutional, and the manner of its formal approval by the Diet. From the roof of the Sanno Hotel, some of us saw student demonstrators provoking the police in an effort to penetrate the grounds of the prime minister's official residence. On June 10, 1960, James Hagerty, who had come to Japan to finalize plans for President Eisenhower's visit to Japan, had to be rescued by a helicopter from a mob of angry demonstrators at the airport. Five days later in the course of a clash between the police and students trying to invade the Diet compound, a coed was killed, either crushed to death by the crowd or strangled by the police, as some asserted. On June 16, Kishi announced that the time was not appropriate to welcome a state guest, and the Eisenhower visit would be "postponed," in effect cancelled.

In the meantime, the American community in Tokyo had looked forward to Eisenhower's visit, and a coterie of Maryland professors with wives and friends had planned to celebrate by viewing the projected ride of the president and emperor through the streets and by a big dinner afterwards. That party was also "postponed."

The security treaty demonstrations in 1960 were the most dramatic and critical event in postwar Japanese politics. Kishi lost the support of his own political party and was forced to resign. About this time, I decided that I should interview a few leading Japanese politicians. First on my list was Katayama Tetsu, who had been the Socialist prime minister between May 1947 and March 1948. Horii would accompany me as my interpreter.

We arrived at Mr. Katayama's office promptly at the appointed hour on July 14, 1960, but had to wait some time for the statesman to appear. When he finally showed up we learned that someone had just stabbed Prime Minister Kishi in the precincts of the Diet Building.

Professor Theodore McNelly interviews former Prime Minister Katayama Tetsu, July 14, 1960

When Katayama took office as prime minister in 1947, MacArthur had made a big thing of Katayama's being a Christian. Katayama told me that he was a fan of the Chinese poet Bai Juyi (772-846) and kindly gave me an inscribed copy of his newly published (1960) book *Hakurakuten: Tōyō no shi to kokoro* [Bai Juyi: The Poetry of the Orient and the Soul]. The book analyzes Bai Juyi's poems and includes Japanese translations and drawings and photographs of places mentioned in the poems. A photograph depicts Guo Moruo (Kuo Mo-jo), China's world famous littérateur, in Beijing handing to Mr. Katayama the manuscript of the book's foreword, which Guo had written. Katayama told me that he did not believe that Japan should recognize the government of Communist China because the Japanese people were naïve about communism. (On Bai Juyi [also spelled Bo Juyi, or Po Chü-i].see Arthur Waley, *The Life and Times of Po Chü-i* [London: George Allen & Unwin,1949].)

On July 21 I delivered to Tanaka Kōtarō, the chief justice of the Japanese Supreme Court, the certificate conferring on the justice an honorary membership in Pi Sigma Alpha, the political science honorary society. The Supreme Court then had its offices in the rambling red brick building that had formerly housed the prewar Navy Ministry. Justice Tanaka cordially greeted me and gave me newspaper clippings concerning recent decisions of the court. On the day before I met him, the court had ruled that certain municipal ordinances that regulated demonstrations, including Tokyo ordinances, were not unconstitutional. As I left the court building, people were starting an illegal demonstration protesting the court's ruling on demonstrations. According to the newspapers, the demonstration, although illegal, was orderly.

During and following the security treaty crisis, Professor Edwin O. Reischauer of Harvard University had been articulating in speeches and writings criticisms of the U.S. government's policies in Japan. He visited Japan in the summer of 1960, and the officers of the Commission of the Constitution invited Professor Reischauer and me to a dinner party on July 28 at the Akahane restaurant, a fancy little place that specialized in wild fowl baked on hot stones. According to my crude notes, Takayanagi Kenzō, the commission's president; Professor Yabe Teiji, the biographer of Prince Konoe; Hosokawa Yūgen, chairman of the subcommittee on the enactment of the constitution; Inaba Osamu, a Liberal Democratic Party official; and Ohtomo Ichiro, secretary of the Commission, were there. Reischauer and I were the only non-Japanese present. The conversation, mostly in Japanese, focused on the recent political crisis as well as on the history of the adoption of the democratic constitution. I felt privileged to be invited to this exclusive affair.

Several months later President Kennedy appointed Reischauer as the new American ambassador to Japan, a position that he held from 1961 to 1966.

On July 28, 1960, accompanied by Mr. Horii, I interviewed Nishio Suehiro, the head of the new Democratic Socialist Party, made up of individuals who had seceded from the Socialist Party. The Democratic Socialists did not approve of some of the Socialists' extraparliamentary tactics or of the policy of cooperation with Communists. Actually, Nishio did not tell me anything that I had not already known from reading the newspapers, but his statements to me were an authoritative confirmation of my understanding of the situation.

LOOKING AHEAD

From the inception of my connection with the Maryland Overseas Program, I did not have the intention of making a career of it, except for a very brief period while I was teaching in Germany. Then someone in the Heidelberg headquarters asked me if I was interested in an assistant directorship in connection with the Far East program. The directors and assistant directors were not peripatetic like the professors, and they could live in more permanent headquarters in or near major cities that they could share with their wives. An administrative appointment would be a welcome change from living out of a suitcase and could be regarded as an upward move. A short time after I had indicated my interest in this possibility, Leslie Bundgaard, a new member of the faculty, was appointed as an assistant director. I believe that temperamentally he was more suited to administrative work than I was. Besides I had other prospects. (A few years later Dr. Bundgaard was appointed to a deanship on the College Park campus and dealt with student unrest there. His sudden death at a young age came as a great shock to everyone.)

Over a period of several years, Professor Walter Posey, whose acquaintance I had made in Wiesbaden, had been writing me to apply for a position at Agnes Scott College, a reputable women's college near Atlanta. I kept putting off giving a definite reply because teaching women in an undergraduate institution appealed to me less than other possibilities, but I did not want to close the door completely to the Agnes Scott possibility.

While at Munich Branch and Chaumont I was making efforts to revise my dissertation for possible publication. At the same time, I applied for several research grants (once on the suggestion of Professor Peffer of Columbia) so that I could devote full time for research, but I was unsuccessful with the applications, because, I believe, I did not have the knack of writing strong proposals.

I was asked to write an article for *Political Science Quarterly*, a leading scholarly journal. I wrote the article and had it typed in the Tokyo office of the university and the article appeared in the June, 1959, issue of the journal under the catchy title "The Japanese Constitution: Child of the Cold War." I bought a supply of reprints and sent them to my relevant department heads in College Park and a list of scholars of Asian studies.

I also regularly sent Christmas cards to the department heads in College Park. Thank you notes from the recipients confirmed that people were still aware of my existence, even when I was teaching near the demilitarized zone (DMZ) in Korea, an academic Siberia.

At least once I met Professor Elmer Plischke, who had succeeded Franklin L. Burdette as head of the Department of Government and Politics, during his inspection tours in Europe.

Of course, I saw him briefly again when I visited College Park while traveling to New York to present my paper at the 1958 meeting of the Association of Asian Studies. I kept Professor Plischke informed of my collaboration with the Commission on the Constitution, of my search for a research grant, and my search for a stateside job.

In Tokyo at a meeting at the International House of Japan I met Shannon McCune of the University of Massachusetts who suggested that I might be considered for a position at his university but that much depended on the needs and views of the chairman of the relevant department. I wrote my mother that there was a possibility that I might get a job at a state university on the East coast.

During my second year in the Far East Program, I had become tired of my constant travel and of the lack of a tenure system in the Maryland program. Phil Wheaton, a colleague who had recently returned to the States, reported that the job situation in the America had improved over what it had been in 1953 when I had joined Maryland. In January 1960, Bob Daly, the director of the Far East Program, asked me in a letter to let him know by January 31 if I was interested in being reappointed for the following year. The letter, however, made it clear that whether one would actually be reappointed depended on "an estimate of the size and solvency of the separate geographic divisions, changes in course demand, and the extent of military support anticipated."

With Wheaton's comments in mind and the thought that I might, while seeking a job, return to Columbia to complete the requirements for the certificate of the East Asian Institute, I made a bold decision. I indicated to Daly that I did not wish to teach an additional year in the Maryland program. I was quitting a job without having another one lined up. It was quite conceivable that at the age of forty I would be unemployed for an extended period of time.

Nothing came of the possible position at the University of Massachusetts, but I received a letter addressed to me at "Misawa Air Base, Northern Honshu, Japan" from Professor Plischke, dated February 3, 1960. He inquired of my possible interest in a vacancy in his department at College Park. "The position is *not of a temporary nature,* and appointment would be intended to be *continuing, with tenure* subject to the usual University conditions [emphasis added]."

This was the answer to my dreams. I telegraphed a reply: I AM INTERESTED IN POSITION DESCRIBED IN YOUR KIND LETTER OF FEBRUARY THIRD PERIOD WOULD GREATLY APPRECIATE BEING RECOMMENDED TO DEAN AND PRESIDENT VERY SINCERELY THEODORE MCNELLY.

At the same time I wrote Plischke a letter (February 10, 1960) of similar import, thanking him for "the privilege to work in an environment so favorable for effective teaching and research." The possibility of teaching at a state university on the East coast that I had previously written my mother about had been realized, but the university would not be Massachusetts, but rather Maryland.

The University of Maryland, College Park Campus, was in a close-in suburb of Washington, D.C. I had found the D.C. area attractive and interesting when I had worked for the Army Security Agency and attended Georgetown University at night during the war. Uncle Ed, Aunt Lois, and cousin Carol lived in nearby Maryland.

While I was teaching in Misawa, William L. Holland, editor of *Pacific Affairs*, a journal published by the Institute of Pacific Relations, asked me to write an article on Article 9 of the Japanese Constitution and the Sunakawa case, cited earlier in the present chapter. I began to collect relevant sources materials. Also Professor Plischke recommended me to Houghton Mifflin as a possible author for a book on Japanese government to be published in a series on comparative politics. Plischke was writing the book on Germany. Richard Clark, the Houghton Mifflin editor, wrote me indicating that the publisher had already begun negotiations for a Japan book with a Stanford professor, but the book the Stanford professor had in mind might not be as suitable as something that I might to write. (Within a few months, it developed that I would be the author of the Japan book.)

I was allowed to transport at government expense something like 4000 pounds of personal effects when moving back to the States. I had a small round lacquer table, that Yoshi Takahashi had helped me to buy, a *tansu* (chest, made of paulownia, a very light wood), two *hondana* (for use as curio cabinets), and a low table (folk art I had bought on recommendation of Frau Mecklenburg), that had to be moved together. (A beautiful Kyoto-style *hibachi*, converted for use as a coffee table, I had previously sent by mail to my mother as a Christmas present.) I had managed to store some of these items in my hotel room, but Yoshi Takahashi generously let me leave some of it with boxes of books at her house during my Okinawa and Misawa stints. It was suggested that I might purchase a stone lantern to take full advantage of my shipping allowance, but I was uncertain of what I would do with it in the States and it was inconvenient to purchase one. Although I failed to use fully my moving allowance, when I arrived at Tachikawa Air Base I had far too much luggage, which included extensive newspaper files. Yoshi Takahashi, who was very generous with her time and help, had accompanied me to the air base, and we reorganized my stuff to reduce the weight of my luggage. She would ship the newspapers to me separately.

According to my incomplete records, at 12:00 noon on August 4 I left Tachikawa (outside of Tokyo) and after stop-overs or changes including Honolulu and Chicago, I arrived in Madison, Wisconsin, at 4:45 PM the next day. I had taught two terms

(16 weeks) in Korea, two terms (16 weeks) in the Tokyo area, two terms (16 weeks) in Okinawa, two terms (16 weeks) in Misawa. I had spent two summer terms in 1959 and 1960 (16 weeks) in Tokyo engaged largely in research. Between assignments or on weekends I had traveled extensively. I had been living out of my suitcase for seven years. Although in the coming fall I would still be teaching for the University of Maryland, it would not be in foreign climes but on the College Park campus close to the capital of the United States. I would be in line for tenure. A new chapter of my life was about to begin.

CHAPTER 13

PARTNERSHIP

In the late afternoon on August 5, 1960, I arrived in Madison. My mother was still living in the Jefferson Street house. Gramma Taylor had passed away the previous January. Mother may have had a student roomer or two upstairs, but there was plenty of room for me. Jimmy and his family were living in Madison, and I enjoyed seeing them. John and his family were in East Lansing, Michigan, where John was teaching and winding up his Ph.D. in journalism at Michigan State University.

I looked up Myra Koehler just about every day. She had been teaching in Minneapolis, but was home for the summer. Her house was near West High School, about a mile from our place. I would either walk over to her house or take a taxi to see her.

Although in the past Myra and I had engaged in and enjoyed wholesome cultural activities together, our relationship had not been particularly romantic. We had many common interests and were good friends. By now, however, my lonely life as a bachelor had completely lost all of its charm, and I felt that I needed Myra around all of the time. We began to go picnicking and swimming together and took pleasure in our physical propinquity.

About a week before I was due to leave for College Park, on a swimming beach on Lake Monona in Madison, I undertook to propose marriage to her. I was too shy to just ask her cold turkey to marry me. My method was to approach the subject gradually, emphasizing my need for her. I began by pointing out that in moving to my new job in Maryland, I needed somebody to help me pack my many books. At this point Myra interrupted: "Well, I have a lot things of my own that have to be packed!" We were on the verge of an argument about who had the most stuff, and my proposal was not going smoothly. But the implication was unmistakable that we had both already decided that we would be married and go to Maryland together. Neither Myra nor I can remember my formally asking her to marry me or her formally accepting my proposal.

I did not want to be "engaged" to Myra. I had known her and her family fairly well for ten years and there was no need for a long engagement. I wanted to take Myra to Maryland with me as my bride. In the back of my mind I was absolutely convinced that Myra was the girl for me and I was afraid that if there was a period of engagement, I might make some stupid mistake and louse up everything. So Myra and I did not get engaged. I did not give Myra an engagement ring. Instead I bought her a wedding ring with four diamonds on it. We got married about a week after our elliptical agreement. (Myra reminds me that several weeks after our wedding, I bought Myra an "engagement ring" with a faux diamond at a drug store for ten cents.)

Myra had sold her Ford in Japan. In Germany she had owned and sold an Opel, a small German-made General Motors car. Back in the United States she bought herself a new Opel, of which she was fond. I would need a car of my own and looked at cars in a used car lot in Madison. I chose a large Plymouth sedan, several years old, with enormous tail fins. In the course of bargaining, I apologized that I did not have a car to trade in, and the salesman immediately lowered the asking price. I persuaded him to lower the price another $35.00 and he agreed, but said this would have to approved by the boss. I said I would buy the car, but the boss vetoed the $35.00 reduction that I had negotiated with the salesman. I bought the car anyway. I later learned that the technique that had been applied against me is known as "low-balling." I drove in my car with Myra to Minneapolis to help her move out of her quarters there. She had taught in the Minneapolis public schools the previous year and now resigned her position there to marry me.

Myra's mother was very active in her church (Christ Presbyterian Church, downtown) and did all of the planning for the marriage ceremony and telephoning of invitations. The wedding was held on Sunday, September 4, 1960, in the newly built Westminster Presbyterian Church in the western part of the city. (The old small church building in my family's neighborhood had been sold.) Reverend Richard Pritchard, who had visited me in the state sanatorium ten years before, presided. The wedding was informal, and rather than wear a tuxedo I wore the black silk suit that had been tailored for me in Tokyo two months previously.

The reception following the wedding was held in the church. Afterwards a number of out-of-towners met at Myra's house. Myra and I did not completely understand the agenda and mistakenly left before we should have, to begin our honeymoon drive to Maryland. We went in my Plymouth; Myra would go back to Madison later to get her car.

My mother surprised me with a new pair of pyjamas for the honeymoon and on her own initiative had made reservations for us for one night at the Oakton Resort Hotel next to Pewaukee Lake, near Milwaukee. After dinner, a Jewish comedian presided over the evening's entertainment. The performer's Yiddish humor eluded our Presbyterian sensibilities and we escaped to our room. The room itself was a disappointment. Its sole window did not overlook the lake, so we just pulled down the shade. We enjoyed each other's company that night.

A Wedding Picture
From the left: Lillie Francis (matron of honor), Myra, Ted, Jimmy McNelly
(Ted's younger brother)

We took the *Milwaukee Clipper*, a ferry, from Milwaukee to Muskegon, Michigan. We visited my brother John and his family in East Lansing, Michigan. We stayed overnight at motels along our route. We stopped in Columbus, Ohio, to say hello to Ulrich and Almut Groenke, who had recently moved there from Germany to take a teaching position at Ohio State University. We stayed one night in Cumberland, in the mountainous Maryland panhandle, where we left my new pyjamas in the motel. We visited the Antietam battlefield.

Our trip ended on Friday in front of the court house in Rockville, Maryland. From there we telephoned Uncle Ed. Ed and Lois put us up at their house in the country for a week while we looked for a place to rent. Every morning Lois cooked up something exotic for breakfast. For the first time in my life I ate scrapple. I have forgotten what other goodies we had.

We ended up renting a spacious apartment in Mount Rainier, Maryland, a working-class suburb of Washington, D.C. and a short drive from College Park and the university. We had to get some furniture for our new abode. Within a few weeks the shipment of my personal effects, including my beloved antiques, arrived from Japan.

Professor and Ruth Lutwack, my friends from Wiesbaden days, made us feel very welcome. After I had been teaching several weeks, at the end of one day I went to the parking lot to get my car, but after much search I could not find it. Discouraged, I called up Myra saying my car had disappeared. After some discussion she confessed that she had been on the campus with Mrs. Lutwack that day and that she (Myra) had moved my car. When I told Lut what had happened he sympathetically observed that I had married a practical jokester. I am relieved to report that following that particular episode, Myra never again played a mean trick on me.

Myra has a lively, if not always subtle, sense of humor. She can sometimes be blunt and outspoken. But she is also a kind and patient person. I think she learned patience from having to deal with her two brothers, each of whom (like me) had distinctive peculiarities.

Myra and I had much in common besides our West High and Presbyterian connections. We both had played music under the direction of Richard Church at West, I as a "lieutenant" in the band, she as concert mistress in the orchestra. For two summers she had played in the Music Clinic Orchestra. She had played not in the University of Wisconsin Symphony Orchestra but in the Madison Symphony Orchestra, where for 35 years her eminent violin teacher, Marie Endres, served as concert mistress under the leadership of Sigfrid Prager. Having majored in art at the University of Wisconsin, Myra had been a commercial artist and had taught arts and crafts in public schools in the United States, army dependent schools in Japan, and army Special Services in Germany. We both love to travel.

SUBURBAN LIFE

During my seven years in Europe and Asia, my habit had been to dine in officers clubs, restaurants, and PXs. Our apartment, Number 303 at 3370 Chillum Road in Mount Rainier, Maryland, was in easy driving distance of downtown Washington. For several weeks we did not eat supper at home but would drive to the Dupont Circle area or to Georgetown for dinner at one or another attractive restaurant. One evening we sighted J. Edgar Hoover dining with a friend in a downtown restaurant. After several weeks of this pleasant activity, I realized that I was running out of money, so we settled on eating suppers at home. This new arrangement was quite acceptable to me, as I had noticed when we had gone picnicking during our recent courtship that Myra was an excellent cook.

During the Christmas holidays in 1960 we drove to Madison in Myra's Opel. (It was not tuned for Wisconsin weather and while in Madison we often had to phone AAA to give us a start.) We had big dinner parties both at the Koehler house on Chamberlin Avenue and the McNelly place on Jefferson Street. These would include my two brothers, my sister, and their families, and Myra's brothers and Karl's family.

A number of old friends lived in the Washington area. We frequently visited Ed and Lois. In those days Lois gave big dinner parties at their place, including many people involved in building and real estate. Myra's high school friend, Kathryn

("Kay") Sanford, and her husband Kenneth Kerst, a Russian expert and diplomat who had attended West High, lived in suburban Virginia, and we saw them from time to time. Of course there were the Lutwacks, whom I had known in Wiesbaden. Janus Poppe and his wife, whom I knew in Japan, lived in Virginia. Janus taught at the Industrial College of the Armed Forces. Ann Demaitre and her husband, whom I had known in Munich, lived in the D.C., and we once had dinner at their place. Lucille Tipple, a neighbor and friend of Myra's in Madison, now lived in suburban Maryland with her husband, Vernon Kirkpatrick, an oboist in the National Symphony Orchestra and a Madison boy who had graduated from the University of Wisconsin School of Music.

Edward Griffin and his wife Jane were very hospitable to us just as we were establishing ourselves in the Washington area. Ed was a student of Hugh Borton, spoke Japanese fluently, and was connected with the State Department. He had yet to finish his Columbia doctoral dissertation and taught part-time at American University. Jane, an expert on Asian art, had been doing graduate work for her doctorate at the University of Michigan

I had met Hattie Kawahara Colton during my Maryland days in Tokyo, and I had known her husband, Kenneth, when he worked in the CIS. He worked in the War Department, earned a doctorate at American University, and in the 1970s taught at Kent State University, in Ohio. (In the newspapers in 1970, I would see mention of Professor Kenneth Colton's efforts to calm the student demonstrations at Kent State. For several years he had to travel between Ohio and Washington, D.C. to keep in touch with his family.) Hattie, with a Ph.D., administered the East Asian program at the Foreign Service Institute of the State Department, and invited me to lecture there several times.

DOUGLAS AND GALE

Douglas was born in the Washington Hospital Center in the D.C. on August 8, 1962. One of my earliest memories of Douglas was looking at him while he was in a glass box recovering from jaundice, with which he had been infected immediately after his birth. Myra had come home weeping because she had to leave her new baby behind to recuperate in the hospital. I looked at the little baby with a touch of resentment. He was a complete stranger to me and was now threatening to take over a large share of my life. My relationship with Myra was very different. After getting to know her fairly well, I *had chosen her* to be my mate. Douglas, on the other hand, was a complete stranger from another world and willy-nilly I was stuck with him. (But Myra has reminded me that unlike me she had become acquainted with Douglas during her pregnancy.)

As a tribute to his Scottish ancestry we assigned to Doug the names Douglas Scot. I had General Douglas MacArthur on my mind and we thought of Scott Koehler, the son of Karl Koehler, Myra's brother.

A fond memory of Douglas was our first picnic. I drove with Myra, Myra's mother, and Douglas to a dam in the Patuxent River. The dam held back the Tridelphia Lake, an area famous for its massed azaleas in the spring. Immediately below the dam is a beautiful park, and we enjoyed our picnic there on a beautiful August day.

Up to this time, our neighbors in the apartment building had paid no attention to us nor we to them. But when the news spread that we had a new baby, some of them became very interested. On August 31, less than a month after Douglas's birth, we moved out of our apartment in Mount Rainier to our newly purchased house in Takoma Park.

In the summer of 1963, when I was teaching at Columbia University, my little family occasionally walked to Grant's tomb, where there were swings for children. There Douglas had his first ride on a swing, which evoked a beaming smile on his chubby countenance. He certainly liked that swing. He was a cheerful baby, with a button nose turned yellow by the carrots that made up a large part of his diet. He had chubby triangular fingers; the bases of his fingers were wider than the tips. He laughed out loud when seeing jello shake and had learned to roar like a lion.

On March 12, 1964, Gale arrived at the Holy Cross Hospital, in Silver Spring. Myra's mother had come from Madison to be present at the occasion. We assigned to our new baby the names Gale, after George Washington Gale, my great great grandfather and founder of Galesburg, Illinois, and Anne, reminiscent of the middle name of Gale's grandmother Koehler.

Gale was a crabby baby with an angry cry until Myra discovered that she did not want to lie on her tummy. After this discovery, Gale was put down on her back and became a happier baby.

DOMICILES

When Myra became pregnant with our first child, we felt that we would need a larger place to live. Believing that I had a future at the University of Maryland, we began looking at houses to buy. The search was more difficult than I had expected, as many of the smaller houses we looked at seemed to have less actual living space than the apartment we were currently renting in Mount Rainier. Finally we found an all-brick home with three bedrooms at 7219 Central Avenue in a pretty neighborhood in Takoma Park, Maryland near Sligo Creek Parkway. Very shortly after Doug's birth we moved to our new house. Takoma Park, which buts on the District of Columbia, had originally been settled by Seventh-Day Adventists, whose churches, college, hospital, and national headquarters were still prominent in the city.

In our three-bedroom house, Myra and I used the largest bedroom, Doug and later Gale as well used the mid-sized bedroom, and I used the small bedroom as an office. When the children became of school age, we assigned the small bedroom to

Gale, and I moved my office from the small bedroom to the basement. My newly located office was unattractive and inadequately heated, and we began searching for a new house. We looked at some homes in University Park, a fashionable area next to the campus of the university, but the houses there seemed beyond our means. We were also thinking of the possibility of enclosing our porch or otherwise remodeling, and it occurred to us that we should see how the houses currently being built were designed and equipped for contemporary living.

We visited a new development, Stonegate, a northern extension of Silver Spring, near the Trolley Museum. These attractive large houses, about 25 minutes drive north of the university, had large lots (½ acre, minus easements for roads) and were less expensive than we had expected. Doug wanted a bicycle, but there was too much traffic in Takoma Park for him, but Stonegate was a much less busy area for bicycling. We picked a nearly completed house (14800 Cobblestone Drive) on a hill that commanded, in the rear, a view of hilly farmland and, in the distance, colorful sunsets and the wooded skyline of Gayfields.

Our home beginning in 1970
14800 Cobblestone Drive, Silver Spring, Maryland.

Our contract was contingent on the sale of our Takoma Park residence, which took several months to accomplish and involved renegotiating our mortgage. We had lived in Takoma Park for eight years before moving into our new home in 1970. The new house had a foyer the size of the dining room in our old house. In addition to a living room, dining room, eat-in kitchen and powder room, the first floor included a family room and a den. On the second floor were, in addition to a master bedroom with bath, three bedrooms and a bathroom. The house had a full basement, unfinished, and a double garage. At the time we bought the house, it seemed unusually large, but in the 1990s substantially bigger houses were being built in nearby developments.

The new house had one disadvantage. It was notably farther from the university and downtown Washington than the old place. In the 1980s the hilly farmland behind our house was covered with new homes, but because of our elevated location, we could see over these houses and enjoy the view of a distant skyline and sunsets.

In the 1990s after receiving a substantial "lump sum" as a part of my retirement settlement, I had vinyl siding installed. This involved changing the color of the upper part of the house from brown with yellow shutters to a more fashionable cream with Williamsburg blue shutters. Also I hired a carpenter to convert the rear patio (a concrete slab) into a screen porch (with a swing) that Myra had been wanting for years. The new porch could be conveniently accessed from the kitchen, so that during the summer it became our custom to eat our suppers on the porch. In 2002 triple-glazed windows replaced our original windows, which had become difficult to operate and maintain.

In her late seventies, Myra found the stairs more and more difficult to negotiate, and we had an additional handrail installed.

BOWL PARTIES

The University of Maryland, not unlike other large colleges, sponsored football and basketball teams that attracted national attention. The Maryland football team more or less regularly participated in one of the minor annual bowl games. Elmer Plischke, chairman of the Government and Politics, began the custom of inviting some of the senior faculty and other friends and their wives to his home to watch the big game. After Plischke retired and moved to Gettysburg, Myra and I began to hold bowl parties at our house, inviting some retired faculty and other friends, including friends of Douglas. These parties would include games involving the Washington Redskins as well as University of Maryland matches. In 2003, the University of Maryland basketball team won the collegiate national championship. Some of our guests were not greatly interested in the games themselves, but the game provided an excuse for a party and informal eating and drinking.

TED AND DELLA AND THE BALL BABIES

Myra's sister, Della, had been married to Edward ("Ted") Ball for about twelve years by the time Myra and I were married in 1960. Ted had been a student of horticulture at the University of Wisconsin and the couple had four children. Ted held positions as a city planner in small cities in Pennsylvania, and Myra and I visited them more than once there. Ted was concerned about the future college education of his children. He and Della were delighted when he got a job in planning in the government of Washington, D.C., and they moved to Bethesda, Maryland, which would make their children eligible for education at the nearby University of Maryland. Myra, I, and the children occasionally dined or attended movies with Ted and Della and the two families enjoyed one another's company.

On a wet icy night in March 1969 Ted and Della were driving from the university after leaving Ted, Jr. at his dormitory. Near the intersection of University Boulevard and Metzerott Road, their Volkswagen collided with a truck, and the Volkswagen caught fire. Ted and Della were seriously burned in the accident and suffered other grave injuries. Della died almost immediately and Ted died a few hours later.

Mrs. Koehler, Myra's and Della's mother, took charge of the four orphaned children at their home in Bethesda while Mr. Koehler, who did not like the arrangement, watched after the Koehler home in Madison. The four children had a meeting where they decided that they did not want to be divided up. After some negotiation, it was decided that the four children would live with Ted's brother, in accordance with Ted's will. A large house was purchased and redecorated and the four orphans moved in with the family of Ted's brother in Orchard Park, near Buffalo, New York.

Ted, Jr. finished a medical degree at the Case Western Reserve University and joined the medical faculty at Dartmouth College, later joining successively the University of Pittsburgh and the University of California at San Diego. His younger brother, Greg, studied oceanography at the University of Bridgeport and became a house painter. Jodie studied art at the College of Wooster, in Ohio, and married a journalist. Wendy married and had two children.

WITH THE FAMILY IN JAPAN

I was awarded a research fellowship by the Japan Foundation for the summer of 1973. As both Myra and I had enjoyed our individual previous stays in Japan, we felt that the children would profit from seeing the country. I sublet the home of Professor Ronald Rich on the grounds of the International Christian University in Mitaka, in the western part of Tokyo. From our house on a clear day one might catch a glimpse of Mount Fuji.

A high point among our adventures was a tour of Hakone conducted in Japanese (not designed for foreigners). Each of the tourists was given a booklet of tickets for use on the successive buses, boats, cable cars, etc. that carried us through the scenic area. Our tour group often mixed among other travelers, but we were supposed to keep up with the schedule of our group. At one point, Gale began to cry. She said that she had lost one of her tickets. It developed that her lost ticket was not essential: it was for a cup of coffee at the end of the tour. She was a very bright and responsible child even at the early age of only nine years.

We also took the "bullet train" (Shinkansen) to sightsee for several days in Kyoto and Nara. In Nara, where the deer were tame and roamed freely, Gale moved close to a doe and her fawn in order to take a picture. The doe, apparently to protect her fawn kicked at Gale, but her feet caught a trash can instead.

Once while we were shopping, Gale was in the middle of the street and a car was rapidly driving towards her. Our shouts to her may not have been much help, as she hesitated briefly before running to safety. She had had a very close escape from a serious injury or death.

At the end of the summer, Myra and the children returned to Maryland while I rented a room at the International House of Japan in Roppongi, Tokyo. Besides engaging in research and discussions with Japanese scholars, I made a trip to Kanazawa, on the west coast of Japan, where my mother had lived as a child. I took a bus tour of the historic city conducted in Japanese. Virtually all of the tourists obviously consisted of Japanese honeymoon couples and the ladies were wearing fancy dress shoes as we tromped through the wet November snow.

At Kanazawa University I talked with several professors who were entertaining but who could give me no clues about the school where my grandfather had taught in the 1890s. However, at the prefectural museum, I was introduced to an aged workman who as a child had played with missionary children. Thus I was able to locate the old school where my grandfather had taught. It was now called the Hokuriku Gakuin, and had several campuses in the city—kindergartens, elementary and high schools, and a junior college. I had discussions with the principal and the two American woman teachers, and showed them pictures of the house that my grandfather had designed and lived in. It was learned that although some of the old Victorian buildings of the school were still in use, my grandfather's house, after a relocation, no longer existed. The principal gave me an informative *Sixty Year History of the Hokuriku Gakuin* in Japanese which describes in great detail the founding of the school by American missionaries.

In the summer of 1977 my family temporarily split up. Myra and the children flew to Europe, where, among other adventures, they visited Myra's German friends and took a tour to Hungary. I went to Japan for research while my Japanese friend, Professor Takemae Eiji, and his wife and son occupied our house in Stonegate. He was engaged in research in the archives at Suitland while his little boy attended the Barrie School, a Montessori institution near Wheaton.

I was again scheduled to do research in Tokyo in 1980. When I had first announced our plan to reside in Japan, Gale was upset. She did not agree with my suggestion that she could attend the School of the Sacred Heart in Tokyo, which the Japanese empress had attended as a young lady. (Internationally, Schools of the Sacred Heart have been favored by the families of American diplomats stationed abroad.)

I leased a house in Koganei, in the western part of Tokyo. Instead of attending the School of the Sacred Heart, Gale went to the famous American School in Japan (ASIJ), located in its new modern building in Chofu, not far from Koganei. This school (at an earlier location) had been attended in the 1930s by, during their youthful years, the actress Joan Fontaine, Professor Edwin O. Reischauer (U.S. ambassador to Japan, 1961-1966), and Reischauer's second wife, Matsukata Haru. Every day Gale, a tenth grader, would bicycle to school, sometimes holding an umbrella with one hand. She took advantage of the permissive policies of the school by returning home early rather than serving out her study hour at the school. She and some of her school friends performed in a Japanese TV commercial. When it came time to return to Maryland, Gale was sorry to have to leave her new friends.

Douglas began his college career as a freshman in the International College of Sophia University, where classes were conducted in English. My friend, Father John Witek of Georgetown University, had kindly written a letter recommending Doug to Sophia University. Doug would take the crowded Chuo line (a principal elevated electric train in Tokyo) to his classes downtown.

We much enjoyed seeing the famous cherry blossoms in Tokyo's Mitaka neighborhood. Myra became interested in making Japanese paper dolls, which are three dimensional. She took a class in doll making at a tiny shop in Koganei. Occasionally Gale would attend the class. After returning to the States, Myra purchased the materials (fancy colored papers, *washi*) from the shop and gave lessons in doll making to some of her friends.

We did much sight seeing in and near Tokyo, taking trains or busses to Kamakura, Yokohama, Odawara, Mt. Fuji, Nikko, and Yokosuka, where we visited Professor and Mrs. Watanabe Hajime. Our longest trip, which took several days, was to Himeji and Osaka (to see the famous castles there) and Kanazawa, a city with many samurai houses, where Ted's mother had lived as a little girl. Ted's grandparents had often spoken of the Kanazawa's famous Kenrokuen Garden, and we enjoyed seeing that.

Once while shopping in Tokyo, Myra and Gale were running to catch a train and Myra fell down, badly injuring her mouth and breaking two teeth. Ted Kidder and his wife suggested to us the name of an English dentist in Tokyo who repaired Myra's teeth.

In the summer of 1984, the daughter of the doll shop owner, Onuki Yoshiko, who had been admitted to Tokyo University, was our house guest. She would ride to the university with Gale and me and would attend my class, not for credit, in American foreign policy.

GROWING CHILDREN

It was almost inevitable that Doug and Gale would take music lessons given their parents' interest in music. Myra played violin in the Prince Georges [county] Philharmonic Orchestra and for several years was personnel manager of that organization, charged with finding substitutes for temporarily absent players. Myra also played in the Friday Morning Music Club orchestra, which performed twice in the Kennedy Center. Gale, Douglas and I regularly attended the performances of the Prince Georges orchestra.

When Gale began piano lessons with Mrs. Helen Beard, she practiced on my out-of-tune harpsichord. This arrangement was unsatisfactory because the technique required for playing the harpsichord is quite different from that for the piano. Myra bought an upright piano from neighbors on our street who had inherited a grand piano. I had lost interest in the harpsichord, which required tuning almost every time one sat down to play on it, and I found pleasure in playing old popular sheet music on the piano. Gale did well in her piano lessons and played in several recitals given by Mrs. Beard's students.

At a concert the family attended, several high school students played solos on their saxophones, and this inspired Douglas to study that instrument. Doug played in the Springbrook High School band. When the family went to Japan in 1980, overwhelmed by the quantity of our luggage, we would have left Doug's saxophone in the downtown Tokyo air terminal if a kind Japanese gentleman had not reminded us that we were forgetting something.

Myra and I had been concerned with the choice of a college or colleges where our children would receive their higher education. We gave some consideration to the new Baltimore County campus of the University of Maryland and to the College of William and Mary, in Williamsburg, Virginia. The University of Maryland at College Park, where I taught, was a huge institution and offered a wide spectrum of courses, including Japanese, a special interest of Gale. The university had a large music program, and Douglas's saxophone teacher, Reginald Jackson, was for a while connected with the university. It would be relatively inexpensive for the children to live at home while attending the university. The program of tuition remission for children of university personnel was an additional advantage of the University of Maryland for Doug and Gale.

After returning from Japan, Doug held a number of jobs, including work in an ice cream store, and then attended the Maryland Drafting Institute for twelve months. I would drive him and Gale, who attended the university, to their classes on my trips to work. For several years Doug worked as a draftsman in Virginia, where he shared a house owned by a friend. Doug began to find the work uninteresting, and when his friend sold the house, he made a change. He moved back home and resumed his college career at Montgomery College (a large junior college operated by Montgomery County) in Rockville. He did well in music there and transferred to the University of Maryland, where he did well in all of his studies, especially in music, and was awarded a Golden Key.

While he was living at home, Doug and I sometimes went biking or hiking together, often in the Maryland section of Rock Creek Park, which had paved hiker-biker trails through the woods.

After earning his B.A. at Maryland, Doug attended the North Carolina School of the Arts, in Winston-Salem, where he studied under James Houlik, a famous saxophonist. After two years of study he was awarded a Masters Degree.

Friends at Doug's church were talking about opportunities in computer science, and Douglas suddenly took a keen interest in learning Oracle. I bought him instructional software. We had a telephone line installed in his bedroom to provide him with an Internet connection. He took and completed an intensive night course in Oracle, and was immediately offered a position as a software engineer. When after a week his first employer lost a major contract and no longer needed Doug, Doug received offers from other companies. As of 2004, for six years he had been employed by Titan Corporation, in Virginia. There he has received several promotions and has bought a new car and a townhouse.

Doug has been interested in evangelical religion and in Republican politics and from time to time plays in amateur concert bands. At the time of writing he was in his early forties and unmarried.

Gale was fond of office work and, while an undergraduate, got a part-time job as an "elf" in the Department of Government and Politics. (At one time, the person in charge of the part-timers was a lady named Elva, and it became customary to refer to her charges as "Elva's elves", or just "elves.")

Gale would ride to the university nearly every day with me and occasionally with a neighbor whose daughter also attended the university. Without discussing the matter with me she decided to major in two subjects, Japanese and criminology. This involved getting two bachelors degrees and attending university longer than the expected four years. Gale graduated cum laude, was awarded the Golden Key, and was made a member of Phi Kappa Phi and Phi Beta Kappa.

While working as an assistant manager of the Waxie Maxie record store in Aspen Hill, on the telephone she became acquainted with a young man who at that time worked in the headquarters of the chain, Mark Bradley, a computer specialist and University of Virginia graduate. They were married in 1990 in a Presbyterian Church on New Hampshire Avenue, not far from our house. Doug played an aria by Bach on the saxophone before the ceremony.

Gale and Mark make a perfect pair, and I was delighted with my new son-in-law. They bought a house in Sterling, Virginia. In 2005 they moved into their new house in Fawn Lake, near Fredericksburg. Mark and Doug are devoted golfers and occasionally play together. Doug, Mark, and I often discuss computers to the disgust of Myra and Gale, who are more interested in other things. Gale works as a secretary to a group of patent attorneys in Alexandria, Virginia. She has recently performed in amateur theatricals, keeps rabbits and a cat, and owns a horse.

Our Children
from the left: Mark (Gale's husband), Gale, and Doug

One of my hobbies has been the study of espionage and for Father's Day in 2003, my children treated me to a visit of the new Spy Museum in downtown Washington. One of the first things visitors see there is a documentary film, in which the convicted British spy, William John Vassall (1924-1996) was singled out. My genealogical research had disclosed that Vassall was our very distant cousin.

PASSAGES

My two brothers and my sister resided most of their lives in Madison, Wisconsin, and were normally physically much closer to mother than I was after I left home in 1942 to teach at Kemper Military School in Missouri. During and after the war, I regularly reported to her on my activities in Arlington, Tokyo, and St. Louis. During much of 1951 I resided with her in our large Victorian house while I wrote my Columbia dissertation. Mother seemed to take a special interest in my activities because of our shared involvements in music and in Japan, where she had been born.

After my grandmother's death in January 1960, and as changes in the neighborhood made keeping the Jefferson Street house more difficult, my mother sold her three houses and moved into an apartment in the new western part of Madison. After a major illness, when living alone in the apartment was no longer practical, the children in Madison urged her to take up residence in Attic Angels, a fashionable retirement home in western Madison. In her letters to me, my mother complained that she did not want to make the move, and there were hints that she wanted my support to resist the urges of her Madison children. However, I believed that the children in Madison had their mother's best interest at heart and that they were in a much better position than I to evaluate the situation. After mother had actually moved to Attic Angels, the tone of her letters changed. It appeared that she very much enjoyed the organized activities at the place and the company of the other residents, and there were no more complaints from her.

Doug and Gale with Their Aunt Lucille, Grandma McNelly, and Grandma Koehler (Madison, August 1979)

In February 1984, I got a telephone call from Madison concerning my mother's serious illness, and there was an implication that she was close to death. So I flew to Madison to see her. The weather was unseasonably warm and pretty for February in Madison. I went with Lucille to see mother, who was bed ridden. She seemed impressed with my leaving my work and the expense of air travel to see her, and I was later told that my visit had improved her morale.

I do not think she ever again left the sick bed until she died on July 8, 1984. She had told Lucille that she wanted to die, a shocking statement from a devout Christian. Given her evidently incurable illness and confinement to a bed, her attitude is understandable. She was over 95 years old when she died. (I flew to Madison for the funeral on July 12.) She was buried next to her husband in Forest Hill Cemetery, near West High School. There was room for four more bodies in the McNelly burial site. After a brief negotiations, two places each were acquired by Jim and me, while Lucille and John opted for monetary compensation.

Surviving my mother were her four children, her brother (Edwin), 13 grandchildren, and 11 great grandchildren.

Ted with Uncle Ed

For several years before he died suddenly in 1990, it was my custom to visit my Uncle Ed on Sunday afternoons. Ed was living alone in his lovely house, next door to his daughter and her family. (Both of the houses had been built by Ed and Lois, but because of the 5-acre lots they were not particularly close to each other.) Ed's wife, Lois, and his sister (my mother) were no longer alive, and Ed enjoyed reminiscing about the past. I was very fond of Uncle Ed and much missed him after his death.

On April 21, 1985, Karl Koehler, the elder of Myra's two brothers, died at the age of 61. He had been the proprietor of a small printing business at the time of his stroke. He was hospitalized at the Veterans Administration hospital in Madison, receiving therapy to restore his speech. He had been famous during his life for his jokes and shaggy dog stories, and it was painful to see him unsuccessfully trying to finish simple sentences.

At the memorial service in a Madison church, Mrs. Koehler, Karl's mother, sat in the first row facing the coffin. Shortly before the formal ceremonies were about to begin, the room was completely still. Mrs. Koehler asked aloud, so that everyone could hear, "Where is Karl?" In her last years the dear lady had been suffering from intermittent dementia. Karl's body had been cremated and Myra suspects that Mrs. Koehler had expected to see her son on display in a coffin. Mrs. Koehler died the following year on March 23.

CHINA

In another chapter, I describe the highlights of Myra's and my trip to India in 1986 (where I presented a paper), including side trips to Agra and Kashmir. Originally we had planned to fly from Bombay to China, to meet a tour group there, but we decided to postpone the China trip when our travel agent was not able to guarantee the connections in Bombay. Myra had long wanted to visit China and was concerned that if we waited too long to make the trip our health might be an impediment.

On May 21, 1988, Myra and I arrived in Shanghai to join a group to make a seventeen-day tour of China. We visited eight cities. In Shanghai we were quartered in an elegant new hotel and saw a commune and an acrobatic show, including a panda that did tricks. After seeing Suzhou, noted for its gardens and factories, we proceeded by boat on the Grand Canal to Wuxi. At Nanjing we saw Sun Yat-sen's mausoleum and the stone animals at the Ming tombs. There I took an individual tour to see the Memorial to the "300,000 victims" of the Nanjing massacre ("rape of Nanking"), which included a gallery of photographs of atrocities committed by Japanese troops, a garden covered with gravel to prevent grass from ever growing again on the site of an atrocity, and human bones—the remains of some of the victims.

We flew to Beijing where we saw the Forbidden City, the Summer Palace, and the zoo. We viewed the Great Wall and finally Xian, where we saw the excavation of life-size terra cotta warriors and horses. I made a private tour to the place where Chiang Kai-shek was recaptured by his kidnappers in the 1936 "Sian incident." (To make this little side trip, I had to forego a luncheon where guests found bits of glass in the food.) At Guilin we saw the famous mountain scenery and took a boat to a village on the astonishingly beautiful Li River. In the village I saw scores of Japanese busses that had brought masses of Chinese tourists to this place.

POLITICIANS I HAVE KNOWN

In the course of thirty years of teaching at College Park, I became acquainted with several individuals who became prominent politicians. During my first year of teaching on the home campus, Steny Hoyer, whom I scarcely knew, upon learning his term grade stormed into my office, outraged that he had not received an A. In the ten years that I had spent in college teaching no student had reacted to a disappointing grade as violently as Hoyer did. Rather than simply asking me the reasons for the grade, he began to bawl me out, as if I were an incompetent subordinate employee. I almost immediately sensed that he was some kind of student politician, accustomed to throwing his weight around.

Mr. Hoyer had not distinguished himself in class discussions. I showed him his numerical grades on his written work. Although he had not done badly, his grades did not place him in the top one fourth of the class, a class which was not notably better than any of my other classes.

Twenty-five years later, I attended a small outdoor gathering at the university where Mr. Steny Hoyer, congressman from the fifth district of Maryland (in which the university is located), was the guest of honor. I doubted that he recognized me and I did not remind him of our earlier encounter.

Donald Devine, a Syracuse Ph.D. who taught in our department, was an outstanding scholar whose publication record clearly earned him a promotion to full professor, although he left the department before being promoted. His scholarly publications and solid grasp of research methodology inspired the respect of everyone. One semester when I was teaching in the night program on the campus I sometimes shared dinner with him in the University College cafeteria, and he told me of his activities in support of Bob Dole and Ronald Reagan. Our wives became friends. As a Republican political consultant he rose to a position one level below cabinet level as Director of the Office of Personnel Management in the Reagan administration.

Once he ran for Congress as a Republican against Steny Hoyer, the incumbent Democratic congressman in Maryland's fifth district. Devine was deeply committed to the idea of reducing the scope of government and shrinking the size of the federal bureaucracy. Hoyer, whose constituency was largely made up of federal government employees, openly declared his adherence to the opposite philosophy: "I am a tax, tax, spend, spend Democrat and am proud of it." Devine lost this contest, but continues to work as a Republican consultant.

In 2003, Steny Hoyer was elected by his Democratic colleagues to become minority whip. Recently, as I was entering Archives II in College Park, the world's largest archival building, I noticed a sign in the foyer referring to the Steny Hoyer Research Room, accompanied by a photograph of the congressman, although this portrait was not as large as was President Bush's. The sight of Mr. Hoyer's portrait in one of my favorite haunts is a constant reminder to me of an earlier encounter. It also reminded me that even the most meritorious public works may serve as pork.

James M. Soles was one of the best and most popular lecturers in our department. He had been hired in the 1960s as an instructor while he was completing his doctoral dissertation at the University of Virginia. Failing to win tenure at the University of Maryland, he got a job at the University of Delaware. Very popular as a teacher, he was able to build a substantial following and in 1974 became the Democratic Party candidate (unsuccessful) for Delaware's seat in the House of Representatives.

Elbert M. Byrd was an assistant professor when I joined the campus at Maryland. He was a competent scholar and was liked by the students. He entered Democratic politics in Maryland running unsuccessfully in the 1962 Democratic primary election for U.S. Senate. Later over a period of years he ran for a series of less prestigious posts. After a number of political defeats, he resigned from his professorship at the university even before his pension had been vested, so that he lost any claim to a Maryland pension. He let me read a copy of the draft of his political autobiography, *The Confounded Truth,* which I do not think was ever published. His fellow faculty members liked him and his wife and were sorry to see him leave, without at the same time finding a regular teaching position elsewhere. He moved to a farm that he bought in West Virginia and became involved in real estate sales, teaching part time. My strong impression was that his primary ambition in life was not teaching and research (he was good at both) but rather public service in elective office. His reserved manner—he was not a happy backslapping kind of politician—was not a help, and he did not do well at raising money. Another of Elbert Byrd's problems was that he was a traditional Humphrey Democrat during the Vietnam War era when a more radical group, such as that surrounding McGovern, came to dominate the party. When repeated attempts to win an elective office in Maryland failed, he chose to leave the state and begin a new career.

When I first joined the College Park campus, although I was close to middle age, I associated occasionally with some of the younger faculty members. These included Parris Glendening, assistant, later associate, professor specializing in local government with a Ph.D. from Florida State University. Once several of us drove together to the American Political Science convention in Chicago, with Parris driving in his car. In those days, Parris looked very young for his age, and in order to get drinks at College Park bars had to show his driver's licence to certify his age. He was deeply involved with a series of attractive girl friends. His positions on internal departmental politics tended to harmonize with mine, and he seemed to get along with everyone. Because of his relative youth, I was very surprised when I noticed that some graduate students and others on the campus began collecting money to support Parris's election to the Prince Georges county council, later to the position as county executive, and finally to the governorship of Maryland, which he won in 1995 with Kathleen Kennedy Townsend (daughter of the late Senator Robert Kennedy) at his side as Lieutenant Governor.

I became accustomed to see Glendening's name as governor on road maps, signs welcoming visitors to the state, and notices of roads and buildings under construction. Elsewhere in this memoir I mention his kindness to me at the time of my retirement.

My brother John would sometimes tell me about his acquaintances at the University of Wisconsin who had become leading politicians. While I was at Maryland I had a similar relationship with politicians. It appears that at least in cases of Wisconsin and Maryland, the state university is an ideal place to launch political careers. Either as a student or a faculty member, the would-be politician can test and improve his political skills on a campus, whose thousands of students and alumni with state-wide influence may be easily contacted and cultivated.

JANE FONDA

After the killing of several students at Kent State University by the Ohio National Guard in May, 1970, student disruptions occurred at many college campuses across the United States. The University of Maryland was no exception. Even before the Kent State affair, there was unrest in College Park concerning the university's refusal to renew the contract of an untenured but popular professor in the School of Journalism. On the day after the Kent State shooting, I noticed several girls on the campus wearing nursing costumes, adorned with red crosses. They would presumably care for the student victims of police or military violence. It was already exciting fun for some of the youngsters. There were demands that the classes be closed to provide for organized "discussions" to be sponsored by academic departments and colleges. The administration capitulated to this demand. Also an ad hoc campus convocation was held in the Cole Field House. Of course, most students did not attend these meetings, but instead chose to enjoy a few days off during beautiful weather.

When I first heard of student disturbances in Wisconsin before they had broken out at Maryland, they struck me as cute and a more or less legitimate mode of idealistic expression. But when rioters on the Maryland campus provoked the police to reply with tear gas, I, and perhaps a substantial minority of other professors, were appalled. My attitude was that American foreign policy should be conducted by our democratically elected officials rather than by cliques of rioting adolescents. It seemed to me that conspiratorial minorities were trying to enforce their views by dint of physical threat and violence against the majority. I had gone to great personal effort and expense to qualify as a professor, and the taxpayers of Maryland were paying me a salary to do my job and to provide for the instruction of the students. Instead the growing anarchy prevented conscientious professors and students from performing their legitimate business.

Of course there were "underlying causes:" (1) controversial issues and procedures relating to the conduct of university business, including grading systems, procedures for promotion and tenure of professors, tuition, etc. (2) debatable political policies regarding the Vietnam War and the military draft, (3) social issues involving real or alleged discrimination against blacks and women, (4) and purported violations of the right of expression. These issues had been coming to a head for decades, while colleges had expanded in size and increased in number as college education ceased to be the privilege of only the rich and the clever but became the right or perceived necessity of the general mass of the population. (Concerning the student movement of the 1970s, I have been greatly impressed by James A. Michner's *Kent State: What Happened and Why* [New York: Random House, 1971].)

At College Park, every day there were rallies on the mall. One side of my office building faced the mall, the other side faced the dining hall. When Jane Fonda was scheduled to speak one noon, my friends and I could easily have gone to a balcony to see and hear this celebrity. But most of us had become bored with revolutionary rhetoric, and we strolled to lunch at the dining hall. One professor said that he would have gone to see Jane if she would take off her clothes, but he did not want to hear her talk. That comment accurately reflected the consensus of our luncheon group.

One afternoon while a speaker, whose every sentence included a profanity, was holding forth, I initiated a conversation with a member of his audience. The student I talked to was not a Marylander, but a visitor from a western state. It was not uncommon for students, that May, to wander from campus to campus looking for excitement. Some of the individuals involved in vandalism at the university were high school students.

At Maryland, as elsewhere, there were confrontations between students and the National Guard, which was engaged in the legitimate activity of protecting individuals and property from violent attack. Once at Maryland during a face-off that I witnessed, an irresponsible person set off a fire cracker, which conceivably could have provoked serious violence.

Some of the professors volunteered to serve as "faculty marshals." They would mediate between the students and the forces of order. I had seen in Japan, during the 1960 security treaty crisis, how faculty marshals had been caught in the crossfire between hostile forces. It would be morally irresponsible of me as the head of a family, including two minor children, to risk my life for the benefit of the know-it-all, self-righteous children on the campus who would substitute mob rule for democratic processes.

A particular problem for the University of Maryland was that it was the largest university in the Washington D.C. metropolitan area, which included the national capital. U.S. Route 1, which connected Washington with Baltimore, ran through the eastern edge of the university's main campus in College Park. Using mob tactics, some agitators managed several times to close down this major national highway. One day I visited the headquarters of the faculty marshals. Faculty members were mimeographing leaflets for the students to hand to motorists, stating, "Honk if you want peace." If the students handed out these leaflets presumably they would not resort to blocking the highway. It seemed to me that the faculty in this instance was engaged in manipulating the students.

One day the morning newspapers reported the state governor's announcement that if on that day students closed Route 1 as they had threatened to do, the National Guard, already mobilized near the university, would forcibly reopen the road. I was afraid, given the stubbornness of the agitators, that there would be shooting. I told an economics professor, famous for her eloquence at campus meetings, that I very much hoped that it would rain, so that the students would not force a confrontation and noone would get hurt. Her attitude was that it would be just as well if a few people did get hurt. "You want the war to end, don't you?" she replied to me. Evidently there were some people on the faculty who would not risk their own necks but would be happy if their students did.

The end of the school year was nearly over. Attendance became spotty and many classes were not held. Ultimately it was decided that the students would not have to attend final examinations provided that they submit letters to their professors indicating why they could not attend. The letters I received were remarkable for their variety if not for their ingenuity. (I am sorry that I did not save them.) One student could not come because he had been mobilized by the National Guard. Another could not come because her parents would not allow her to risk her life by going to the campus.

The students having closed Route 1 more than once, I became pessimistic that discipline could ever again be restored on the campus.

When Nixon negotiated an end to American military involvement in Vietnam, the "anti-war" movement faded away on American campuses, even though the war (without American participation) continued full blast while Communist forces undertook the conquest of South Vietnam, a conquest largely made possible when Congress (responsive to the "anti-war" movement) refused to continue economic aid to the South.

Campus idealists at College Park continued their struggles. There were "smoke-ins," where the students publicly smoked marijuana. There was a big demonstration with the slogan "Narcs off campus," which demanded that state authorities not enforce drug laws in state-owned property, including the campus dormitories. I sensed that not many faculty members sympathized with this movement.

Back in Madison, Wisconsin, college students were pushing automobiles into Lake Mendota and attacking the police. My brother Jim was a policeman in that city of scholars. My mother was so upset by the student violence against the police, that one night she got up, removed all of her dishes from her cupboards, and washed them all.

LUNCHEON BUDDIES

During my first few years in College Park, I and a few departmental colleagues frequently lunched together at the Main Dining Hall, which was near our offices. Sometimes Elmer Plischke, the department head, would assemble a little group and drive us over to the nearby International House of Pancakes on New Hampshire Avenue. At one such meeting, for example, he told us about the salary increases that he had included in the proposed departmental budget. In the late 1960s Elmer stepped down from the headship.

During the controversy over the Vietnam War, the College Park campus was afflicted by much of the same turmoil as other universities. The department grew in size, and democracy and contention replaced the congenial atmosphere that I had originally enjoyed.

Frequently in the 1970s and '80s Professor Enver Koury, Professor Hsueh, and General William Wadsworth would lunch with me either in the Main Dining Hall, or occasionally in the cafeteria of the Center of Adult Education, which had its own campus adjacent to the College Park campus. The center administered the off-campus, evening, and overseas programs, and its attractive cafeteria served as a convenient refuge for those seeking escape from the sight of obnoxious colleagues on the College Park campus.

Professor Plischke was a strong advocate of area studies, and in late 1964 we were on the verge of hiring a bright Indian with the Ph.D. from our department. However, at an academic convention in Washington, D.C. I met Professor Chun-tu Hsueh, who was planning to return to the University of Hong Kong after a sabbatical leave in America. Hsueh had earned his Ph.D. at Columbia University, was elegantly dressed, and made a strong impression on me. Professor James Morley at Columbia strongly recommended him as one of the leading authorities in America on modern China. After Hsueh had met and favorably impressed the senior members of our faculty, Plischke hired Hsueh instead of the Indian scholar mentioned above. Because of our common interest in East Asia and our Columbia connections, Hsueh and I became life-long friends and were frequently in touch after both of us had retired.

Professor Enver Koury had a habit of breakfasting at a restaurant with Wadsworth. One morning when Koury failed to show up for breakfast, Wadsworth went to Koury's apartment. When Koury failed to answer the door, Wadsworth called the police, who entered the apartment and found Koury dead on the floor.

I had first met General William Wadsworth at a lunch with Walter Jacobs, the Columbia Ph.D. who was our Soviet expert. During hand-to-hand combat in Korea, Wadsworth had been captured and imprisoned by the Chinese Communists. In my mind he was a war hero, but his strong conservative views, which he publicly and loudly proclaimed, antagonized some people. He was fond of telling jokes and we frequently enjoyed hiking together in parks in Maryland.

He had attended the University of Maryland on the GI bill after the Korean War and had become the graduate assistant to Professor Gordon Prange, a leading expert on Pearl Harbor and author of *At Dawn We Slept: The Untold Story of Pearl Harbor* (New York: McGraw-Hill, 1981). Wadsworth had served in U.S. Army intelligence in Europe in the late 1940s and liked to discuss all aspects of World War II.

Wadsworth was short in stature and he nearly always wore a gray suit. Once when I was lunching with Wadsworth in the Howard Johnson restaurant near the university, a middle-aged waitress told him that she was going to kiss him. Later during our meal when no one seemed to be watching, that is what she suddenly did. He looked younger than his age, he was jolly and outgoing, and I could easily understand that women would find him attractive.

For months Wadsworth was plagued by telephone calls from a woman who was stalking him claiming that he had been her lover. He got a restraining order against her. Her husband became involved in the controversy, and for months this situation was a worry for Wadsworth.

Wadsworth and I frequently lunched at the Roy Rogers at Beltway Plaza, as it was closer to his apartment in Prince Georges county than were most of the places where we ate. In the early '90s he traded in his tiny old Chevrolet for a Prizm Metro, a small red hatchback. (The car was not equipped with an air conditioner, a virtual necessity in Maryland's sweltering summers, because the motor was not sufficiently powerful to support such an appliance.) One day (I was not present to witness the incident), a man tried to hijack Wadsworth's little car while Wadsworth was still in it. Fortunately the police arrested the culprit before any serious damage was done. At the trial, where the general waited an entire day to testify, the defense successfully argued that Wadsworth's identification of the hijacker was not credible because he was not wearing his eyeglasses at the relevant moment. Wadsworth became very bitter at the inefficiency of the system of justice.

General Wadsworth was plagued with medical problems and was sometimes treated in the Bethesda Naval hospital. During his last surgery he was equipped with an artificial anus (colostomy). I could hear that he was in tears when he told me on the telephone how a doctor had informed him that he had only ninety more days to live.

He was estranged from his brother for many years. Apparently on my urging he reconciled with his brother, who lived in the Midwest. The brother, however, had cancer and was unable to visit the general or even to attend his funeral when Wadsworth died in 1996.

Other luncheon buddies during my retirement have been Professor Hsueh, Professor Emeritus Wayne Cole (Department of History), Professor Emeritus Thornton Anderson (Department of Government and Politics), who died in December 1997, and my neighbor and hiking companion, Robert Gilroy, a retired official of the General Accounting Office.

MY SEVENTY-FIFTH BIRTHDAY

In December 1994, Myra's sister-in-law Anita Koehler, and Anita's daughter, Susan, flew from Wisconsin to visit us. Two days after Christmas, on my birthday, Anita, Susan, and I spent the day at the National Zoo, where we had a good chance to see, among other wonders, the panda bear.

When we got back to our house at supper time, we were surprised by the presence of many of my friends and relatives. This was my 75th birthday party. It had been arranged by Myra and Gale. The Plischkes had come down from Gettysburg. My niece, Carol Oakey, and her sister, Jane, and Jane's daughter were there. Professor and Mrs. Wayne Cole came. Also Professor and Mrs. Anderson, and Andy's beautiful daughter. Professor Hsueh and Cordelia Hsueh and General William Wadsworth were there. Dr. Walter Hohenstein (a former overseas professor then connected with the university administration) came with his German wife, Heidi. Jane's husband, Jerry, came late, from Annapolis.

I was flabbergasted. That birthday party was a high point in my sunset years. By the year 2006, Professor Anderson, Professor and Mrs. Plischke, Doctor and Mrs. Hohenstein, Cordelia Hsueh, and General Wadsworth, over one third of the eighteen guests, had died.

SEEING AMERICA

Before she married, Myra had enjoyed living and working in both the Midwest and the West and felt that I should become acquainted with the Rocky Mountains and Yellowstone. In late September 1995 we took a deluxe bus trip sponsored by Tauk Tours, beginning in Rapid City, S.D. We saw Mt. Rushmore, the Big Horn mountains, Yellowstone Park (with nights at Yellowstone Lake and the Old Faithful Inn), the Grand Teton Mountains, and Salt Lake City, where the tour ended. From Salt Lake City we flew to Filer, Idaho, (near Twin Falls) to visit Myra's cousin Marinette, whom she hadn't seen for forty years, and Marinette's husband, Jack Jordan. On the way home we stopped in Denver to visit Myra's long-time Madison friends, Vonnie and Gil Hill.

In May 1996 Myra and I flew to Madison to attend our university class reunions. The largest reunion was that of the class of 1946, Myra's class and also that of my brother John. The fiftieth reunion dinner filled the grand ballroom of the Student Union, the very place where in 1950 I had first been introduced to Myra and where she had made a very strong impression on me. The fifty-fifth reunion of my class of 1941 was celebrated with a dinner and a musical program followed by group singing led by my Lancaster and Madison friend Orville Shetney, a professor of music at Wisconsin.

DIABETES

In June 1996, I had some painful headaches, which for me are rare. Dr. Michael Barth gave me some tests and insisted I had giant cell arteritis, or temporal arteritis (inflamation of the artery in the temple). Temporal arteritis can lead to blindness if not checked. He prescribed medication (prednisone) and told me to get a biopsy.

A doctor at Holy Cross Hospital, Dr. Eric Oristian, performed the biopsy. I was given local anesthesia and was conscious throughout the procedure and I engaged him in a conversation. When he said he had interned at George Washington University Hospital, I asked him if he had been there when Reagan was brought in after being shot in front of the Washington Hilton Hotel (in 1981). He said yes, he was the first doctor to see Reagan, and he was the doctor who sent Reagan to a brain specialist. My biopsy was positive for temporal arteritis.

In a few weeks, my gait became unsteady, and having lost much of my sense of balance, I could no longer ride my bicycle. My eyebrows and beard, which had lost their hair several years previously, began to grow back. After a few months I had a heavy beard and had to shave every day. I told the doctor about these miracles and he joked that perhaps we had discovered a cure for baldness.

One day in September, I fell into a coma, and Myra called Dr. Barth's week-end number but was unable to contact him. Finally she called 911. An ambulance took me to the Montgomery General Hospital. I heard later that I had shouted "Save my sight" frequently as I was being checked into the hospital. My concern seems to have been that I did not want my medication for temporal arteritis to be halted.

I was under intensive care for a week and was told that I was diabetic. Five or six doctors were assigned to my case. I was prescribed insulin injections 3 times a day, and five times a day I had to measure my blood sugar level using device to prick my finger. After I returned home, a nurse visited the house each day to teach Myra how to administer insulin to me. When my hands became less shaky, I could learn to do it myself. It was a tricky procedure, involving the mixing of two kinds of insulin for each injection.

During a routine checkup, Dr. Innerfield, who was in charge of my case, became concerned about an abscess on my buttocks, and sent me directly to the hospital, which was across the road from his office building. I got pneumonia while in the hospital. I was put in an isolation room, was hitched to an oxygen tank, was fed and given antibiotics intravenously and subjected to numerous tests. After two weeks in the hospital I was finally released. After I got home nearly all of every day was taken up with my medications, tests, dietary meals, and snacks. I was weak and had to walk with a walker, and then with a cane.

In January, 1997, I had two insulin shocks, so I was taken completely off insulin. Dr. Innerfield put it in writing that my steroid-induced IDDM (insulin-dependent diabetes mellitus) had been "resolved."

Needless to say, I was deeply grateful to Myra for the attention and care that she had given me during my long bout of diabetes. As a tribute to her in September 1997 I made a modest donation to the Monona Terrace Community and Convention Center, designed by Frank Lloyd Wright, in Madison. One of the tiles to be installed on the rooftop garden floor of the center would bear the inscription: "MYRA & TED MCNELLY."

MORE TRIPS

After my recovery from diabetes, Myra and I took a second bus tour of the West in May and June of 1997. The Coles had recently taken this tour and recommended it. About half of the members of the tour group were English, whom we found very congenial. (Saga Tours had a large English clientele.) We visited Albuquerque and Santa Fe. I especially enjoyed riding the perilous narrow-gauge railway from Durango to Silverton. We saw Canyonlands, the Arches, Bryce Canyon, Grand Canyon, and Mesa Verde National Parks, Lake Powell, Scottsdale, Oak Creek Canyon, Montezuma's castle, and Phoenix.

In July, we visited Mark's parents in Bucks County Pennsylvania, seeing New Town, Peddlers' Village, and Washington Crossing. In September, Myra and I attended a reunion of Myra's cousins on her mother's side in Lancaster, Wisconsin, and visited relatives in Madison.

I was invited to speak at the forum on the fiftieth anniversary of the Japanese Constitution in Tokyo in November 1997, as described in chapter 15. I wanted Myra to come with me, but she said that she had seen enough of Japan. To sweeten the trip for her, I set up a side trip to Taiwan, which she had never seen. The day after the forum we went sightseeing in Kamakura with the Nishis, who took us to a fine outdoor restaurant for a tempura dinner. In Taiwan we joined tour groups to see the National Museum, the Chiang Kai-shek memorial (our guide, a bitter critic of Chiang, insisted that Chiang had been responsible for murdering many fine people), a geyser and waterfalls in the countryside, and music and dancing by native (non-Chinese) Formosans in the mountains. In the evening in Taipei I enjoyed seeing the shops near our hotel but because of my defective eyesight was afraid to cross the street with its heavy traffic. After returning to States, I had the cataracts removed.

In September 1998, after I had chaired a panel on E. Herbert Norman at the American Political Science Association in Boston, Myra and I took a one-day bus excursion to Plymouth. There at the reconstructed village of the Pilgrims, I talked with several of the actors who impersonated the original settlers. I conversed with Miles Standish and Mary Brewster, and asked questions about my pilgrim ancestors, William White and Richard Warren. The weather and scenery were beautiful.

Shortly after our Boston-Plymouth trip, between September 25 and October 6, Myra and I took a bus tour of Canada's maritime provinces. We flew to Halifax and checked into a hotel near the Citadel. On my own I climbed a steep hill to the fortress, which had sophisticated historical exhibits and commanded a fine view of the harbor. However, I had a headache and felt giddy, apparently the result of the steep climb, and briefly feared that our trip would have to be cut short. We went for a bus tour of the city of Halifax and saw Peggy's Cove and the Citadel, which I had just seen on my own.

On a later day we drove via a causeway to Chéticamp on Cape Breton Island, where we spent the night. French-Canadians entertained us with their vigorous Acadian step dancing and fiddle playing. We drove the next day to Ingonish on the east coast of the island and stayed overnight at the elegant Keltic Lodge, which commanded a splendid view of the coast.

The following day we went to Prince Edward Island. We had lunch at the Green Gable house (made famous by L. M. Montgomery's novel, *Anne of Green Gables*, which we had seen dramatized on Public Television). We took a ferry to New Brunswick and visited the Acadian country made famous in Longfellow's *Evangeline*. Then another ferry to Nova Scotia, where we had a farewell lobster dinner party.

Myra was the chauffeur for the Coles and me when we went to Gettysburg to visit Elmer Plischke on October 19. Myra's cousin Forbes Koehler and his wife visited us later in the month. From November 16 to 20 Myra and I were in Ocean City, which by this time of the year was cold and largely deserted. However we had fun eating out and I especially enjoyed the bracing Ocean air.

Professor Hsueh hosted a party in honor of my seventy-ninth birthday on December 27, still 1998. The Coles and the Shulmans were there as well as the Hsuehs and McNellys. We had dinner at a Chinese restaurant.

In 1999, Myra and I made an exciting trip to Finland, described in another chapter. Myra's back surgery the following year reduced our options for travel, but in 2000 Myra was able to drive us and the Coles to Gettysburg to visit Elmer Plischke. In October she and I drove to Ocean City, where we enjoyed four days where we had a balcony overlooking the Atlantic Ocean. When Jim and Liz came to visit us in April 2001, Myra drove Liz, Jim, and Douglas to see the sights of Gettysburg.

ALASKA

Our American travels came to a climax in August 2001, when we flew to Fairbanks, Alaska, to begin a tour with the Holland America line. We took a one-day cruise on the Tanana River with stops to see native villages, huskies pulling sleds, and wildlife. We took a train to Denali National Park, where we stayed overnight and took bus rides into the wilderness. The next day, as we were reboarding our train, a moose strolled along the tracks to say goodbye. From Anchorage we took a bus to Seward, where we boarded the *m. s. Statendam.*

Our stateroom had a large picture window and a veranda. As Myra had difficulty walking and as the weather was either cold or rainy or both, we were able to see a great deal from our quarters without having to venture on the open decks. There were many activities on board, including gambling, shops, movies, stage shows, a piano bar, a beauty parlor, and fitness programs. Myra could not attend most of the stage shows as the theater was on the far end of the boat and it was unsafe for her to walk when the sea was rough. She was unable to see a hilarious ventriloquist performance (Patrick Murray and Matilda, his sassy Jamaican dummy), so I ordered a video of the act to be mailed to us in Maryland.

Myra and Ted at Mendenhall Lake and Glacier, Alaska

On our 41st wedding anniversary (September 4, 2001) we cruised Glacier Bay. Twice we took small ships to see otters, seals, sea lions, and whales. We took an excursion to Mendenhall Glacier. At Ketchikan in a driving rain, we visited a native village to see Indian dancing and totem poles. We disembarked in Vancouver on September 9, and from there we flew to Toronto to change planes, arriving in Baltimore at 11:30 PM.

A taxi brought us home in the early morning of September 10. While I was watching the 7:30 A.M. news the following day, I saw live pictures of the 9/11 attack on the World Trade Center. If our Alaskan tour had lasted a day longer, we might have been seriously delayed trying to reenter the United States from Canada.

Life in Stonegate was not particularly exciting, and Myra and I spent three days in October in Ocean City.

HEALTH PROBLEMS

During our family's residence in Japan in 1980, Myra found walking increasingly painful, and after our return to the States, she had the bunions on both her feet surgically removed.

Arthritis had so ravaged her knee joints that in 1991 walking became excruciatingly painful. She had both her knees replaced by a surgeon affiliated with Johns Hopkins Orthopedics at Good Samaritan Hospital in Baltimore. (The alternative would have been confinement to a wheelchair.) The knee operations were successful, but in 1992 and 1993 her left and right kneecaps respectively had to be replaced. In 1999 at the time of arthroscopic surgery on her right shoulder, it was discovered that she had no rotator cuff in that shoulder, and in 2002 she was told that there was no rotator cuff in her left shoulder. She is unable to reach most of the dishes in the kitchen cupboard.

In 1999 she was operated on for a ruptured disk. While she was home under my care recovering from the last operation, she began to run a fever and became very weak. Unable to cope, I called 911 in the middle of the night. She was hospitalized and a doctor at Holy Cross Hospital later told me that Myra had almost died of pneumonia. In February 2000 she was again operated on to relieve her of severe sciatica.

In 2002 while traveling with Myra to attend the 65th year reunion of the class of 1937 of Madison West High School, I fell with a broken right hip in the Cleveland airport. On July 11 Dr. Mark Panigutti gave me a partial hip replacement at the Southwest General Health Center in Middleburg Heights, Ohio, near the Cleveland airport. The personnel at the hospital seemed much more committed and caring than the staffs at the hospitals in the Washington area. During my two weeks of treatment and therapy in Ohio, Myra resided in a nearby motel and visited me every day. (The motel gave Myra a reduced rate, the motel's bus driver watched after her, and the hospital provided her with a wheel chair for her comfort during our visits.) Back in Maryland, after several months I could walk without a cane, without pain, and without a limp.

In December 2002, during a periodic examination for diabetes, Dr. Innerfield noticed an irregular heartbeat and sent me directly from his office to Holy Cross Hospital for an examination. I was diagnosed with atrial fibrillation, placed on medication, and released from the hospital after five days. In April and May 2003, I received cardioversions at Holy Cross Hospital, but neither treatment had any lasting effect. I was prescribed coumadin to prevent clotting.

About midnight on November 22, 2003, as she was entering our bedroom, Myra fell down. I phoned 911. She was taken to Montgomery General Hospital. Instead of operating on her there, it was considered expedient to move her to Holy Cross to place her under the care of her orthopedic surgeon, Dr. Antoni Goral, who had recently made repairs on her left knee. Dr Goral found that she had broken both bones of her lower left leg and damaged her knee replacement. Following an elaborate operation and therapy at Holy Cross Hospital, Myra returned home on December 18. Because our only available bed was too low for her to get up from, we rented a hospital bed which we kept in the family room. For several weeks she had home care, with a therapist and bath lady each coming about once a week. She was fitted with a brace for her leg but was still unable to climb stairs. During the weeks of Myra's recovery at home, I did all of the cooking and shopping. Myra is remarkably aware, well organized, and not hesitant to ask for help. She will need further surgery to repair her knee and leg.

In February 2004, I was diagnosed with a bilateral inguinal hernia, and an operation ("repair") was performed on March 11 by Dr. Eric Oristian. Six weeks after the operation my two incisions no longer pained me and I had no complaints. In 2005, because Myra could not longer climb the stairs, the downstairs den, which had served as Myra's office, became our master bedroom, and a shower was installed in the powder room.

A SISTER AND TWO BROTHERS

My sister Lucille did not complete university and for a while worked for the telephone company. She fell in love with and married Charles Oakey, who had played basketball at West High. While helping Lucille to bring up their children, Charles earned a law degree at the University of Wisconsin. He passed the state bar examination, but was unable to find a position as a lawyer. For a while he sold paint for a wholesale firm and because of his asthma moved his family to Texas. In 1960, Charles found a good position in an insurance company in Madison and his family, which included two girls and two boys, moved back to Madison. My mother sold the three houses she had inherited from Gramma Taylor, and Charles and Lucille bought the house on Regent Street which had been built by Grampa Taylor. I was pleased see that beautiful home kept in the family. Charles, afflicted with Alzheimer's disease, died in 1991. Lucille has four children, six grandchildren, and three great grandchildren.

Carol Oakey, Lucille's oldest child, was briefly a Peace Corps volunteer in Africa and for a while taught school in the District of Columbia. She married David Van Horn, a landscape architect in Boston. They had two children, Theodore ("Teddy") and Amy. When David got a job in Maryland they moved to Silver Spring. David and Carol divorced, and in 2003 Carol retired from her work in the editorial staff of the *Washington Post*. Teddy became a nuclear engineer and Amy earned a law degree.

Steve Oakey, Lucille's second child, became a sports referee and newspaper reporter. From time to time Lucille flies to San Diego to visit Steve's family. John Oakey, Lucille's third child, is married, lives in Madison, and has a daughter, Tyler-Rose, who is learning to play the cello. Jane Oakey, Lucille's fourth child, is now married to her second husband, Jerry Chambers, and commutes from their country home near Annapolis to College Park to edit a trade journal. Their daughter Katie, who majored in cello under the virtuoso, Evelyn Elsing, at the University of Maryland, recently won a scholarship to study at the San Francisco Conservatory of Music.

My brother John, a retired professor of the University of Wisconsin, and his wife, Pamela, are the parents of a daughter, who has never married, and a son, who has a daughter by his second wife. My brother Jim, a retired policeman, and his wife, Patricia, a nurse and an officer in a nursing organization, have four sons and a daughter. Jim and Pat have spent several of their retirement years traveling about the United States in their large RV, sometimes visiting their children in the Madison area. They continue to maintain a permanent residence in Florida, and have decided to remain there rather than return to Madison, where the climate is too severe for Pat.

My first cousin, George McNelly, was for twenty-one years dean of the School of Technology at Purdue University, and is now retired and living with his wife in a home on the shore of a lake in Michigan. In the course of my genealogical research, I became acquainted with Mahlon McNelly, Jr. ("Mike"), a first cousin of my father. While a soldier in World War II, Mike survived an airplane crash off the coast of Japan.

CHAPTER 14

THE JAPANESE CONSTITUTION

In the fall of 1960 I was immediately involved in the graduate as well as the undergraduate program, at College Park, conducting seminars and supervising master's theses and doctoral dissertations in the Department of Government and Politics, in the College of Business and Public Administration. Like the other professors in the department, I was required to teach one or another of our two mandatory introductory courses, i.e., government of the United States or introduction to political science. (I preferred and was assigned the latter). In addition, I taught a wide variety of courses, including international relations, U.S. foreign policy, comparative politics (introductory and advanced), and Asian politics, as well as Japanese politics. Sometimes I would teach more than one section of introduction to political science. I sometimes participated in doctoral examinations administered by other departments, and often taught in summer sessions. Committee work took much time.

In addition to our day jobs, some of the professors in the department taught in the night program, which, like the overseas programs, was administered by the College of Special and Continuing Studies (now known as the University College). As the courses in the night program were apt to duplicate those we taught during the day, the night classes would not involve preparing completely new lectures.

Professor Elmer Plischke, the head of the Department of Government and Politics, persuaded me to teach a night course in international relations at the Pentagon once a week, which would supplement my income. I was not then familiar with the roads and traffic patterns of the Washington area, and for a whole semester took a long circuitous route to the Pentagon, which had to be reached by driving from suburban Maryland through downtown Washington, D.C. and taking a bridge to the Virginia side of the Potomac River. Twice, after reaching Virginia I completely missed the proper turnoff to the Pentagon. As a result of this confusion I arrived at my first Pentagon class over an hour late. To my amazement, the class was still there, at least fifty students in the auditorium were waiting patiently for my arrival. In day school, if a professor is late by fifteen minutes, the students are free to leave. But at the Pentagon, as in the Maryland Overseas Program, the students consisted largely of military personnel, who had been trained to be patient about such things.

Plischke and I had served in the military administrations in Germany and Japan respectively. Plischke especially, I think, felt that participation in the Maryland's Pentagon program was a part of his patriotic effort to win the war and ensure the peace. The Pentagon courses sometimes included graduate-level seminars. Many of the night courses were held on the College Park campus, in buildings that were being used for the day program. Some classes were held at nearby military bases. For several terms I taught at Fort Meade, a huge base that included the National Security Agency (NSA), successor to the Army Security Agency. The students at Ford Meade were excellent, but I disliked the drive to get there. It involved the late afternoon rush hour between Washington, D.C., and Annapolis. In the return drive at night I would sometimes get lost in the base itself or on the roads homeward, that looked completely different at night. I would leave home late in the afternoon and sometimes eat supper at a fast food restaurant in a small town outside the base. For years I taught in the night program because I needed the extra pay, but I became increasingly aware that it was cutting into time that could otherwise be used for research and recreation.

TEXTBOOKS

In the months just before my return to the United States in 1960, I had begun correspondence with Houghton Mifflin Company concerning the possibility of my writing a textbook on Japanese politics. This book would be in a series of textbooks on comparative politics under the general editorship of Professor Dayton D. McKean of the University of Colorado. January 9, 1961, is the date of a formal "agreement" with the publisher that I would write the manuscript for *The Contemporary Government of Japan.*

When the manuscript was two-thirds complete, Professor Plischke, who was hoping to promote me, asked to see it, and I was happy to show it to him. I became an associate professor with tenure shortly before the book was published in 1963.

Myra typed the final draft of the manuscript, but, she reminds me, she was never given the pair of shoes that she had been promised. While wrapping the manuscript for mailing, at the last moment I included several editorial cartoons from Japanese newspapers. The manuscript was mailed the following day, and permissions to include the cartoons were promptly obtained. They enlivened the text. I dedicated the book "To My Mother."

Houghton Mifflin published the 228-page volume in the spring of 1963, and simultaneously Allen and Unwin published a British edition. It was adopted at many colleges and universities, including the University of California at Berkeley. The London *Times Literary Supplement* (August 6, 1964) had kind words to say about the book:

> This is a minor *tour de force*. Professor McNelly has produced a work of interpretative scholarship within the framework of the kind of superior textbook justly cherished by dons, school-teachers, university student and the brightest sixth-form boys . . . . the author is invariably accurate, clear and judicious . . . . There is really no fault to be found in this admirable, compact, little study.

When I was invited to teach Japanese politics at Columbia University in the summer of 1963, I made the first use of the book in my classes.

In 1971 Esduck in Cairo published an Arabic translation of the book by Ali Abdel Kader.

Houghton Mifflin published the second edition, under a new title, *Politics and Government in Japan*, in 1972. The Houghton Mifflin comparative politics series was allowed to go out of existence, but in 1984 the University Press of American published the third edition. The publication of the last two editions of the book involved substantial new research and writing. (In the 1980s, I became acquainted with the daughter of the translator of the Arabic version of the book. She was a graduate student at College Park.)

In the 1960s college textbook salesmen frequently asked individual professors about their plans for publication. The success of *Contemporary Government of Japan* stimulated me to think of writing more textbooks. In my large personal collection of books and research files on the Far East, there were ample materials to compile a book of readings suitable for college courses in history and political science related to Asia. Under contract with Appleton-Century-Crofts, I produced such a textbook: *Sources in Modern East Asian History and Politics,* which was published in 1967. The project took me much more time than I had anticipated. I had to obtain permissions to use copyrighted materials, which sometimes involved locating the heirs of the original authors. The section on Vietnam had to be continually revised as the war there was ongoing. A section on India was eliminated to sharpen the focus of the book. At the end of the volume, I included a "correlation chart" which indicated the precise pages in fourteen currently used textbooks on the Far East relevant to each of the thirteen chapters of the book of readings. This chart was intended to help teachers who assigned the book to supplement the core textbooks used in their courses.

The publisher provided an attractive cover for the book, mailed brochures to relevant professors, and distributed examination copies. The book was adopted at a fair number of colleges. Once it found its way into research libraries it proved to have a shelf-life longer than that of most textbooks, and used copies continue to be advertised by on the Internet. On the other hand, editing this book took much of my time and attention, distracting me from my research specialty on the Japanese constitution and from critical political developments in the Department of Government and Politics and the Committee on East Asian Studies, of which I was the first chairman.

(While I was teaching the introductory course in political science in the auditorium, I had all of my lectures tape-recorded with the idea that the lectures might be readily converted into a textbook. The course focused heavily on political theory and comparative politics. Efforts to convert part of the tape record into a chapter of a college textbook revealed how time consuming it would be to do the massive research and editing necessary for an acceptable scholarly product, and I ultimately abandoned the project.)

A major textbook published by Harper and Row, *Introduction to Comparative Government,* under the general editorship of Michael Curtis of Rutgers University, did not contain a section on Japanese politics, and I was asked to write the Japanese section for the second edition. The book consisted of country studies by well-known specialists, including Michael Curtis and Jean Blondel, both of them leading comparativists. I was happy to join the group as a contributor to the second, third, fourth, and fifth editions, which appeared in 1990, 1993, 1997, and 2003. The fourth and fifth editions were published by Longman. I was an emeritus professor when I wrote for the last three editions. My section on Japan in the last edition was 64 double-column pages long.

From time to time, I served as a "referee," one of the specialists consulted by editors who were considering the possible publication of manuscripts on the occupation of Japan or textbook manuscripts. Publishers who compensated me for my advice on manuscripts include the Congressional Quarterly, Dorsey Press, Harper and Row, Oxford University Press, Princeton University Press, University of Chicago Press, the University of Georgia Press, and the University Press of Colorado. My critiques usually included suggestions for the improvement of the manuscripts, suggestions on which the authors sometimes acted.

Although college administrators frequently make public declarations about the priority that their institutions place on teaching, the reality may be otherwise. It is not easy to evaluate a professor's teaching ability (school administrators virtually never monitor classrooms), but in the competition for jobs, promotions, and salary increments, the professor whose scholarly publications attract favorable attention to his department and college is more apt to be a winner than one whose brilliance does not reach beyond the classroom. At one departmental faculty meeting the chairman frankly told us that the best way to get a promotion in his department was to come up with a job offer from another institution. With impressive publication records and astute networking, some professors are in a much stronger position than others to get promotions or job offers from outside. Finally, at major research-oriented universities, a minimal publication requirement may have to be met even to keep one's job, let alone get a promotion. The mantra "publish or perish" pretty well sums up the truth about academic careers in major universities in the United States.

RESEARCHERS

The reader may recall that when I arrived in Tokyo in August 1958 to teach in the Far East Program of the University of Maryland, Satō Isao and Satō Tatsuo, who were drafting the reports of the Japanese Government's Commission on the Constitution, contacted me, pointing out that I was the American author of a work paralleling theirs, namely of a narrative and analysis of the adoption of Japan's new constitution. The commission had already published in June 1958 a Japanese translation of the paper that I had presented at the Association for Asian Studies meeting in New York in the preceding April, "The Japanese Constitution in the Cold War," (translated by Kobayashi Shōzō, *Kempō Chōsakai Jimukyoku, Kenshi* No. 22,). I was invited to a meeting of the subcommittee on the enactment of the constitution meeting in Hakone, where copies my Columbia dissertation were discussed and I was asked questions concerning it. The commission published a Japanese translation of major portions of my dissertation.

The Washington, D.C. area was the most favorable location in the United States for research on the origins of Japan's postwar constitution. A number of retired Occupation personnel resided in Washington. It was here that the bulk of the records of the Occupation of Japan are kept. Initially they were stored in the torpedo factory in Alexandria, Virginia (here torpedoes had been manufactured for the first World War), and Professor Robert E. Ward of the University of Michigan and I (in the 1960s) both consulted the records there. This enormous collection was later moved to the National Records Center in Landover, Maryland, and finally deposited in the newly constructed Archives II, in College Park, Maryland. In the meantime, the relevant files of the late Charles L. Kades and Justin Williams are deposited in the University of Maryland McKeldin Library. (Many of these records have been copied and are maintained in Japan's Diet Library.)

On November 20, 1961, I became directly acquainted with a principal American author of the Japanese Constitution. In Japan I had copied the notes of an American Army officer who had heard Rodman Hussey lecture, and from these notes as well as my other research I had a fair idea of Hussey's important role. He proposed that we lunch together at the famous Yenching Palace restaurant on Connecticut Avenue. I would recognize him by his stocky build, his gray hair, and his mustache. When I saw him he reminded me very much of a stereotypical

British colonel. As he had aspirations to publish an article or book himself on the Japanese constitution and as I had similar aspirations, he seemed to regard me as a competitor and was reluctant to tell me very much. Also at that time, he may still have been employed by the CIA. He had read Robert Ward's famous article in the December 1956 *American Political Science Review*, which had criticized the American occupiers for imposing their draft constitution on the Japanese. He had contacted Ward and explained to him the constraints under which the Americans had operated and the need to act expeditiously. Hussey said that he had succeeded in persuading Ward to agree with him. Hussey was thinking about engaging in a scholarly polemic with the critics of the Japanese constitution.

Our conversation became more pleasant as we savored the wine and the Chinese cuisine. After saying goodbye, I thought it prudent to remain in my parked car to allow the effects of the drinks to wear off and to write a summary of our conversation. (It is evident from the Hussey papers at the University of Michigan Library that Hussey had been working on his papers with the intention of writing a book. However he never did publish a book or a journal article, even though he had written the section on the new constitution for the 1949 SCAP publication, *Political Reorientation of Japan*.)

Early in the 1960s Osborne Hauge, one of the American authors of the Japanese constitution, invited Myra and me to a dinner party at his home in Virginia which Robert E. Ward also attended. There I first met Dr. Justin Williams. At that time, Williams, who had served in SCAP's Government Section, was joining the administrative staff of the University of Maryland. (Before World War II, Williams had been a professor of history and head of the department of social science at the University of Wisconsin at River Falls.) Williams and I became friends, and I assisted him in connection with the publication of one of his articles on the Occupation appearing in the *American Political Science Review*, and with various aspects of his book, *Japan's Political Revolution under MacArthur* (University of Georgia Press, 1979). I regret that I unreasonably failed to accept his kind invitation to me to write a preface for this informative and insightful book on the Occupation. Williams was in contact with General Courtney Whitney and General MacArthur in New York and encouraged me to continue my research on the Occupation. I persuaded him to present a talk on MacArthur at an initiation dinner of the Pi Sigma Alpha political science honorary society at the University of Maryland. (Dr. Williams died in 2002 after a long illness in Florida.)

Japanese and Americans researching the Occupation of Japan who came to the Washington area for their research would from time to time contact me. Sometimes their research proposals agenda formally designated me as a collaborator. In particular, Amakawa Akira, Inumaru Hideo, Nishi Osamu, and Takemae Eiji, leading Japanese authorities on the formulation of the postwar Japanese constitution, collaborated with me when engaged in research in the Washington area. Other visitors were Furukawa Atsushi, Kawai Yoshikazu, Kobayashi Naoki, Okudaira Yasuhiro, Ōnuma Yasuaki, Sugihara Seishiro, Tsuji Kiyoaki, Tsunoda Jun, Watanuki Jōji, and Yoshida Yutaka.

In March 1963, Professor Satō Isao, of the Commission on the Constitution, visited the Washington, D.C. area. The cherry blossoms were then in full bloom. He joined Myra and me for dinner at our apartment in Mount Rainier, Maryland. (Little Douglas rocked his little rocking chair too vigorously and rolled over forward with it onto the floor, but was unharmed.) Satō, Myra, and I had luncheon at the Cosmos Club with Paul M. A. Linebarger, the China expert who headed the School of Advanced International Studies. (I later learned that Linebarger, during the war an expert on psychological warfare, had ghost written parts of Ambassador Joseph Grew's wartime *Report from Tokyo* and was also the author of esteemed science fiction under the pen name Cordwainer Smith.) Linebarger once told me that although he and Owen Lattimore (the Johns Hopkins professor and principal target of Senator Joseph McCarthy) took opposite sides during the debate over recognizing Communist China, the two men were good friends and had sometimes substituted for each other's classes.

I drove with Satō to New York to a meeting of the Association for Asian Studies. There we encountered Cyrus Peake, one of the authors of the Japanese constitution. Satō, Peake, and I, joined by David Titus and one or two other scholars, had a Chinese dinner, where I made notes of our conversation on the menu.

In May 1963 Dr. Alfred Oppler, the eminent jurist who had served in SCAP'S Government Section while the proposed democratic constitution was being debated in the Diet, visited Washington. He kindly spoke to my advanced class in comparative government at the University of Maryland. At my house in Takoma Park he spotted my harpsichord and played by memory a little piece by Bach. He later wrote a memoir on the Occupation: *Legal Reform in Occupied Japan: A Participant Looks Back* (Princeton University Press, 1976).

PUBLISHING

James Morley, an authority on Japanese politics then director of the East Asian Institute, kindly invited me to teach at Columbia University during the summer of 1963. I could choose between teaching either two classes or one class. I chose to teach only the course in Japanese politics so that I might have time for research in the university library. I was especially interested in the Oral History Collection, which included interviews with American officials in the Occupation of Japan. For the Columbia class, we used my brand new textbook on Japanese politics, *Contemporary Government of Japan* (Houghton Mifflin, 1963). This book, of course, heavily emphasized the importance of Japan's new constitution.

I was one of the "eminent political scientists" invited to contribute articles (in my case on 20 specified subjects) to Joseph Dunner, ed., *Dictionary of Political Science* (New York: Philosophical Library, 1964).

The editor of *Current History*, a publication sponsored by the *New York Times*, in 1965 asked me on very short notice—one of their proposed authors was unable to fulfill his obligation—to write an article on "Japan's Role in South Asia." I promptly produced my article (*Current History*, Vol. 49, No.291 [November 1965], pp. 284-293). The Mayfair Subscription Agency published a bulletin announcing "Ten Outstanding Magazine Articles Selected by a Council of Librarians, November 1965," which included my *Current History* article as one of the top ten. Among the other authors cited were Tom Wicker and Hubert Humphrey.

I was forced to keep well informed of current events in Japan in the course of writing a substantial article on Japan for every annual issue of the *World Topics Yearbook* (Lake Bluff, Illinois: United Educators, Inc.) from 1968 to 1987. I contributed articles concerning the Japanese Constitution to *Japan: An Illustrated Encyclopedia* in two volumes (Tokyo: Kodansha, 1993), a subsequent one-volume version, a CD ROM version (1999), and an online version, www.ency-japan.com (2002).

In the 1960s the emerging ideological dispute between the Soviet Union and China was beginning to affect communist movements throughout the world. The Japan Communist Party appeared to be splitting up, and I began researching this issue. I presented a paper on this topic on December 28, 1966, in a panel sponsored by the National Institute of Social and Behavioral Science at the annual meeting of the Association for the Advancement of Sciences in Washington, D.C. (The paper is summarized in *Science*, Vol.155, No. 3764 [17 February, 1967], p.886, and was presented at a meeting of the Columbia University Seminar on Modern Japan.)

THE JAPAN-AMERICA SOCIETY AND THE COLUMBIA SEMINAR

Shortly after arriving in Maryland, I become interested in the activities of the Japan-America Society of Washington. The society would give receptions and dinners for Japanese prime ministers, Japanese ambassadors to the United States, and American diplomats going to Japan.

At a reception Mr. Akatani Genichi, cultural attaché at the Japanese embassy, in a conversation with me offered to donate books in English on every aspect of Japanese civilization to the University of Maryland library. I was asked to select the books we might want from a large catalog that Mr. Akatani sent to me. After conferring with Mr. Howard Rovelstad, the director of libraries at the university, I selected titles of books that the library did not already possess. In November

1964, the Japanese Ambassador Takeuchi Ryuji came to the university and formally presented the books at a ceremony attended by university President Wilson Elkins, as well as Mr. Akatani, Mr. Rovelstad, and me.

PRESENTATION OF JAPANESE BOOKS TO THE UNIVERSITY OF MARYLAND
From the left: Mr. Akatani Genichi, cultural attaché; University of Maryland President Wilson H. Elkins; Ambassador Takeuchi Ryuji; Professor McNelly; Mr. Howard Rovelstad, director of libraries at the university.]

I was invited to see the emperor of Japan on the lawn of the White House during his visit to the United States in September 1975.

The guest of honor at one Japan-America Society reception was Fukuda Takeo (prime minister 1976-78). When I mentioned to him that I was a professor of political science, he asked if I had any suggestions for him. I was so surprised that such an astute statesman was asking for my advice that I was speechless.

For several years I chaired a lecture series of the society, which every month sponsored a talk on Japan by an authority. We met in private homes and during one academic year at the American University. I later was elected to the Board of Trustees of the society, once serving as chairman of the nominating committee to propose names for the society's president. I became especially acquainted with former Ambassador William Sebald when he was president of the society and his memoirs were published.

Mike Masaoka as president of the Society especially impressed me. As a Nisei (second-generation Japanese-American), he was a principal leader of the Japanese-American community in the United States. One might wonder about possible conflicts of interest that might make it difficult for him to give his full devotion to one side or the other, but he was an unusually polished speaker and could get along with all kinds of people, including prominent retired bureaucrats and diplomats.

When I was appointed chairman of the scholarship committee, the task of launching the scholarship program became too much of a burden, and I found it necessary finally to decline re-election as a trustee. (The trustee meetings were held at luncheons in downtown Washington once a month, and travel to and from the meetings seemed to consume entire days.)

During the 1960s I became a member of the Columbia University Seminar on Modern Japan. The seminar met once a month for dinner at the Columbia University Faculty club. Papers were distributed in advance of the meetings. For several years I attended regularly, although the round trip by train or bus was very tiring. Sometimes I made reservations at hotels so that I would not have to travel back to Maryland right after the meeting. The dinners (especially the authentic Manhattan clam chowder) and the company of other professors of Japanese studies were very enjoyable, but sometimes because the traveling was stressful I had to struggle to stay awake during the discussions.

THE FOREIGN SERVICE INSTITUTE AND THE JAPAN FOUNDATION

In Japan while employed by MacArthur's Civil Intelligence Section, I had become acquainted with Kenneth Colton, and later when connected with the Maryland program in the Far East came to know his wife, Hattie Kawahara Colton. The Coltons were hospitable to Myra and me in Washington, where Hattie became chairman of East Asian Area and Country Studies in the State Department's Foreign Service Institute, which trained diplomats in preparation for foreign assignments. On several occasions Hattie invited me to lecture at the Institute, and in April 1967, when she had to be absent for a week, I served as her co-chairman of a three-week course on East Asia. My task was to recruit and/or introduce visiting lecturers, give one or two lectures myself, and preside over discussions. This experience made it possible to become acquainted with some of the leading authorities on Asia who served as our guest lecturers.

In 1973 I received a fellowship from the Japan Foundation for six months of research in Japan. During the summer months I was joined by my family, and the four of us lived in a professor's house we sublet on the campus of the International Christian University. Professors Takemae Eiji and Amakawa Akira, who were researching the Occupation, interviewed me at the house. In the fall, Myra and the children returned to Maryland and I resided at the International House of Japan. In another chapter I described our experience as a family living in Tokyo.

Although the most famous feature of the Japanese constitution was the ban on war and arms, the Japanese government, encouraged by the United States, was engaged in building up its "self-defense forces." I contributed an article on "The Constitutionality of the Japanese Defense Establishment" to a book edited by James H. Buck, *The Modern Japanese Military System* (Beverley Hills, California: Sage Publications, 1975), pp. 99-112. This article was reprinted in *Perspectives on Japan's External Relations: Views from America*, edited by David J. Lu and published in 1982 by the Center for Japanese Studies at Bucknell University.

BINATIONAL RESEARCH ON THE OCCUPATION OF JAPAN

Professor Robert E. Ward of the University of Michigan and Professor Sakamoto Yoshikazu of Tokyo University obtained substantial grants from the Social Science Research Foundation and the Japan Society for the Promotion of Science for a binational study of the Occupation reforms in Japan. This project supported my research in Japan for several months. The participants had two meetings in the Royal Lahaina Hotel, Kaanapali, Maui, Hawaii. The objective of the first meeting (November 29-December 2, 1975) was to get acquainted and refine our research objectives and the objective of the second (July 16-22, 1978) was to discuss one another's papers and the results of our studies.

The preparation of two books, one in English and one in Japanese, was itself a major project. At our second meeting we were told to make draconian cuts in the length of our papers. Professor Ward, who edited the English volume, was for a while invalided and involved with other projects. The papers of the Japanese participants had to be translated into English, while the papers of the American participants had to be translated in Japanese. As the text was largely concerned with complex legal and ideological issues, the task of translating proved too challenging even for the professional translators originally contracted. As a result, for example, Mrs. Sakamoto, who knew English well, produced the Japanese translation of my paper. (Unfortunately revisions in my paper which I had sent to professor Ward did not reach Mrs. Sakamoto, so that the Japanese version of my paper disagrees on some points with the English version.)

Sakamoto and Ward, although collaborating on the first chapter, were unable to agree on the conclusion, so that the English and Japanese editions of the book were somewhat different in content and tone. The University Press of Tokyo published the Japanese edition, and the University of Hawaii Press published the English edition. Because of the difficulties I have mentioned, it was not until 1987, nine years after the last meeting of our group, that Robert E. Ward and Sakamoto Yoshikazu, eds, *Democratizing Japan: The Allied Occupation* (University of Hawaii Press) was finally in print.

The thirteen scholars listed as contributors to the book were Amakawa Akira (Yokohama National University); Hans H. Baerwald (University of California, Los Angeles), who had served in MacArthur's Government Section, was an expert on the purge, and had written textbooks on Japanese government; Theodore McNelly (University of Maryland); Ota Masahide (University of the Ryukyus), member of a prominent Okinawan family and later governor of Okinawa; Ōtake Hideo (Tōhoku University); T. J. Pempel (Cornell University); Susan Pharr (Harvard University); Sakamoto Yoshikazu (Tokyo University); Kurt Steiner (Stanford University), who had served in the International Prosecution Section in MacArthur's Tokyo headquarters and had published a book on local government in Japan; Takemae Eiji, probably Japan's premier authority on the Occupation, whose 751-page book in English was published in 2002: *Inside GHQ: The Allied Occupation of Japan and Its Legacy* (New York: Continuum); Tanaka Hideo (Tokyo University), an expert on Japanese law who had taught at Harvard and published in English the 954-page *The Japanese Legal System* (University of Tokyo Press, 1976); Uchida Kenzō (Hōsei University), a distinguished journalist; and Robert E. Ward (Stanford University), then the leading American student of the Occupation, who later became president of the American Political Science Association. Three of the six Americans (Baerwald, McNelly, and Steiner) had served in MacArthur's headquarters during the Occupation, but their research assignments were not directly related to their duties in the Occupation.

ADVENTURES IN HAWAII

Our few days in Maui were completely taken up with our business, but in the evenings we took in the picturesque sights of the island, including the old whaling village Lahaina at the end of the narrow-gage railway (once used to transport pineapples) that stopped near our hotel. And still ringing in my ears are the haunting strains of Joseph Lamb's "Ragtime Nightingale," beautifully played by the pianist in the hotel bar.

My fondness for sightseeing had been rather frustrated by our busy schedule at the first Maui meeting, so that for the second meeting I planned to visit the "Big Island" (Hawaii) before proceeding to Maui. On the Big Island I asked a concierge to reserve a place for me on a conducted bus tour of the island that I had seen advertised. The tour evidently was executed only when a minimum number of participants signed up. The people at my hotel phoned neighboring hotels and were able to recruit enough tourists to justify the tour company to lease a bus and contact a guide. The tour was interesting as we circled the island, seeing a famous ranch, hot springs in the volcanic mountains, a coffee plantation and factory, and historical sites. One side of the island was blessed with lots of rain and resembled a tropical forest. The opposite side of island was extremely dry, and only sparse vegetation grew in the lava remaining from a century-old eruption.

At about 4:00 AM the following day I was awakened by people talking excitedly as an earthquake had rocked the hotel. A few hours later a severe second shock cut off the electricity in the building. The guests were directed to remain in their rooms and not enter either the elevator or the stairs. I became panicked that because of the earthquake I might not be able to catch my morning flight to Maui and would miss the meeting of researchers there. If I failed to appear at the conference, I might have trouble collecting compensation for my round trip to Hawaii. At about 9:00 AM a siren sounded. Actually the siren was supposed be an alert for the tidal wave. The earthquake had cut off the electricity intended to power the siren. Only some hours later when the electricity was restored did the siren sound the alarm. I noticed that the first floor of the new hotel across the street from ours, not yet in operation, had been flooded by the tidal wave.

I read later that a group of boy scouts had set up a camp on the beach, and when the tidal wave struck, although the boys were saved, their scoutmaster who had gone for help had been drowned. The quake had provoked volcanic activity, some of the parks were closed, and falling rocks had made it necessary to close parts of the highway that circled the island. It would be a while before anyone would take the island tour that I had enjoyed the day before the earthquake.

The scenery in Maui was splendid. One morning before dawn, some of us took a bus to the top of a mountain. When the sun rose in the east, its round reflection could be clearly seen in the sky on the western horizon. After viewing this unusual phenomenon, during the bus ride down the mountain all of the Japanese passengers were sleeping and thus failed to enjoy the view of the beautiful tropical forest on the mountain side. The beach at our hotel in Kaanapali commanded a view of the nearby island of Lanai. After swimming, while relaxing in the sun we could watch the activities of the tiny crabs living in the sand. Susan Pharr, our youthful female participant, was not the least of the attractions on our little beach.

A REVIEW OF OUR BINATIONAL BOOK

Chalmers Johnson (formerly at Berkeley, but later at the University of California at San Diego), possibly the premier Japanologist among American political scientists, wrote a long review of the Ward-Sakamoto book for the *Journal of Japanese Studies* (Vol. 14, no. 2 [Summer 1988], pp.472-480). He dealt with each of our essays separately and was kinder to me than to some of the other authors. He mentions my "expert retelling" of the writing of the Constitution of 1946, which he believed was "the best available treatment of this subject in English."

McNelly, he said, "is persuasive on the linkage between preservation of the emperor and article 9 [the renunciation of war and arms]" in the new constitution. Chalmers then quotes me at length (the only long quotation in the review):

> A principal objection to the emperor system among the Allies was that the throne had been used to justify militarism and aggression. By banning war and arms, the draft constitution would remove this objection to the perpetuation of the monarchy. Under the new constitution the emperor would no longer exercise military prerogatives; rather he would be the symbol of a pacifist state. On the basis of the logic of the situation and statements made by some of the formulators of the new constitution, I incline to the view that a principal purpose of article 9 was the preservation of the monarchy.

OTHER RELEVANT RESEARCH

The most controversial provision of the Japanese Constitution is Article 9, in which war and arms are banned. Supporters of the article praise it for preventing the possibility that Japan would go to war. Critics fear that it will make it difficult or impossible to defend Japan; they advocate making the necessary changes in the text. There is also a controversy over the origins of Article 9. Some claim that it was MacArthur's idea and that he imposed it on the Japanese. Others, citing statements by both MacArthur and Baron Shidehara, claim that Shidehara originally suggested it. The wording of the article suggested that its authors had in mind the Kellogg-Briand pact of 1928, which had outlawed war. I began my analysis of the origins of Article 9 by studying the history of the movement to outlaw war and of the Kellogg-Briand pact and relating this history to the legislative history of Japan's constitutional provision.

With financial support from the Ward-Sakamoto Japan Occupation project and the Interuniversity Seminar on Armed Forces and Society, I was able to spend the summer of 1976 on research in Japan. I was invited to participate in the Fourth Kyushu International Cultural Conference, sponsored by the Fukuoka UNESCO Association, August 1 to 4, 1977. There were fifty non-Japanese and about eighty Japanese reportedly in attendance.

Among the Japanese participants were leading academic authorities on Japanese culture and society, including Ishida Takeshi, Katō Shūichi, Nagai Michio (the former minister of education, next to whom I was for a while seated), Nakamura Takafusa, and Sakamoto Yoshikazu, while many of the non-Japanese were leading

Japanologists from universities throughout the world. These included Ronald P. Dore, Ezra Vogel, and Donald Keene. At receptions and during a bus tour that some of us took of western Kyushu, there were ample opportunities to become acquainted. I got to know K. Kesavan (Jawaharlal Nehru University), who had difficulty adjusting to Japanese food, and whom I later would meet in Washington and New Delhi; William P. Malm, musicologist at the University of Michigan, who borrowed a samisen from a geisha and sang Japanese songs for us; Lee Farnsworth from Brigham Young University, who told us how he had managed to bring his large family to reside in Japan.

My paper, "The Origin and Meaning of the Disarmament Clause of the Japanese Constitution," is printed in the report of the meeting (pp. 187-202) together with a Japanese translation (pp. 281-292).

I was asked to be one of the speakers at the closing ceremony of the conference. I protested that I did not speak Japanese well but was told that I spoke it "very clearly." With the help of a friend I wrote a little speech in Japanese. Page 373 of the conference report includes a photo of me speaking together with the text of the speech. Following the conference, thirty-nine of the international participants enjoyed a three-day bus excursion that took us to Hirado, Sasebo, Nagasaki, and Shimabara, historic sites that I had never before visited. The excursion included a performance by geisha who played rhythmic tunes on their samisen and a "stunt night."

The Summer 1977 issue of World Affairs (Vol. 140, No. 1, pp. 58-66) carried my article on "American Political Traditions and Japan's Postwar Constitution." The relevant traditions were the constitution as the supreme law, popular sovereignty, civil liberties, civilian control, judicial review, and universalism. (This particular issue of World Affairs was dedicated to the memory of Franklin Burdette, who, when head of Maryland's political science department, had been involved in my recruitment into the overseas program in 1953. He died on August 8, 1975.)

For two academic years, 1978-1980, Professor Furukawa Atsushi of the Tokyo College of Economics was a visiting scholar at Maryland working in cooperation with me on the Japanese constitution and the Occupation of Japan. Products of our collaboration included Furukawa's article in the law journal, Hōritsu Jihō (May 1979) concerning American perspectives on Japan's rearmament (pp. 159-166) and Professor Furukawa's translation into Japanese of my article on the origins of Article 9 in the same journal (pp. 178-181). The original English version of my paper is appended as a reference (pp.256-260 of the journal).

During Furukawa's stay in the United States, his family and mine became well acquainted and together saw the fireworks at the planned city, Columbia, Maryland, one fourth of July. He bought a used car, toured the United States, and gained a fluent command of spoken English language as well as producing publishable research.

Professor Furukawa Atsushi, his son, and Professor McNelly

On the request of the editors of the student daily newspaper, the *Diamondback,* for that paper I wrote two long articles on American politics: "Carter's Foreign Policy Is Projecting Weakness (January 31, 1979), and "The Reagan Record: Foreign Policy (January 27, 1982) The article on Reagan was translated by Duck Kim, a graduate student, and published in the Korean journal, *Tongil* (April 4, 1982, pp. 96-99)

Nostalgic for Europe, I submitted a paper on "Implications for Teaching in the Differences between Adult and Adolescent Students of Political Science," for presentation at the International Conference on the Improvement of University Teaching in Aachen (Aix-la-Chapelle), West Germany, July 26-29, 1978. While asking for travel funds from President Ben Massey of the University College, I failed to notice that the sofa on which I was sitting did not have arms and I inadvertently slid onto the floor. Although I was not physically hurt, this mishap may have worked in my favor in the mind of the sympathetic president, and he granted me the travel subsidy. My paper was reported in the proceedings of the conference, and the trip to Germany provided me with a chance to view Charlemagne's tomb and visit my old friend, Ulrich Groenke, in Frankfurt.

RESEARCH ON A FULBRIGHT GRANT

With the support of Sakamoto Yoshikazu, I was awarded a Fulbright grant for research in the Faculty of Law, University of Tokyo, during my sabbatical leave for the spring of 1980. I went to Japan late in December 1979 and was assigned office space at the University of Tokyo and living quarters in that university's guest facility in the Shirogane neighborhood of Tokyo. When my family came to Japan in January 1980 we leased a house south of the Higashi Koganei station on the Chuo Line. (In Chapter 13 I described our family life in Tokyo.)

As the Fulbright grant allowed me a full year in Japan, I was able to persuade the Fulbright officers in Tokyo to allow me to return to Japan for the summer of 1981. By using my sabbatical semester plus two summers, I was able to enjoy the full extent of my one-year Fulbright grant while at the same time minimizing the amount of salary lost at Maryland.

PROFESSOR SHIDEHARA MICHITARO

My most important research accomplishment was a long interview on the afternoon of April 22, 1980, with Professor Shidehara Michitaro, retired from Dokkyō University. Professor Shidehara was the son Prime Minister Shidehara Kijuro, the alleged originator of Article 9, the ban on war and arms in the postwar Japanese Constitution.

Professor Shidehara, who spoke English fluently, insisted that while his father was a strong advocate of peace and disliked war, he would never have advocated that Japan disarm itself unilaterally. Shidehara was unequivocal in his contention that his father could not have been the originator of the ban on weapons in the constitution. He repeatedly reiterated this view throughout our conversation which lasted for over four hours.

As reported in the Rowell papers, in his talks with General MacArthur Premier Shidehara had objected that if Japan gave up its military forces other countries might not follow Japan's example. Thus Shidehara Michitaro's statements to me corroborated the objections to Japan's unilateral disarmament that Premier Shidehara had expressed to MacArthur in 1946.

While I never doubted the sincerity of Premier Shidehara's devotion to peace and I had no reason to believe that he opposed the ban on *war* in the constitution, I had never been convinced by statements made by either Shidehara or by MacArthur that Shidehara had initiated the ban on *armaments* in the constitution. My doubts about Shidehara's purported advocacy of the unilateral disarmament of Japan in the constitution were a distinguishing feature of my writing on the formulation of Japan's basic law. I believed that Colonel Charles L. Kades and General Courtney Whitney may have been the actual initiators of Article 9 and that it was they who may have influenced MacArthur to insist on this provision for Japan's new constitution. My long interview with Shidehara's son constituted powerful evidence in support of my point of view.

The September 1980 issue of *Keizai Jidai,* includes a long article (pp. 42-47) by Professor Shidehara entitled "Concerning Professor McNelly's New View That Puts an End to the Fabrication that Shidehara Proposed Article 9 of the Japanese Constitution [my translation]." In the article, Professor Shidehara adduces substantial evidence corroborating my thesis.

I presented a paper on "The Japanese Experience with Constitutional Disarmament and Its Relevance for the Elimination of War" at the 20th International Conference of Orientalists in Japan, held May 9, 10, 17, 1980 in Tokyo and Kyoto, sponsored by the Tōhō Gakkai (the Institute of Eastern Culture. (A summary appears in the *Abstract of Papers,* published by the Tōhō Gakkai, p.49.)

At the meeting I met a professor at the Defense Institute in Tokyo, who invited me to address the institute, which I was happy to do. I insisted that as a Fulbrighter I could not accept an honorarium. However the institute kindly gave me a large quartz-activated clock in a rustic wooden frame, which now graces a wall of our kitchen.

The *Japan Times,* Tokyo's daily newspaper in English, on June 8, 1980, published my article, "'Peace Constitutions' Can't Bring End to World's Wars: Simultaneous Universal Disarmament Unlikely—Even Japan Maintains Costly SDF [Self-Defense Forces]."

PROFESSOR NISHI OSAMU

Professor Nishi Osamu of Komazawa University, who specializes in defense law studies, took an interest in my research and arranged for me to give several lectures before Japanese groups. A version of one of these lectures was published as an article on the Japanese constitution and disarmament in *Bōeihō Kenkyū* (Vol. 5 [September 1981], pp.121-138, translated by Yasuda Hiroshi). Myra and I recall with particular pleasure our visit on July 3, 1980, to the National Defense Academy in Yokosuka, where I spoke on the origins of Article 9.

Professor Nishi took me on July 21, 1980, to visit the base of the Japanese Air Defense Force at Hyakuri, near Tokyo. He introduced me to the officers of the base, and they executed a scramble (a launch of aircraft) said to be in honor of my visit. I was invited to try out the seat of one of their fighter jets (but I did not fly in it), and I told the people there in my clumsy Japanese about how my mother had been born of missionary parents in Kanazawa. The weather that day was beautiful, and I was astonished at how welcome the officers there made me feel.

Professor McNelly Inspects Japanese Fighter Plane (Hyakuri Air Base, 1980)

In January 1981, I presented a paper on "Constitutional Disarmament and the Global Abolition of War; The Meaning of the Japanese Experience," at the meeting of the Southeast Conference of the Association for Asian Studies, at Washington and Lee University and the Virginia Military Institute in Lexington, Virginia. My paper was one those chosen for publication in *Annals* of the Conference (Vol. III, pp.22-36).

On June 8, 1981, I presented a formal paper on my topic at the general meeting of the Asiatic Society of Japan in Tokyo under the title "General Douglas MacArthur and the Constitutional Disarmament of Japan."

ETŌ JUN

In the August 1980 issue of *Shokun!* the particularly featured article is (I am translating the title into English) "The 1946 Constitution: Its Constraint," by Etō Jun, referring to taboos concerning free discussion of the constitution in Japan. He discusses the three articles that I had published about the Japanese constitution in the *Political Science Quarterly* as well as articles by Robert E. Ward. He points out that Ward and McNelly freely write about the critical role that American Occupation authorities played in the writing of the Japanese constitution and that the Japanese are largely unaware of the circumstances under which the

constitution was brought into being. Allied censors during the Occupation had
prohibited any mention of the American authorship of the constitution, and also
any mention that the Americans were censoring the Japanese press.

Etō gave me an inscribed copy of his 1980 book, *1946 Constitution: Sono
Kōsoku* [The 1946 Constitution: Its Constraint] (Tokyo: Bungei Shunju), in which
he again cites my research. (The Constitution of Japan was promulgated by the
emperor on November 3, 1946, became effective on May 3, 1947, and has been
variously referred to as the "1946 constitution," the "1947 constitution," the
"new constitution," the "postwar constitution," and the "Peace Constitution.")

In August 1981 Etō invited me to join him for breakfast at the International
House of Japan, where we had a pleasant conversation. (In 1999 I was shocked to
read of Etō's suicide following the death of his wife from a long and painful
experience with cancer.)

THE COLUMBIA SEMINAR

Back in the States the following September I was invited to present the paper on
General MacArthur and the constitutional disarmament of Japan at the meeting
of the University Seminar on Modern Japan at Columbia University. For the
Columbia presentation the seminar chairman accepted my suggestion that Charles
L. Kades, the principal drafter of article 9, serve as my discussant. Kades, a
distinguished lawyer, distributed to the listeners a carefully reasoned printed version
of his discussion of my paper.

Kades' extended critique of my paper at the Columbia seminar was concerned
with the interpretation as well as the origin of the constitution, and on my suggestion,
when my paper was published by the *Transactions of the Asiatic Society of Japan*
(Third Series Vol.17, October 1982) the Kades paper was printed together with
mine.

RIO DE JANEIRO

The Research Committee for Comparative Judicial Studies of the International
Political Science Association sponsored a panel at the Twelfth World Congress
of the International Political Science Association in Rio de Janeiro, Brazil,
August 9-14, 1982, where I presented a paper on civilian control in Japan. In
the same year, my paper, "Disarmament and Civilian Control in Japan: A
Constitutional Dilemma," was published by International Peace Research
Institute at Oslo in the *Bulletin of Peace Proposals*, vol. 13, no. 4, pp. 355-364.
The paper was reprinted with an update in the *Occasional Papers/Reprints Series
of Contemporary Asian Studies* (No. 8-1982) of the School of Law, University of
Maryland.

I made an intensive analysis of the international and domestic contexts of Prince Konoe's efforts in 1945 to revise the Japanese Constitution. The results of this study was a long paper, "Civil-Military Relations in Tokyo, August-December, 1945; The Konoye-Atcheson-MacArthur Triangle and the Japanese Constitution." This paper was published in the *Proceedings of the Fourth International Symposium on Asian Studies, 1982* (Hong Kong: Asian Research Service, 1982, pp. 297-328. A revised version would later appear in 2000 as a chapter in my book, *The Origins of Japan's Democratic Constitution.*)

Between March 1984 and March 1985, Professor Nishi Osamu of Komazawa University (Tokyo) was engaged in research at the University of Maryland in consultation with me and at Princeton University in consultation with Professor Walter Murphy. On Nishi's kind invitation I wrote the foreword for his book in English, *The Constitution and the National Defense Law System in Japan* (Tokyo: Seibundo, 1987).

My article on "The Study of Japanese Politics in the United States" appeared in *Participation: Newsletter of the International Political Science Association*, Vol. 8, No. 1 (Spring 1984), pp.16-21. This article was reprinted in the *Newsletter of Research on Japanese Politics*, XI (March 1985), pp. 3-13

PARIS AND AMSTERDAM

In July 1985, Myra and I flew to Paris, where I would present a paper on "The Renunciation of War in the Japanese Constitution: Its Significance for Peace and Security in Asia" at the meeting of the International Political Science Association on July 17. Before stopping in Paris we visited Jim and Liz (Myra's brother and sister-in-law) in England. In France while I was attending meetings, Myra visited Monet's residence in Giverny.

We saw the palace at Versailles and took a bus tour lasting several days of the principal chateaux on the Loire River, including Chenonceaux, which Myra had never seen before. One morning, after an overnight and breakfast in Tours, I took a short walk and heard someone in the vicinity of our hotel desperately calling for help. I wondered about this, but I was a foreign tourist and did not want to be involved. It turned out that the caller was our bus driver, who had inadvertently locked himself into his hotel room.

Then we went to Germany, stopping in Cologne to visit Ulrich and Almut Groenke, and to see Myra's old friends in Heidelberg and Karlstadt.

The Paris paper was printed in *Armed Forces and Society* (Vol. 13, No. 1 [Fall, 1986], pp. 81-106).

The journalist Frank Waldrop wrote in 1942 that General MacArthur had "always been and always will be, a priest of his cult, a philosopher of militarism." In 1957 Samuel Huntington declared that MacArthur had "emerged as the nation's most eloquent advocate of the abolition of war." At the Ninth Annual Scientific Meeting of the International Society of Political Psychology in Amsterdam in June 1986 I presented a documented paper on "MacArthur's Idealistic Obsession," summarizing the conclusions of my study. The paper, under a new title, "General MacArthur's Pacifism," was later published in *The International Journal of World Peace* (vol. vi, no. 1, [January-March 1989], pp. 41-59), and a revised version is included in my *Origins of Japan's Democratic Constitution.*

INDIA AND KASHMIR

My paper on "Military Occupations and Social Revolutions: The Cases of Germany and Japan" (59 pages long in its final form) was accepted for presentation at the world congress of the International Sociological Association (ISA), meeting in New Delhi, August 18 to 23, 1986. Myra would accompany me on the trip.

Marge Moore, a friend of Myra's who had come to know India, warned us that standards for public lodging in India were lower than in European countries and that we should stay in only the very best hotel. We reserved a room in the Kanishka, which was high on a list suggested by the convention organizers. In India we were repeatedly warned to drink and brush our teeth only with bottled water or water that had been boiled. The Kanishka's lobby and coffee shop were of yellow stone in art deco style and at one time must have seemed elegant. But in the middle of every morning the floors were washed with strong smelling antiseptic that did not enhance the ambience. We found the place passable, but noticed that the carpets in the hallways were warn and black with dirt that had accumulated notwithstanding the daily vacuuming. When we had returned to Maryland, Mrs. Moore told Myra that the Kanishka was exactly one of the hotels that she would not have recommended.

We had several meals in the Imperial Hotel nearby. One side of the dining room consisted of large windows overlooking an attractive row of palm trees. The waiters all wore turbans and red Rajasthani uniforms. It was a very pleasant place to dine. Nearby was a small bazaar where Tibetan refugees peddled their colorful wares.

Before the academic sessions took place, we took a bus tour with overnights in Jaipur and Agra, to see the Taj Mahal. A guard at the Taj Mahal examined the contents of everyone's handbags, and later a guide borrowed Myra's little flashlight to illuminate details on the marble coffin. A festival was being held at the shrine, and a crowd of Moslem visitors attired in white garments surrounded the long reflecting pool. The beauty of the Taj Mahal fully lived up to its advance billing.

Following the ISA meeting we flew to Srinagar, Kashmir, where we were scheduled to live on a houseboat. At the airport in Srinagar, our passports, which had been collected by someone in authority, were all dumped in a pile on the table so that everyone could retrieve his passport. I was shocked at the casual way these valuable documents were treated, as anyone might either by mistake or intent make off with someone else's passport. (Fortunately we had no problem on this score!)

Our houseboat, the *New Ruby*, was shared with two ladies who had also attended the ISA meeting, one an Indian lawyer from South Africa, the other a Polish professor. One evening after dinner, the two ladies modeled their beautiful new saris for us. Our meals, English cooking, were prepared in a boat moored near ours. Every morning we could hear a loudspeaker calling Moslems to prayer. One afternoon we took a boat ride in the canals surrounding the lake, stopping at the docks of various shops. We had wondered before coming to India about what kind of currency to use, but all of the shops bore signs "We accept VISA." We also took long sightseeing tours by bus or taxi in the surrounding hills and mountains, and were impressed with the charm of the ponds and fountains of Shalimar, the clarity of the fast flowing mountain streams, and distant views of the world's highest mountains.

By contrast to India proper, which was deathly hot in August, Kashmir was like Wisconsin in the summer. Each morning, before breakfast, I would stand wearing a light jacket on the boat's porch. A small boy who sang gently as he paddled his *shikara* (a small boat), would be going to the shore, possibly to get groceries. Mist would rise from the water, partly obscuring the nearby hills. We were able to visit with Professors Chopra and Kesavan in their homes shortly before we left the India. The flight home from Delhi took twenty-nine hours.

Part of my paper for the New Delhi meeting was later published under the title "War Crimes Trials in Comparative Perspective," in Stuart S. Nagel, ed., *Research in Law and Policy Studies* (Vol. 4, 1995), published by Greenwich, Connecticut: JAI Press, pp.3-24.

THE CIS MICROFICHE COLLECTION

Around 1988 I was asked to serve as the editorial adviser for a collection of documents in English concerning Japan's postwar constitution to be published on microfiche by the Congressional Information Service of Bethesda, Maryland. The editorial staff of the publisher had a long and distinguished record of producing documentary collections, and working with my suggestions incorporated in the Japanese constitution project materials from the State Department, the War Department, the Far Eastern Commission, from the papers of Charles Kades and Justin Williams in the University of Maryland McKeldin Library, and Rodman Hussey papers.

In the course of my work on the project, I decided to interview Charles L. Kades. I had over the years exchanged letters with him and when I mentioned the possibility of an interview, he and his wife, Phyllis, graciously invited Myra and me to spend a weekend at Kades' home in rural Massachusetts. The Kades' hospitality and generosity were such that I feared that the introduction of my tape recorder might seem intrusive and spoil the ambience of cordiality among us, so that I did not use my recorder at all during our visit. Instead, at the end of each day before retiring, I wrote down as accurately as possible the gist of our discussions. After the visit I gathered my notes together and organized the material according to the topics discussed. I sent a copy of this summary of our discussions to Mr. Kades asking him to correct any errors. He found virtually nothing wrong with what I had written, so that I felt confident in the accuracy of the material. A complete copy of this summary of our discussions was included in the CIS collection on the constitution.

I had in my files the massive complete English translation of the debates in the two houses of the Imperial Diet concerning the adoption of the constitution. (Dr. Justin Williams had given me this material.) I lent this material to CIS, whose staff found it more convenient to photograph my copy in their own facilities rather than photograph the same material in the National Archives or at the University of Maryland.

Cyrus Peake, a principal author of the constitution, knowing of my research interest (and unhappy with the attitude shown him by another researcher), had in the course of disposing of his files, sent me several large manila envelopes containing his papers relating to the Japanese constitution. The content of these files included materials never before made public and add much to our knowledge of his views concerning the new constitution, its interpretation, and subsequent efforts to change it. The CIS collection includes relevant papers from the "Peake Collection," which is incorporated in my personal files.

When completed, the CIS collection included copies of 1,970 documents on 420 microfiche. The collection, *Framing the Constitution of Japan: Primary Sources in English, 1944-1949*, was accompanied by a printed guide in which all of the documents were assigned reference numbers and indexed. I wrote an introduction to the guide, which listed the collections from which the documents had been obtained and included a short bibliography of relevant books and articles. The comprehensive index was prepared by Joan Sherry, who by coincidence had been a student in a graduate seminar of mine at the University of Maryland. The guide, two hundred ten 8 ½ by 11 inch pages, mostly printed in three columns, was a *tour de force* of classification and indexing and indicated the subject matter of every document. The collection was published in 1989. (The price for the collection in 1991 was $2,490; the guide alone, $350.)

In 1992 Suzuki Akinori, a Japanese maker of documentary films for TV, interviewed me and several of the American authors of the Japanese constitution at great length when making a documentary on the drafting of the constitution in

GHQ. He had with him many photocopies of documents in the CIS collection. The 1½ hour documentary was shown on Japanese television by Asahi Hōsō on November 5, 1993. After additional research with the assistance of Jean Gordon Cocienda, Suzuki authored a well documented book: *Nihonkoku kenpō o unda misshitsu no kokonoka kan* [Nine days in a secret room where the Constitution of Japan was born] (Tokyo: Sogensha, 1995). Mr. Suzuki interviewed me again in 2004 when he was compiling a documentary on proposed revisions in the Japanese constitution.

LECTURING IN TOKYO

In June and July 1989 I engaged in research in Japan on a grant from the Northeast Asia Council of the Association for Asian Studies, primarily to study the House of Councillors election to be held that year. Sugihara Seishiro, an expert on Japanese education, arranged to have me lecture (in English with an interpreter) on constitutional democracy and women's rights at Josai University, speak on comparative war crimes trials at Meisei University, where I would lunch with the president, and lecture on the constitution and world peace at Soka University. The lectures were well attended by students whose questions indicated that they were interested in what I had to say.

A Japanese version of one of these lectures was published in the September 1989 issue of the monthly journal, *Seiron*, pp, 224-232. ("Ima sensō saiban ni nana wo manabu ka: Nurenberuku to Tokyo hikaku shite" [What Do We Learn from the War Trials? Comparing Nuremberg and Tokyo], translated by Yamamoto Reiko).

"AT THE HEAD OF THE STATE"

Furukawa Atsushi (now at Senshu University), who had been engaged in research with me at the University of Maryland for two academic years, kindly arranged my meeting on July 23, 1989, with a group of specialists on the Japanese Constitution. On a rainy night we met at a sushi restaurant in Shinjuku. Amakawa Akira, Takemae Eiji, and Sodei Rinjiro were among those present. Koseki Shōichi (Dokkyo University), gave me an inscribed copy of his book *Shin kenpōno tanjō* [The Birth of Japan's New Constitution], (Chūo Kōronsha) which had been published in the preceding May. This book won the Yoshino Sakuzo prize in 1989, and an English version was translated by Ray A. Moore (Amherst College) under the title of *The Birth of Japan's Postwar Constitution* (Boulder, Colorado: Westview Press, 1997).

Also present was Nakamura Masanori, a distinguished historian who was studying the constitutional status of the monarchy in Japan. Much of our discussion centered on the meaning of MacArthur's written instruction to his staff that "the

Emperor is at the head of the state." This statement by MacArthur had been interpreted by many Japanese to mean that the emperor would be the "head of state." My view was that MacArthur may not necessarily have intended to mean that the emperor be the legal "head of state." Instead, as indicated by his use of the preposition *at*, he likely intended that the emperor be "at the top of the state." We also discussed the origins and meaning of the phrase in the new constitution that the emperor was the "symbol of the state and the unity of the people." These issues are thoroughly and competently discussed in Nakamura's book, which mentions his discussion with me. See Nakamura Masanori, *The Japanese Monarchy: Ambassador Joseph Grew and the Making of the Symbol Emperor System*, trans. Herbert P. Bix, Jonathon Baker-Bates, and Derek Bowen (Armonk, New York: M. E. Sharpe, 1992), pp. 98-104.

I reported on the 1989 House of Councillors election at the annual meeting of the American Political Science Association in Atlanta, August 31-September 3, 1989. This paper, "Scandal and Transition in Japanese Politics: The 1989 House of Councillors Election in Japan," was published in the *Asia Pacific Review* (Vol 2, No. 2 [summer, autumn, 1990], pp. 29-48.

In 1989, a 524-page compilation of previously unpublished documents in English with Japanese translations and commentary concerning the formulation of the Japanese constitution was published by the Dai-ichi Hōki publishing company in Tokyo. The principal editor of the book was my friend Inumaru Hideo, and Nishi Osamu was one of the four other editors. I was honored by being asked to write the foreword to the work, which appears on pages i and ii. (Inumaru Hideo, Yasuda Hiroshi, Murakawa Itarō, Nishi Osamu, and Ōkoshi Yasuo, comps., *Nihonkoku kenpō seitei no kei-i: Rengōkoku shireibu kenpō bunsho ni yoru* [Stages in the Enactment of the Constitution of Japan: Documents of the Allied Headquarters]).

Professor Lawrence Beer asked me to serve as one of the translators of Japanese court decisions concerning the constitution. As the issue in this instance concerned the constitutionality of Japan's self-defense forces, I agreed. My translation, "Ministry of Agriculture, Forestry and Fisheries v. Ito et al (1976): The Naganuma Nike Missile Site Case II," appears in Lawrence Beer and Hiroshi Itoh, *The Constitutional Case Law of Japan, 1970 through 1990* (Seattle: University of Washington Press, 1996), pp. 112-122.

CHAPTER 15

RETIREMENT

My contract to teach at College Park, dated 1960, provided for compulsory retirement at the age of seventy. In 1990, although recent federal legislation had banned compulsory retirement in some professions, college professors could still be required to retire. In the case of Maryland, it was explained to me that I could continue to teach full-time one year beyond the age of seventy if I reapplied for my position as full professor and was deemed to meet all the current prerequisites for the job. Actually, I had no strong desire to continue full time after the age of seventy, and, in any event, I thought it beneath my dignity to go through the procedure for reappointment. I decided to retire at seventy, with the understanding that I would complete the academic year during which I became seventy. Thus, although I became seventy on December 27, 1989, I would continue working until June of 1990.

The Department of Government and Politics sponsored a beautiful retirement reception in my honor in the afternoon of May 18, 1990, in an attractive room in the Center for Adult Education, attended by departmental faculty and friends whom I had invited. Professor George Quester, the departmental chairman, presided. Professor Wayne Cole (of the history department) and his wife were present, and later provided Myra and me with photographs of the occasion. I was presented with a letter addressed to me and signed by the governor of Maryland, William Donald Schaefer, offering his "heartfelt thanks for the many years of service you have dedicated to the University of Maryland." "Throughout the years, you have influenced many lives with your outstanding knowledge of European and East Asian government," the governor wrote, adding, "I enthusiastically applaud your commitment to education and acknowledge the good will that has been established in the international community because of your work."

In addition to the letter from the governor I received "A Proclamation" signed by Parris Glendening, the county executive of Prince George's County, Maryland, which cited particularly my 37 years of service in the overseas program and College Park campus of the University of Maryland, my chairmanship of the committee of

East Asian Studies, and my membership in the university senate. Supplementing the proclamation was a personal letter from Mr. Glendening recalling that we had been colleagues in the Department of Government and Politics for a number of years. (In 1994 Parris Glendening, with whom I had been closely associated in the department, was elected as governor of Maryland, with Kathleen Kennedy Townsend, a daughter of the late Senator Robert Kennedy, as lieutenant governor on the same Democratic ticket. In 2002, when Glendening's term as governor ended, Mrs. Townsend ran for the governorship, but was defeated by the Republican candidate, Robert Erlich.)

Also among my mementos are cards signed by departmental colleagues, members of the committee on East Asian studies, and other faculty members and university officials. The East Asian Studies committee gave me a large framed picture, colored in the style of the French impressionists, of the campus in full bloom in the spring. An inscription in Chinese refers to my honorable retirement on May 18, 1990.

Finally the department presented to me, following a custom, a beautiful captain's chair, enameled black with gold accents, with arms of cherry wood and (on the back of the chair) the university seal printed in gold. I must say that in my case the reception, unmarred by long speeches, was a thoroughly happy event, enlivened by the presence of my family, including my recently engaged daughter with her fiancé. (They were married eight days after my retirement reception.)

William E. Kirwan, President of the University of Maryland at College Park, wrote me on June 15, 1990: "I am pleased to inform you that I have approved the recommendation of your colleagues in the College of Behavioral and Social Sciences that you be appointed as Professor Emeritus in the Department of Government and Politics, effective upon your retirement."

Later President Kirwan, sent me a letter enclosing a formal printed "Certificate of Retirement Awarded to Theodore H. McNelly In appreciation of 37 years of faithful service to the University of Maryland, July 1, 1990."

I also received in the mail a large certificate, suitable for framing, of the "Governor's Recognition of Distinguished Service," awarded to Theodore H. McNelly "in appreciation of 36 years of distinguished service to the people of Maryland." The certificate, dated 1 July, 1990, bore the signatures of Governor Schaefer and of the secretary of state together with the great seal of the state of Maryland.

On November 5, 1990, a reception and banquet was held in the ballroom of the student union at which newly appointed professors emeriti of the College Park campus were individually recognized and honored, and each was presented with an elegant wall plaque.

On the next to the last payday in June 1990 I transferred from the old state teachers "retirement system" to the new "pension system." As a result, I received a smaller pension than if I had stayed under the old system, but in compensation I received a "lump sum" amounting to several hundreds of thousands of dollars, even after huge bites had been taken for taxes. (In addition, the deferred compensation scheme paid me something over a thousand dollars a month, and there was social security.) The administration and investment of this small fortune would take me much time and energy during my retirement, but the money made it possible for Myra and me to continue living in and maintaining our large home in Silver Spring, add a screened porch, send Douglas to study for his master's degree at North Carolina School of the Arts, and take conducted tours in the United States and an Alaskan cruise. My income was now greater than it had been before I had retired, and the capital slowly continued to grow. I was fortunate that my investments were not decimated by the collapse of the dot com bubble at the turn of the century.

Because I had little notion of how I would fill my days following retirement, I did some part-time teaching for several semesters and a summer school. I enjoyed this part-time teaching much more than my earlier full-time teaching, as I now had more time to polish my lectures and become personally acquainted with my students. Gradually, however, new research projects attracted my attention, and I was happy to give up teaching completely.

AN APPEARANCE ON TELEVISION

The Pacific Basin Institute in association with KCTS/Seattle produced a series of ten sixty-minute videos entitled *The Pacific Century*, a part of the Annenberg/CPB Collection. Number 5 of the series, "Reinventing Japan," concerned the Allied Occupation of Japan. I had been consulted about who might be interviewed for this production, and I appear in the program as one of those interviewed. The *Pacific Century* (copyrighted in 1992) was broadcast on public television throughout the country, and a friend of mine told me that he had seen me on TV in Florida. The video was made available for sale to the public. I showed the video to one of my classes without forewarning them of my appearance, and they were surprised to see me on the TV screen.

PEARL HARBOR REVISITED

In December 1992, Professor Sugihara Seishiro sent me a copy of a book by a Sugita Makoto that reviewed the media coverage in Japan of the fiftieth anniversary of the Pearl Harbor attack (Sugita Makoto, *Sōtenken: Shinjuwan 50 shunen hōdō— Nani ga doko made wakatta ka* [Tokyo: Morita Shuppan, 1992]). Sugihara wanted me to translate the book and find an American publisher for it. I calculated that I would be able to translate one chapter a month. He would pay me an honorarium which, at the time, seemed attractive. I wrote to Sugihara that I was willing to translate the book but would like to be provided with the copies of the original English language versions of the American documents that were frequently quoted in the book. Sugihara began sending me the requested English material, and the project was underway. After several months had passed, Sugihara wrote me that I might have already correctly suspected that Sugihara himself was the actual author of the book.

I found the project fascinating as I was learning much about the diplomatic and military background of the outbreak of the Pacific War that I had not previously known.

For a while we had a strong difference of opinion over Sugihara's desire to see the Japanese final note (the one the Japanese diplomats delivered to Secretary of State Hull after the war had already broken out) referred to as "declaration of war." I refused to refer to that note as a "declaration of war," if only for the reason that the note made no reference to war or to hostilities of any kind. It did not even explicitly state that Japan would formally break diplomatic relations with the United States. On this issue and several minor ones I ultimately had my way, so that I was satisfied that my accurate translation did not contradict what I considered to be the historical facts. At the same time, Sugihara was generous with his help in the romanization of the names of the authors and publishers of the books that he cited and reviewed.

The book was essentially a critical review of the Japanese literature published on the fiftieth anniversary of the Pearl Harbor attack and would likely not find a wide readership among non-specialists. Indeed, one or two publishers, on seeing the manuscript, seemed not to understand the purpose of the book. Sugihara's book strongly contended that Roosevelt had prior specific knowledge that the Japanese would attack Pearl Harbor. (I myself did not subscribe to this view, although it seems to be held among some Japanese scholars.) One American editor was so shocked by Sugihara's strong criticisms of Franklin D. Roosevelt that she rejected the manuscript on the grounds that it was anti-American.

It took me a year to finish the translation of the book. I arranged with the Asian Research Service, publisher of the journal *Asian Profile,* to publish the book in 1995, with a modest subsidy from Sugihara (Seishiro Sugihara, *Japanese Perspectives on Pearl Harbor: A Critical Review of Japanese Reports on the Fiftieth Anniversary of the Pearl Harbor Attack*, trans. Theodore McNelly [Hong Kong: Asian Research Service, 1995] This book (ISBN 962-234-061-0) is for sale by Asian Research Service, 140-5671 Minoru Boulevard, Richmond, B.C., Canada V6X 2B1, Fax: (604) 276 0813, price: US$20.00).

On Sugihara's request, I mailed copies of the book to every United States senator, virtually all of whom replied expressing their thanks to the author.

I contributed a "research note" entitled "The Joys (and Tribulations) of Translation," in *Japan Political Research: An Annual Review* (Vol. XXV, March 1994, pp. 4-8).

THE ATOMIC BOMB

I was asked to present a paper at a conference on World War II sponsored by the Air Force history program, held July 20 and 21, 1995, at the Bethesda Naval Officers Club. My topic: "The Final Weeks: The Decision to Drop the Atomic Bomb and Japan's Surrender."

To prepare my paper I had to review the principal literature (mostly secondary) on both the creation of the atomic bomb and the decision to use it against Japan. The events involved were controversial, but most educated people of my generation had some knowledge of the facts and the topic was by no means a new one. My research, however, focused on recently published American cryptological intelligence emphasizing Japan's preparation for an American invasion of Kyushu, Japanese attempts, with German help, to develop an atomic weapon, and the Japanese Emperor's recently discovered "monologue," which helped to explain the emperor's slowness to order a Japanese surrender. This newly revealed material helped provoke the interest of the audience.

At the time of my study of the atom bomb decision, the controversy concerning the *Enola Gay* exhibit at the Smithsonian Institution in Washington was raging at its height. The issue had to do with the possible display of materials showing the suffering of the people of Hiroshima as a result of the A-bombing. Professor Wayne McWilliams invited me to join him at Towson State University on April 26, 1995, in a "Debate on the decision to use the Atomic Bomb on Japan in 1945." Williams, whose wife was Japanese, attacked Truman's decision, which I defended.

CHARLES LOUIS KADES

On a beautiful June morning in 1996, Myra and I watched as a horse-drawn wagon bearing a flag—covered coffin wended its way through a shaded road in Arlington National Cemetery. Accompanying it were soldiers in dress uniform and a riderless horse, and following this military procession was a line of automobiles carrying the family and friends of the deceased. Colonel Charles Louis Kades, the principal draftsman of Japan's democratic constitution, was being carried to his final resting place. (At the age of 90, Mr. Kades had died of a heart attack on June 18 in a hospital in Greenfield, Massachusetts.)

The procession halted and pallbearers in dress uniform slowly moved the casket to a grassy place covered with green velvet. A rabbi made brief remarks, citing Mr. Kades's record of service to the United States in peace and war, and recited a Kaddish in Hebrew. The rabbi sprinkled dust on top of the casket. A contingent of soldiers fired a salute of three volleys. Taps were played. While a military band played "America, the Beautiful," the flag was ceremoniously folded into a triangle, and presented to Mrs. Kades.

Following the ceremony, Mrs. Beate Sirota Gordon, who had authored the women's rights provisions in the Japanese constitution, placed on top of the casket a purplish brown scarf. On this scarf was printed, in a number of different languages, Article 9 of the Japanese constitution, the famous peace clause, by which Japan renounced forever war and the maintenance of war potential.

THE FIFTIETH ANNIVERSARY OF THE CONSTITUTION

In Japan it was customary for the strong advocates of the democratic constitution to celebrate its establishment with lectures and seminars annually on May 3 (Constitutional Memorial Day). The ruling Liberal Democratic Party, whose members included strong advocates of the revision of the constitution, did not normally hold such celebrations. However, in 1997, the large conservative Federation of Diet Members for the Establishment of a Constitutional Studies Committee sponsored a "Forum Commemorating the Fiftieth Anniversary of the Constitution of Japan." The aim of the sponsoring organization seemed less to celebrate the constitution than to air criticisms of its substance and the manner of its adoption. Many of the critics held the view that the democratic constitution, enacted when Japan was under the military occupation of the Allied Powers, had been "imposed on Japan," and that the Japanese should now take the matter into their own hands and autonomously adopt revisions in the document that would reflect Japanese beliefs and traditions and that would be suitable for Japan's well-being in the twenty-first century. These conservatives advocated the enhancement of the position of the emperor, provisions for strengthening Japan's defense, and restoring the importance of the family in the constitution.

A central feature of the full-day forum was the participation of Americans involved in the Occupation. Professor Nishi Osamu of Komazawa University was the principal organizer of the forum. Three of the American speakers had, in MacArthur's Headquarters, participated in writing the initial draft of what later became the Constitution of Japan. These Americans were Milton J. Esman (Cornell University), Richard A. Poole (State Department, retired), and Beate Sirota Gordon (the Asia Society). I and Richard B. Finn were asked to present the "keynote addresses." Finn, a prominent State Department official, in addition to being involved in the Occupation and the reversion of Okinawa to Japanese rule, had authored a magisterial book on the Occupation (*Winners in Peace: MacArthur, Yoshida, and Postwar Japan* (University of California Press, 1992).

During the months preceding the meeting in question, my vision had become impaired by cataracts. In order to help me present my comments, my typewritten manuscript was greatly enlarged by a photocopier. However, when I stepped behind the podium and looked at the poorly lighted manuscript, I was unable to read a word. After a moment of panic, I realized that the script was not really necessary. Besides, the interpreter had a copy of my speech and could somehow make out.

During my speech I presented a brief narrative of the American contribution to the Japanese Constitution. I noted that the forum organizers had insisted that I include my suggestions for improvement of the constitution. I said that the constitution was a *Japanese* document, they had been living with it, and that as a foreigner I was uncomfortable about making suggestions for its change. (Indeed, in the back of my mind was the notion that the Americans had already had their turn with the Japanese Constitution and had done enough.) But I added that if I had to make a suggestion it would be to change the title of the *emperor* to *king*. [In the Chinese and Japanese languages there are approximate equivalents for these English words.] My suggestion, which in effect would demote the emperor, floated like a lead balloon. It incited no enthusiasm among people who believed that the emperor should be declared "head of state" rather than "symbol of the state and the unity of people" as provided in the democratic constitution.

In the one-page summary of my thoughts printed in the brochure of the forum, I expressed the view that rather than refer to the new constitution as a foreign "imposition," it might be more correct to say, as suggested by Alfred Oppler, that it represented an "induced revolution."

I concluded:

> Nuclear weapons are proliferating, and third world countries and terrorist groups may soon be equipped with the weapons of mass destruction. *[I made this prophecy five years before the American-led invasion of Iraq intended to find and destroy weapons of mass destruction.]* The Japanese must cope with this reality . . . . Although the Japanese people may be much more pacifistic than is understood in the international community, they must take care that constitutional revisions, however necessary or desirable, do not appear to symbolize Japan's revival as a threat . . . . At the same time, in so far as possible, it is necessary in a democratic state that the people play a role in the formulation of their constitution and laws and that government is by consent of the governed.

After the conference I gave a lecture to professors and graduate students at Waseda University. I was driven back to my hotel by a Waseda professor who was tutoring the younger brother of the crown prince on the constitution. I hinted that since the crown prince and princess had not yet produced a male heir, one might entertain the *kibō* (hope) that the younger brother might someday become emperor.

American Experts on the Japanese Constitution
From the left: Professor McNelly, Mr. Richard Finn, Mr. Richard Poole, Professor
Milton Esman, Mrs. Beate Sirota Gordon

Professor Nishi with Ted and Myra at Hase Shrine in Kamakura (1997)

While shopping with my wife in Tokyo during our brief stay in Japan, I was gratified to note that a book that I had very substantially contributed to was now on display for sale in a major store. *Eigo de yomu nihonkoku kenpō: The Constitution of Japan* was part of the educational Bilingual Books series (in Japanese and English) published by Kodansha. The bulk of the book consisted of the Japanese Constitution in both Japanese and English, and captioned illustrations of events of constitutional significance. The last one fourth of the book contains my essay on "The Constitution of Japan: One View" in English together with a Japanese translation. This essay succinctly summarized my research on the origins and significance of Japan's democratic constitution.

HERBERT NORMAN: SPY OR VICTIM OF McCARTHYISM?

During my retirement, I had plenty of time to indulge my fascination with espionage, and in particular with the famous Cambridge Spy Ring (Burgess, Maclean, Philby, Blunt, and Cairncross). I acquired several shelves of the relevant books. I began to notice that a number of the leading books on the Cambridge Ring mentioned that E. Herbert Norman, a Canadian student at Cambridge, had been recruited as a KGB spy. When Norman committed suicide while ambassador to Egypt in 1957, the authors assumed that the suicide was in effect an admission of guilt. Norman had distinguished himself as one of the leading historians of modern Japan and the tendency among academics was to believe that, notwithstanding views he may have held as a Cambridge undergraduate, he was a loyal civil servant being unjustly persecuted by McCarthyites.

Norman had briefly held a very influential post in MacArthur's Civil Intelligence before I had joined that organization, had been a confidant of MacArthur, and been the Canadian representative in the Occupation of Japan. I was an admirer of his famous *Japan's Emergence as a Modern State*. But I could not lightly dismiss the charges made against him by leading writers on British espionage. To enlighten myself farther, I proposed a panel, which I would chair, to discuss the Norman case at a forthcoming meeting of the Association for Asian Studies.

Although my proposed panel included some leading names my proposal was not accepted by the AAS. However the Japanese political studies group accepted it for the meeting of the American Political Science Association meeting in Boston in 1998. At the last minute, the panelist whom I had expected to present the problematical aspects of Norman's associations withdrew and I hastily wrote a paper myself that emphasized a critical view of Norman. The panel included, besides myself, Eleanor Hadley and Richard Finn, both of whom had known Norman personally and had written books about the Occupation of Japan, John Hilliker of the Canadian Ministry of External Affairs, and Roger Bowen, author of a scholarly book that defended Norman's reputation as a loyal public servant, *Innocence Is Not Enough: The Life and Death of Herbert Norman* (Armonk, New York: M.E. Sharpe, 1988).

A week before the panel was to appear at the convention, Richard Finn suddenly died, to everyone's great shock, and Roger Bowen agreed to present Mr. Finn's paper.

My paper was published on the Internet as were many of the papers presented at the convention. On October 7, 2000, I presented a revised version of the paper at the meeting of the Washington and Southeast Regional Seminar on Modern Japan at George Mason University in Fairfax, Virginia. Hayden Peake, an American intelligence officer very knowledgeable about the Norman case, served as the discussant for my paper. (Hayden Peake is related to Cyrus Peake, one of the American authors of the Japanese constitution. Hayden Peake is the coauthor, with Rufina Philby and Mikhail Lyubimov, of *The Private Life of Kim Philby: The Moscow Years* [New York: Fromm International, 2000].)

THE MOORE-ROBINSON PROJECT

One day in the 1980s when Professor Nishi Osamu of Komazawa University was visiting Washington, D.C., he invited me to meet him at the Cosmos Club. As we were chatting about our studies of the Japanese constitution, we chanced to make the acquaintance of the only other person in the lounge, Donald Robinson, Charles N. Clark Professor of Government and American Studies at Smith College. Professor Robinson told us of a project in which he was engaged with Professor Ray Moore, of Amherst College. Ray had been a longtime student of the Occupation of Japan, having organized an international academic conference on that topic in August, 1980.

I was asked to serve on the advisory board or committee for a documentary collection to be published on CD under the direction of Ray Moore and Donald Robinson. Also serving on this committee were Professors George Akita (University of Hawaii), Doi Masakazu (University of Kyoto), John Dower (Massachusetts Institute of Technology), E. Dick Howard (University of Virginia), Igarashi Takeshi (University of Tokyo), Kyoko Inoue (University of Illinois at Chicago), Koseki Shōichi (Dokkyō University), John Maki (University of Massachusetts), Walter Murphy (Princeton University), and Susan Pharr (Harvard University). When Donald Robinson made several trips to Washington D.C., we discussed the project at an Irish-American pub near the Wheaton, Maryland, subway station. (Sadly, the pub, famous for its beer and Irish chowder, has since been demolished to make way for a small park.)

The Moore-Robinson collection on CD ROM, published by Princeton University Press, in 1998, contained 523 documents (about 8,000 typescript pages). It included material not previously published, and with a computerized index and hypertext cross references, was easy to use. However it contained many fewer documents than the CIS microfiche collection with which I had been associated, described in an earlier chapter.

A FINNISH INTERLUDE

The opening of Archives II in College Park, Maryland, adjacent to the campus of the University of Maryland, and the transfer of documents of MacArthur's Tokyo headquarters from Suitland to Archives II in the 1990s were very welcome developments for me. Archives II, the largest archival building in the world, was only a twenty-minute drive from my home in Silver Spring. Although I had completed my research in the Tokyo documents before they had been moved to Archives II, I had frequent opportunities to meet researchers who were working on the Occupation of Japan. We would have long chats during and after lunch at the attractive cafeteria, which overlooked flower gardens and a woods. Also from time to time relevant lectures or documentary films were presented at Archives II. One day in the late 1990s I met with Henry Oinas-Kukkonen, a scholar at the University of Oulu, Finland, who had been doing research in the records of MacArthur's Civil Intelligence Section, where I had worked in 1946-1948. He was particularly interested in the American policies towards the Japan Communist Party. I was surprised that the relevant files had been declassified.

I was happy to read the chapters of Henry's dissertation as he was completing them (they were sent to me as .pdf files in email), and when asked by his university if his work was ready for a defense, I certified it. Later I was asked to be the "opponent" in the oral defense of the dissertation and agreed to do so. On August 25, 1999, Myra and I left Baltimore-Washington airport on our way to Oulu, Finland, with changes at Gatwick (London), and Helsinki (Finland). Henry met us at the airport in Oulu and while he was driving arranged on his cell phone for the transfer of part of our luggage, which during the confusion had been left in Helsinki.

The defense consisted of a two-hour session in an auditorium at the university. Only three people were on the stage: Henry, the doctoral candidate, his major professor, Olavi Fält, who was "custos" and chaired the meeting, and me, the "opponent." Everything was in English. It was the custom that all of the three participants wear tails, but Americans could wear academic gowns. I wore my Columbia doctoral robe. After I had grilled Henry for half an hour, I suggested that it was Fält's turn to ask questions, but was told that Fält would not be asking questions and that I was to continue my interrogation. Henry did beautifully. His English was fluent and he was thoroughly acquainted not only with the documents and the factual background but also with the bibliography on the Occupation of Japan.

A luncheon was served following the defense. In the evening, a *karankka*, (banquet) formally in my honor (the printed menu named the candidate and the opponent) was held at the Ravintola Franzen, a venerable restaurant in Oulu. Henry's family and many relatives were there to honor Henry and enjoy the splendid cuisine.

On the following day, Henry gave us a tour of Oulu, and we enjoyed the university's fine arboretum. We saw where the university was raising reindeer. The deer were then shedding their antlers, and in some instances, to help them along, the antlers were sawed off. One of the keepers gave us a huge pair of male antlers and small pair of female antlers. The male antlers were so large and awkward that they required special handling every time we changed planes on our trip back to Maryland.

Henry also took us to see his home and local attractions in Muhos, a small city about thirty-five kilometers east of Oulu.

From Oulu we flew to Rovaniemi, Finland, near the Arctic Circle, as we had originally planned, largely to see the reindeer for which it is famous. Because it was not yet Christmas season, Santa Claus Village, a short bus ride from Rovaniemi, was not fully operational, but we did see Santa Claus in person and the thick books where he kept records of the behavior and misbehavior of the world's children. The Arctic Circle is a white line about eighteen inches wide which crosses the central square of Santa Claus Village. We took photos of each other standing on this famous line, on which is printed in black letters "Arctic Circle" in English and French.

Myra and Ted Standing on the Arctic Circle at Santa Claus Village, Finland

From Rovaniemi we flew to Helsinki where we checked into an expensive international hotel for a week. We had expected to take tour buses to neighboring attractions, most notably Sibelius's home. However in Finland the tourist season ends completely on August 31, and these tours were not available. (Because of Myra's difficulty with walking, I felt that it would be impractical to use any transportation other than an organized bus tour.) We did take a conducted bus tour of Helsinki, which was very interesting, and we spent several days loafing in the Esplanada, a kind of Champs-Élysées with trees, cafes, expensive shops, and street performers. Our hotel was near one end of the Esplanada, the busy Helsinki harbor was at the far end. Meals at our hotel and at a restaurant on the Esplanada were excellent, but expensive, and we had one or two lunches at a nearby McDonalds.

In the center of Helsinki there is a large square adjoining a white domed building looking for all the world like an American state capitol building. Actually it is the Lutheran cathedral. In the middle of the square is a statue of the Russian Czar, Alexander II, under whose reign the Grand Duchy of Finland had enjoyed substantial self-rule. On a hill, overlooking the harbor is the red-brick cathedral of the Russian Orthodox Church.

On our thirty-ninth wedding anniversary (September 4, 1999) we took a catamaran (a speedy double-hulled passenger ship) across the Gulf of Finland to Talinn, the capital of Estonia, where, as I had arranged, we were met by a private guide and a chauffeured automobile. The guide, Nadja Solodjankina, was a woman graduate student, a Russian, who spoke fluent English and knew the area intimately. The medieval city walls and public buildings and churches, with tall steeples, had not been damaged by World War II, and were charming in every way. We ate dinner at a restaurant which specialized in medieval cuisine. At the end of the day we again boarded the catamaran for the return trip to Helsinki.

MY BOOK

Until 1991 my 444-page Columbia University doctoral dissertaton, *Domestic and International Influences on Constitutional Revision in Japan, 1945-1946,* was the only book-length treatment in English on the origins of the postwar Japanese constitution. I owned the 1952 copyright, and those wishing to acquire a copy of the book could order it from University Microfilms in Ann Arbor Michigan, in the format of a paper-bound book (printed on demand) or in microfilm. This format met the publication requirement for Columbia Ph.D.s. Negotiations with the Columbia University Press for publication in a more conventional format ended as I pleaded for time to make revisions and updates.

Robert E. Ward's article ("The Origins of the Japanese Constitution," in the *American Political Science Review,* Vol. L, No. 4 [December 1956], 980-1009), which cited my dissertation, spurred me to begin working on revisions while I was teaching in the University of Maryland Munich Branch, but progress was very slow. Of course my contacts with the Japanese Government's Commission on the Constitution while I was in Japan with the Maryland Far Eastern program in 1958 to 1960 were a powerful stimulus for more research and resulted in a second article in the *Political Science Quarterly.* The commission published in 1959 the sections of the dissertation that I felt would be most interesting to Japanese readers (*Nihon kenpō kaisei ni taisuru kokunaiteki, kokusaiteki eikyō).* Kobayashi Shōzō, a young professor at Waseda University, was the translator.

In 1999, Norton published my friend John Dower's magnum opus on postwar Japan: *Embracing Defeat: Japan in the Wake of World War II.* This book, which won a Pulitzer Prize and a National Book Award, contained much material on the Occupation of Japan and in particular on the formulation of Japan's postwar constitution. I was gratified to note that Dower had made extensive use of my Columbia dissertation and published articles on the constitution, as indicated in his frequent references to my work in his endnotes.

One day at lunch with Wayne Cole and Chun-tu Hsueh, I called their attention to Dower's references to my work, and it was decided then and there that I should publish a book on the Japanese constitution.

Reviewing my efforts at revising the dissertation, I discovered drafts of important but previously unpublished material, which, when incorporated with some of my articles and conference papers, would provide a connected narrative of the formulation of the Japanese constitution. I was determined to see my book in print before potential health difficulties might sabotage my effort—I was then eighty years old—and whipped my manuscript into shape.

The University Press of America had published the third edition of my *Politics and Government in Japan* (1984). They had recently issued Wayne Cole's book, *Determinism and American Foreign Relations During the Franklin D. Roosevelt Era* (1995) in a handsome binding. They promptly agreed to publish my book in both hard cover and paperback editions. It would be advertised in some of their widely distributed specialized catalogs. The 223-page volume was published in 2000 in both soft and hard cover, entitled *The Origins of Japan's Democratic Constitution.*

The first chapter of the book describes how American personnel in MacArthur's Government Section authored a model democratic constitution for Japan, how MacArthur persuaded the cabinet of Baron Shidehara to adopt its basic principles, how MacArthur fended off interference by America's wartime allies, and how MacArthur's staff oversaw the enactment of the constitution by the Imperial Diet. The second chapter details the struggle for power in Tokyo at the end of the war; a struggle among the Allied Powers and within the United States for the control of

Japan, rivalry for authority between Government Section and representatives of the State Department in Tokyo, and competition among factions in the Japanese government. A third chapter details personal rivalries and debates among the American constitution drafters. The role of the monarchy in Japan's modernization is described in the fourth chapter. The fourth and fifth chapters describe in detail the roles of MacArthur and his staff in the formulation of the renunciation of war and arms in the Japanese constitution and General MacArthur's changing views on how world peace might be established. The effects of the "peace clause" of the Japanese constitution on Japan's foreign and defense policies and the consequences for international politics are analyzed in a final chapter. At the end of the book are an index and the text of the model constitution drafted in MacArthur's headquarters.

I sent complimentary copies of the book to American and Japanese researchers on the constitution and to professors specializing in Japanese politics. The book can be most conveniently bought on the Internet from not only the publisher (univpress.com) but also, of course, from Amazon.com. I have noticed on the Internet that the book has rapidly found its way into the libraries of leading universities.

My colleagues in the field had kind compliments for me. I was particularly moved by a letter from Professor Marius Jansen of Princeton University, who was at that time engaged in the final preparations for the publication of his last great book. On August 20, 2000, he wrote me that he had lost his core vision to macular degeneration and an embolism, and being unable to annotate his copy-edited manuscript had to type out laboriously nearly 400 pages of commands. He said that he was able to credit me in footnote and bibliographical notes, "conceivably your first citations."

Needless to say, I was much moved by Marius' kindness to me at a time when he was struggling under great physical handicaps to see his own book to final publication. It came as a great shock that on December 10, only a few months after he wrote the thoughtful note to me, Professor Jansen died. The obituary distributed by his family noted, "His latest book, The Making of Modern Japan, Harvard University Press (2000) was published a week before his death, affording him great satisfaction."

Two prominent young Japanese professors have each told me of his enthusiasm for my book and of his wish to translate it for publication in Japan. Arrangements are being made with a leading Japanese publisher for the issuance of a Japanese edition.

In 2003, the fifth edition of *Introduction to Comparative Government,* under the general editorship of Professor Michael Curtis, of Rutgers University, was published by Longman. I was the author of the section on Japan, appearing on pages 260 to 323. Together with suggestions for further reading, I list a number of relevant websites for the study of Japanese politics.

At the meeting of the Mid-Atlantic Region of the Association for Asian Studies held in October 24-26, 2003, in Washington, D.C., I chaired a panel on "The Constitutions of Asia."

A GENETIC PREDISPOSITION FOR CONSTITUTIONALISM?

During retirement I became interested in genealogy, a study greatly facilitated by the relevant family histories: William Elmer Gillingham, comp., *Thomas Gillingham Descendants* (Richland Center, Wisconsin: Richland Observer, 1973); William Lincoln Hart, *Hart Family History: Silas Hart, His Ancestors and Descendants* (Alliance, OH: William Lincoln Hart, 1942); Dena D. Hurd, *A History and Genealogy of the Family of Hurd in the United States* (edition published by Rutland, VT: Tuttle Antiquarian Books); Sophie Selden Rogers, et al, *Selden Ancestry: A Family History* (reprinted by Salem, MA: Higginson Book Company); and Ruth Wilder Sherman, et al, comp. *Mayflower Families Through Five Generations*, Volume 13, *Family of William White* (Plymouth, MA: General Society of Mayflower Descendants, 1997).

My middle name is Hart, and my parents led me to understand that I was related to John Hart, a signer of the Declaration of Independence. However, the *Hart Family History*, cited above, which lists my name on page 163, makes it clear (on page 13) that the line of Harts to which I belong (descendants of Deacon Stephen Hart of Hartford), is not the line of Harts to which John Hart, a signer of the Declaration of Independence, belonged. My researches have failed to find any connection between me and John Hart, the signer.

Nevertheless I have been impressed by the number of my direct antecedents who were involved in the development of constitutional government in America. These included most notably my direct ancestors Richard Warren (died in 1628) and William White (died in 1621), both of whom signed the "*Mayflower* Compact," sometimes referred to as America's first constitution.

My tenth great grandfather, John Vassall (1544-1625) was an alderman of London who outfitted and commanded two ships in the English fleet that defeated the Spanish Armada in 1588. His son, my ancestor, William Vassall (1592-1655), was one of the twelve members (including John Winthrop and Richard Saltonstall) of the Massachusetts Bay Company who mutually swore to reside in the new world, taking with them the company charter and establishing their government in the new colony thus protecting the company from interference by royal authorities in England. William Vassall later reportedly authored a petition ("the Child petition") protesting against political discrimination practiced in New England by the reigning Congregationalists against Episcopalians and Presbyterians. As a polemicist who advocated religious toleration, he was attacked in a pamphlet by Governor Edward Winslow (of Plymouth) as "New England's Salamander." (Governor Winslow was the second husband of my ancestress, Mrs. William White.)

Deacon Stephen Hart (about 1605-1681) and Thomas Selden (1616-1655), my direct ancestors, were named as the founding freemen of Hartford, Connecticut, on a monument erected about 1837 "to the Founders of Hartford and the Makers of the Constitution of Connecticut." Selden's name was associated with the "Fundamental Orders of Connecticut" of 1638, one of America's earliest constitutions.

William Collier (died about 1671), my direct ancestor, was a principal organizer of the United Colonies of New England, being one of the eight signers of the articles of confederation that created that organization in 1643. He was one of the two commissioners representing Plymouth in the confederation.

My direct ancestor Valentine Hollingsworth, Sr. (1632-1710), was a member of the assembly of the province of Pennsylvania and signed the "Frame of Government of Pennsylvania" (1683), which had been authored and signed by William Penn.

My great great grandfather George Washington Gale (1789-1861) was the leading founder of the city of Galesburg, Illinois, and of Knox College.

Descendants other than myself of some of my ancestors include some prominent individuals who, of course, may be counted among my more or less distant cousins. They include Presidents Franklin D. Roosevelt and Ulysses Grant, descendants of Richard Warren. Descendants of John Vassall, who also are evidently my quite distant cousins, include Elizabeth Vassall (1770-1845), who married Henry Richard Fox, the third Baron Holland (1773-1840), a Whig leader in England. As Lady Holland she became famous as a political hostess and was a friend of Napoleon, who left her a gold snuff box in his will. (Lord Holland was the nephew and admirer of Charles James Fox, the advocate in the British parliament of the cause of the American revolutionaries and the abolition of slavery.)

Charles Richard Fox (1796-1873) was the first son of Lord Holland and Elizabeth Vassall, born before the couple was married. He became a member of parliament and a general. (He was evidently my fifth cousin five times removed. He married Lady Mary Fitzclarence [1798-1864], one of King William IV's ten illegitimate children by Mrs. Dorothea Jordan, an actress who had already born seven children before her liaison with royalty. The expenses of raising Mrs. Jordan's brood were partly defrayed by the mother's earnings on the stage. The indefatigable Mrs. Jordan finally removed to France, where she died in poverty. King William IV produced, in addition to his ten illegitimate children, two legitimate daughters, who died in infancy, so that the British royal throne did not succeed to any of his numerous progeny but rather to his niece, Victoria, who reigned respectably from 1837 to 1901.)

Another of my remote cousins, John Vassall, was a wealthy royalist who fled Massachusetts during the American revolution. His home in Cambridge (now known as the Craigie-Longfellow mansion) was used as a headquarters by General George Washington, and later acquired by the poet Henry Wadsworth Longfellow as a gift from his father-in-law.

The American minister to China during the Boxer Rebellion in 1900 and the subsequent diplomatic negotiations was Edwin Hurd Conger (1843-1907), my first cousin twice removed.

The seventh chief justice of the United States Supreme Court, Morrison Remick Waite (1816-1888), a descendant of the above mentioned Thomas Selden, was my second cousin, three times removed. The vice president of the United States (1877-1881), William Almon Wheeler, was a distant cousin.

Alfred G. Taylor, my maternal grandfather, was serving as a Presbyterian missionary in Japan when the Imperial Constitution was promulgated by the Meiji Emperor in 1889. It was my grandfather who, when I was still a boy, first told me about the Meiji constitution and its undemocratic provisions. The Japanese constitution was thus a part of my early environment, but in view of my lineage, one might wonder whether my fascination with politics and constitutions was not at least partly determined by my biological heredity.

However, in 1962, my very distant cousin, John Vassall (William John Christopher Vassall, 1926-1997), was convicted and imprisoned in England as a spy of the KGB. His infamy is chronicled in Rebecca West's *The New Meaning of Treason* (New York: Viking Press, 1964), pages 316-332, and her *The Vassall Affair* (London: Sunday Telegraph, 1963). John Vassall wrote a memoir that incidentally discusses his ancestry: *Vassall: The Autobiography of a Spy* (London: Sidgwick & Jackson, 1975), especially page 11.

CHAPTER 16

LOOKING BACK

I began writing this autobiography with only two purposes: (1) as an undemanding diversion for myself in my old age before my cataracts were removed and other pleasures were not available to me, and (2) as a resource for historians and genealogists, who want to fill in gaps that are left when other sources are unavailable. Consciously, and perhaps unconsciously, I have avoided discussions of topics and events that have been and remain excessively painful or embarrassing to myself or to others. Aside from the selectivity of my memory, for the sake of the historical record I have aimed to be accurate and truthful.

Writing this memoir has stimulated me to analyze the course of my life in a more systematic way than before. From an informed perspective, I can perceive my weaknesses and strengths, my successes and failures, and account for them.

Looking at my childhood, I am struck by the fact that although my family was far from wealthy, actually we were firmly rooted in the middle class. My mother had come from what would be called a "good family," a line of clergymen, political leaders, and scholars, and my father, although very poor as a child, had risen in the world through dint of his natural talents and hard work to become a public school administrator. Presidents Truman, Nixon, Reagan, and Clinton had come from poorer, less promising families than I and as children had not had my advantages.

Thinking back on it, I was blessed with somewhat better than average talents in music, scholarship, self-discipline, and ambition. I believe that I was held back by psychological complexes, which were too embarrassing to describe in these memoirs. (1) A kind of inferiority complex drove me to scatter my efforts, trying to succeed in too many things at once, and failing to follow some projects through to successful completions. (2) I have usually been too reluctant to ask for help from other people. I am sure that if I had asked for more help in many cases I could have gotten it, because people actually liked me more than I had imagined. (3) In the course of two decades as a bachelor, I became involved sentimentally with a number of attractive and intelligent ladies (the number today surprises me) and mismanaged some of my romantic involvements with embarrassing consequences. (All of that is now past, of course, and I am what is often termed "a happily married man." Such men, statistics show, are in the majority, but one would never know it from watching television shows that depict factual and fictional accounts of marital disasters. I attribute much of my present contentment to my wife, who seems to be completely free of negative complexes.) (4) At critical stages in my career, I made strategic mistakes, mistakes that I might not have made if I had had a constant mentor.

It should be said, however, that some of my weaknesses were attended by partially compensating strengths. For example, my reluctance to ask for help was complemented by a strong sense of self-reliance and forced me to accomplish a great deal independently. The scattering of my energies had the positive effect of broadening my horizons and opening possibilities that I would not otherwise have imagined.

Had it not been for my family connections with Japan—my mother having been born there—and the outbreak of war with Japan, it seems unlikely that I would have acquired a life-time commitment to Japanese studies and political science. I might very well have remained committed to French studies, working towards a Ph.D. and college teaching in that field. In the lives of many Americans of my generation including myself, World War II was a defining event.

In the course of writing my autobiography, I became more aware than I had been of the influence of particular individuals on my life. These individuals affected my life in distinctive ways. Among these people were:

- Miss Caroline Young, teacher of French at Madison West High School, whose effective "direct method" of teaching and enthusiasm for the study of French culture, provided the motivation and ability that made it possible for me to excel in French at the University of Wisconsin and prepare me for Japanese language studies.
- Mr. Richard Church, of Madison West High School and later of the University of Wisconsin, whose friendly encouragement and direction helped me to develop my skills as a musician and an actor.
- Professor Germaine Mercier, of the Department of French and Italian at the University of Wisconsin, who introduced me not only to French literature and drama, but also to the universe of ideas.
- Professor Elmer Plischke, of the University of Maryland, who hired me to teach political science in his dynamic department and constantly supported my applications for research grants.
- My mother, who was my first music teacher.
- My father and my maternal grandfather, who by their example taught me the values of devotion to family, discipline, self-reliance, and work.

• My beloved wife and mother of my beautiful children, Myra, whose level-headedness and common sense have kept me sane and brought much joy into my life.

I attended a first-rate high school and the best universities, Wisconsin, Georgetown, and finally Columbia, where I was awarded a doctorate of philosophy. My family was protected from the ravages of the Great Depression by my grandfather's prudent financial management. Apparently it was my involvement in signal intelligence that saved me from the peril of combat during the Second World War. One could say that I lived a charmed existence during a very challenging period of history. I have had my fair share of health problems, including bouts of tuberculosis and diabetes, but my life has been prolonged by favorable genes, the miracles of modern medicine, and timely calls on 911.

During much of my life, I kept my nose to the grindstone, and was so engrossed in my own individual problems and activities that I tended to regard myself as self-made and give myself credit for earning the good things in my life. After researching and analyzing my life history, I have arrived at the humbling conclusion that the talents and efforts in which I have found pride and pleasure are products of a heritage and an environment that have been unusually favorable to me. It is impossible for me not to feel a sense of gratitude to a Providence that has so graciously blessed me.

INDEX

Note: As a rule, in this book, when a Japanese individual is mentioned, the family name precedes the given name.

Y